C00 139 895X

D1375452

Stagecoach

Stagecoach

*A classic rags-to-riches tale
from the frontiers of capitalism*

Christian Wolmar

ORION
BUSINESS
BOOKS

Copyright © 1998, 1999 Christian Wolmar

All rights reserved

The right of Christian Wolmar to be identified
as the author of this work has been asserted by
him in accordance with the Copyright,
Designs and Patents Act 1988.

Paperback edition first published in Great Britain in 1999
by Orion Business
An imprint of The Orion Publishing Group Ltd
Orion House, 5 Upper St Martin's Lane,
London WC2H 9EA

A CIP catalogue record for this book
is available from the British Library.

ISBN 0–75283–088–0

Typeset by Deltatype Ltd, Birkenhead, Merseyside
Printed and bound in Great Britain by
Clays Ltd, St Ives plc

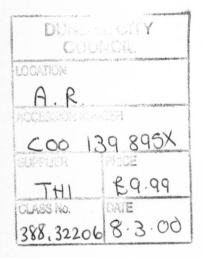

DUNDEE CITY
COUNCIL

LOCATION

A. R.

ACCESSION NUMBER

COO 139 895X

SUPPLIER   PRICE

THI   £9.99

CLASS NO.   DATE

388.32206   8.3.00

Contents

Stagecoach chronology

1976 Ann and Robin Gloag set up caravan-hire business.

1980 Brian Souter, Ann Gloag and her husband Robin form Gloagtrotter partnership to run coach services between Scotland and London, taking advantage of Transport Act 1980 deregulation. Name soon changed to Stage-Coach.

1982 Robin Gloag leaves partnership. In April 1983, business becomes Stagecoach Limited company, operating coach services throughout Scotland as well as to London.

1985 Transport Act passed deregulating bus services.

1986 Launches Magicbus in Glasgow.

1987 Buys three companies from National Bus Company (NBC) privatisation: Hampshire, Cumberland and United Counties.

1988 First overseas operation, in China, providing buses in exchange for advertising.

Summer 1988 Blockades Keswick town centre in protest at local council turning down development plan.

December 1988 Private placement through Noble Grossart raises £5 million and gives Stagecoach £50 million bank facility. Ewan Brown of Noble Grossart becomes first Stagecoach non-executive director.

March 1989 Buys majority stake in United Transport Malawi.

1989 Buys East Midland, Ribble and Southdown, all ex-NBC companies, from management teams.

August 1989 Sells Stagecoach Express coaching operations to National Express.

1990 First problems with regulators over minor acquisitions in Portsmouth and Hastings, both of which result in ministerial requirements to divest.

1990 Ann Gloag is made Veuve Clicquot Businesswoman of the Year.

October 1990 Buys Gray Coach Lines in Canada.

1991 Buys two Scottish Bus Group companies at privatisation: Northern Scottish and Fife Scottish.

May 1991 Public Accounts Committee reports on NBC privatisation highlighting the large profit made by Stagecoach on sale of Southampton bus station.

November 1991 Buys bus operations in Nairobi and Mombasa, Kenya.

1992 Ann Gloag becomes one of the European Women of Achievement for the year.

May 1992 Stagecoach Rail launched, operating seat service between Scotland and London.

July 1992 Gray Coach Lines files for protection from bankruptcy and soon after Stagecoach sells out of Canada.

October 1992 Acquires Wellington operation in New Zealand. Brian Cox and Barry Hinkley promoted to main board.

April 1993 Floats on Stock Exchange valued at £134 million.

July 1993 Buys East Kent for £5 million.

October 1993 Stagecoach Rail service ends with losses of at least £700,000.

October 1993 Keith Cochrane joins as group financial controller and becomes finance director in March 1996 at the age of thirty-one.

November 1993 Buys Grimsby–Cleethorpes and Western Travel for total of £14 million.

June 1994 Buys Busways in Newcastle for £28 million, biggest purchase so far, Western Scottish for £6 million and soon after buys 20 per cent stake in Sheffield Mainline for £1 million but later forced to divest.

September 1994 Buys two London former LT subsidiaries for total of £42 million.

November 1994 Battle of Darlington and Stagecoach swamps town with free buses and local municipal company goes out of business. MMC announces enquiry.

November 1994 Buys 20 per cent stake in Glasgow's main company, SB, but later forced to divest.

June 1995 Buys stake in Portuguese bus company.

August 1995 MMC calls Stagecoach's behaviour in Darlington 'predatory, deplorable, and against public interest'.

December 1995 Becomes first outside company to win rail franchise, South West Trains, the largest on the network. Bids for all other 24 franchises but gets only tiny Island Line.

February 1996 Transport Secretary, Sir George Young, rides on inaugural privatised train.

February 1996 Buys Greater Manchester Buses South for £42 million, and later launches competition against itself with Magicbus.

August 1996 Announces two biggest acquisitions so far: Swebus, with 3500 buses throughout Scandinavia for £233 million and Porterbrook, the train leasing company, for £826 million.

February 1997 South West Trains fiasco.

April 1997 Launches attack in Glasgow on FirstBus, which retaliates in Fife and Ayrshire, but all-out war is avoided.

July 1997 Completes purchase of Transit Holdings, which includes operations in Oxford and Australia.

December 1997 Acquires Sheffield Supertram operation.

April 1998 Appoints Mike Kinski as chief executive, taking over part of Brian Souter's role. Buys Glasgow Prestwick Airport for £41 million and acquires a 28 per cent holding in Road King, a toll road company in China for £107 million.

June 1998 Souter announces tie up with Richard Branson by taking 49 per cent investment in Virgin Rail Group for £158 million. Stagecoach becomes one of Britain's top 100 companies, by joining FTSE-100 index, and shares reach £15 later in the summer.

August 1998   Buys Yellow Bus in Auckland for £35 million giving it an integrated system in the City after the August purchase of majority holding in Fuller's Ferries.

September 1998   Leaves Africa by selling Kenya subsidiary to management buy-out.

November 1998   Kinski appoints Stagecoach's first in-house PR man, Robert Ballantyne, a former *Times* journalist, and also fills two new posts, head of IT and head of human resources.

March 1999   Buys Citybus, Hong Kong's second largest bus company for £181 million, after failure in a bid for Hong Kong Motor Bus which was won by rival FirstGroup. Citybus is later taken off the Hong Kong stock exchange as it becomes wholly owned subsidiary.

June 1999   Acquires 45 per cent stake in Sogin (Sita), Italy's largest private bus operator for £32.5 million and then makes its biggest ever purchase, Coach USA, the largest bus operator in the US for £1.2 billion.

June 1999   Announces pre-tax profits of £219.9 million in the year to April 30 1999, up 39 per cent.

The rise and rise of Stagecoach

Year (to end April)	Turnover £m	Pre-tax profits £m
1984	2.7	0.2
1985	3.5	0.2
1986	3.3	0.3
1987	4.0	0.3
1988	26.2	4.3
1989	36.8	3.5
1990	98.4	2.3
1991	103.4	2.5
1992	140.7	8.2
1993	154.3	13.0
1994	191.0	18.9
1995	337.7	32.6
1996	501.2	43.6
1997	1152.8	120.5
1998	1381.5	158.5
1999	1584.4	219.9

Acknowledgements

This book was written with the active co-operation of Stagecoach's senior executives but it is not an authorised biography. The responsibility for the text is mine alone. However, it is thanks to Stagecoach's co-operation that such a detailed and comprehensive book could be produced. In particular, Brian Souter gave his time for a series of lengthy interviews and has been helpful throughout, despite his initial doubts about the idea. In particular, I am grateful that he understood throughout that the commentary and views in the book are the prerogative of the author. I would also like to give special thanks to Derek Scott for his due diligence. Not only did he go through the history of the company in great detail during a series of interviews, but he also was always available to help sort out details, and he read the draft with a conscientious eye, spotting mistakes worthy of a *Mastermind* contestant.

Several other Stagecoach executives and board members helped extensively: Sandy Anderson, Ewan Brown, Michael Chambers, Keith Cochrane, Ben Colson, Brian Cox and Barry Hinkley.

I would also like to give particular thanks to John Mair of Mair Golden Moments, who let me use his extensive archives from his television programmes and provided advice and insights throughout the project.

Other people who helped include: Gavin Booth (for historical insights), Caroline Cahm, Stuart Cosgrove, Roger Ford, Chris Green, Richard Gardner, Robin Gloag, Richard Hannah, Keith A. Jenkinson (whose bus-spotters' guide was incredibly useful), Michael Morgan, David Myrrdin-Evans, Steve Norris, Veronica Palmer, Gordon Prentice MP, Randeep Ramesh, Patrick Shergold, Ann Christin-Sjolander, David Souter, Graham Stevenson, Stuart Turner (for an excellent analysis of Manchester), David Watson, Peter White, Birgit Wolmar (for the Swedish translations) and many others who must remain anonymous or whom I have forgotten to mention.

Particular thanks are due to Martin Higginson and Doug Jack, who read the draft and picked up many mistakes and errors. Penny de Abreu typed up the interviews with astonishing accuracy and clarity.

There are lots of Stagecoach workers who gave me their views, necessarily anonymous and in particular a group at Burnley & Pendle who showed me the sharp end, all of whom are due thanks. A number of bus users and former workers also kindly responded to my requests for help.

The project was originated by Martin Liu at Orion Books who, I hope, feels his patience has been rewarded.

Finally, I would like to thank my partner, Scarlett MccGwire, for casting her critical eye over the draft and for being helpful and supportive throughout the project, and our children, Molly, Pascoe and Misha, for lighting up my life.

Prologue: The man who lost £15 million

On the day Brian Souter met me to discuss arrangements for this book over lunch, he was £15 million poorer than when he had shaved that morning. Indeed, he looked like a man on his uppers. He was hunched, appearing tentative and unconfident as he came into the hotel reception, apologising for his lateness. His beige woollen jacket had a cracked button and clashed dreadfully with his blue-and-yellow-checked cowboy shirt. The Tesco plastic bag he was carrying in lieu of a briefcase was on its last legs, as it was bulging with papers and it had already endured a flight from Edinburgh.

But we were in the Palm Court Restaurant of the Waldorf in London's Aldwych where thin sandwiches are £7.95 and tea is £5 for two and Souter was decidedly chirpy. He seemed completely oblivious to his morning's loss, which had been caused by an overall 7 per cent fall in the stock market, resulting in a 40p drop in Stagecoach's price. Souter holds 33.6 million shares, a 14 per cent stake in the company, worth around £350 million, and he had retained them despite knowing the Stock Exchange was overvalued.

He smiled, and those sharp grey-blue eyes twinkled: 'I knew there needed to be an adjustment. I had been expecting it. It's nothing to do with our company. I think you will find the underlying trend for Stagecoach is good.' Indeed, the fall on that autumn day in 1997 was just one of those periodic hiccups in the Exchange, a couple of days of panic that might have presaged another Black Monday but in the event did not.

The clothes and the plastic bag have become Souter's trademark and they are now part legend, part disguise. He says that one of the reasons he left his first job, with Arthur Andersen, the accountants, was because he hated wearing a suit all the time. He had been frowned upon the first day when he wore a jumper under his jacket. He has never felt obliged to dress in a conforming way in order to please his associates. He admits that, in the early days, 'I wore a suit to go see the bank manager when we needed a loan. I didn't want Stagecoach to be affected by my eccentricities.'

Indeed, when the company floated in April 1993, his City advisers, UBS, made him wear smart clothes and carry a briefcase for a month during the run-up to the flotation. But now, with the shares over ten times higher than at flotation, there is no such pressure on him. When he had to go and see a City banker recently, he asked whether he should wear a suit.

'Oh, no, don't,' he was told by a City adviser. 'They know all about you.' Indeed, if he were to wear a suit, his advisers feel it would suggest he had bad news to impart.

As for the plastic bags: he hates briefcases and since he flies so much, finds them inconvenient: 'You can't get a briefcase under your seat on a plane. And it's easier to get through security.' He spends his hours on planes working his way through vast amounts of paperwork, most of which he leaves dumped in the pocket in front of his seat.

He says the downdressing is not a disguise: 'I didn't set out to fool them by wearing casual clothes.' But clearly the idea has occurred to him since. Being underestimated, having your opponents take you for a naive, out-of-town hick, is a powerful weapon.

Money is not his motivation and that is why he can shrug off his morning loss of £15 million: 'I can't say I'm not interested in it. It is a measure of success but I've never been tempted to, say, get a Rolls-Royce, to show that I've reached the top.'

He has, instead, a high-mileage Jaguar: 'It's not tax-efficient to have a company car since I only use it to go to the airport and back.' He bought the car off the company but 'if I lost it tomorrow, I wouldn't care'.

Balding, short and hunched, hesitant and unrelaxed with strangers, with a whiff of Bob Mortimer of Reeves and Mortimer about him, he must have fooled many neighbouring passengers on those endless shuttle flights to Heathrow into thinking that he could not afford a taxi from the airport rather than that he was rich enough to be able to buy the aircraft – and a few others – on which they were seated. The skin of his face is pockmarked but those clever eyes and the little mouth which breaks easily into a smile give him an easy charm that wins over almost everyone he talks to: 'I don't think I have many enemies' he says disarmingly. He pauses, thinking. 'John Mair [who has produced four highly critical documentaries about Stagecoach] just kept on trotting out the same people. He couldn't find any others. You can talk to all the people I've done deals with, people who have left the company and none of them will say that I have ever done anything dishonourable.'

He was not entirely happy about co-operating with the book and spent an hour at an earlier meeting grilling me about my personal circumstances and views before agreeing to help with it. He also convinced his fellow directors – who were even unhappier – that it was a good idea. 'The publicity has been so awful that we can't lose.' Indeed, Stagecoach has, so far, been much more famous for its battles with the authorities and its reputation for aggression, than for its phenomenally successful performance.

Souter had been late for lunch but lingered at the end: 'I was late for you and I can be late for them.' But eventually he rushed off, grateful that I had offered to pay the bill, the least I could do for a man who had lost £15 million in a morning.

Two decades ago, Brian Souter barely had £1,500 to his name, let alone £15 million. Stagecoach started as a tiny business with a couple of coaches, a few thousand pounds in capital and the energy of its brother-and-sister team who created it, Brian Souter and Ann Gloag. It was like thousands of tiny businesses across the country, many of which go bust every week.

But right from the beginning Stagecoach was different because it had Brian Souter, with his exceptional business brain, at the helm. Brian Souter made Stagecoach. Of course a lot of people helped on the way, most notably his co-founder, Ann Gloag, who worked as tirelessly and hard as Souter and shared in all the vital business decisions. But as a City analyst put it, 'Without Brian, Ann could have built up a sizeable regional operation but it took Brian's genius to make Stagecoach into a major concern which is likely to reach the FTSE 100.'

So this book on the rise and rise of Stagecoach has, also, to be the story of Brian Souter. Because he is wary of the media and an outsider who lives in Perth, the extent of his achievement has been greatly underreported. For a long time, he was also overshadowed by his sister, who was, at times, deliberately put forward by Stagecoach as the front person for the company, partly in a vain effort to give it a softer image and partly because, as a woman, she attracted most publicity.

Despite Gloag's achievement in becoming Businesswoman of the Year in 1990, it is Souter who was primarily responsible for the exponential growth of what was to become Britain's largest start-up company since the arrival of Margaret Thatcher in 10 Downing Street. It was Souter who saw the opportunities as successive rounds of legislation opened up the coach market, local bus services and then the rail industry. Thanks to his foresight, Stagecoach got in first at every stage. The company was the first to try to run long-distance bus services in the early 1980s against the established monopoly operators, it was the first outsider to buy one of the National Bus Company concerns, and it became the first company to win a rail franchise. These processes of deregulation and privatisation resulted in the creation of hundreds of small companies run, mostly, by former bus workers and managers, and the vast majority have gone back to coaching or been bought up by larger concerns. Yet Stagecoach survived and flourished thanks, in no small part, to Souter's vision.

All this happened in an industry as unfashionable as Brylcreem and hot pants. To say that the bus industry was a Cinderella of the transport sector was to exaggerate its potential. At least she became a princess. Buses were thought to be a dying industry, on their way to becoming as redundant as, well, stagecoaches. The industry was caught in a vicious cycle of decline. Every year there were fewer passengers and increased subsidies. Buses were being killed by the car. For every household that acquires a car owner, its members take 200–300 fewer bus journeys per year. As fewer people used buses and the services became increasingly uneconomic, fares went up, further reducing usage by anyone who had an alternative. Worse, the cars that these former bus passengers started to drive clogged up the streets, increasing the journey times of the remaining buses. It seemed like the industry from hell, not one for budding entrepeneurs.

Because this grim scenario deterred the interest of many potential rivals and because Souter was confident he knew the industry from his experience working as a bus conductor, Stagecoach was able to take advantage of the situation created by the new legislation without having to face fierce competition. No one else was very interested in this industry where the customers were mostly women, pensioners and schoolchildren, and, God forbid, the poor. Or as Souter put it in his London Transport lecture in October 1997, the best customers are those living above the line between the Bristol Channel and the Wash who are 'the beer-drinking, chip-eating, council-house-dwelling, Old-Labour-voting masses'. Not much scope, there, for the marketing men and the City whizz kids.

Stagecoach is interesting for many other reasons apart from the fact that it is an archetypal rags-to-riches story (in any case, while the riches are indeed real, the rags are metaphorical since Souter's parents were solid, respectable blue-collar stock). The bus industry was a test bed for a remarkable Thatcherite experiment during the 1980s. The idea promoted by the late Nicholas Ridley, in the 1985 Transport Act, was to create a free market in bus services. The result was very different from the plan, with the inevitable result that few players survived and Stagecoach's role in this process was key, undoubtedly hastening the maturing of the bus market by pushing out some of its competitors and buying up others.

Through press coverage of Monopolies and Mergers Commission referrals and reports, Stagecoach became notorious, an emblem of the excesses of Thatcherism. The association of highwaymen and stage-coaches made for a lot of easy punning by newspaper headline writers, ignoring the fact that it was the Dick Turpins who did the robbing and stealing and that the stagecoaches and their occupants were the victims. Stagecoach's PR, or lack of it, did not help, nor did Brian Souter's big little mouth, particularly when he berated people complaining about the service from South West Trains because they were wasting their employers' time, telling an Adam Smith Institute conference, 'SWT receives forty thousand complaints a year. That means more than eight hundred people a week get off our trains, go to their work and write a letter of complaint to us. What I want to know is this: do their bosses know?'

Through such media coverage, Stagecoach became the company that everyone loved to hate, particularly Labour politicians. Yet, although the company was a child of Thatcherism, its very existence being owed to her antipathy to anything state-owned and state-regulated, Souter, and his senior executives did not embrace the Lady's ethos. Gordon Brown, the Chancellor after the 1997 General Election, describing a meeting with Souter at a business dinner in the early 1990s, recalled that the Stagecoach Chairman was the only other person at their table who shared his views on the Tories' social policies. Indeed, Souter defines himself as 'left of centre' and has never voted Tory.

When he was a bus conductor, he went on strike several times out of class solidarity, abiding with a majority vote even though he often disagreed with the decision to take industrial action. In April 1998, Souter became the first private-sector employer to address the Scottish TUC and sang a bowdlerised version of 'The Red Flag', Labour's anthem, to rapturous applause, much warmer than that accorded to Donald Dewar, the then Scottish Secretary. And he must be the only chairman of a billion-pound quoted company to insist on writing 'Not for Trident' on the cheque for the company's 1987 Corporation Tax payment, in line with his pacifist views. The Revenue ignored the endorsement and banked the money regardless. Souter sends his children to state schools, believing that 'education should be universally provided and the level of provision should be adequate for everyone'. He is supporting the Labour govern-ment's welfare-to-work proposals, seeking to develop a special company scheme which will maximise the number of potential trainees and increase the chances of success. As Andrew Smith, the minister in charge of the scheme, said to me on the day he met Souter, 'unlike some businessmen, Brian really understands what it is like for twenty-three-year-olds who have never had a job'.

Souter is not interested in the trappings of wealth, although he has bought himself a nice pile in Crieff, near Perth and drives his Jaguar. His sister, however, has indulged herself rather more, famously buying herself Beaufort Castle near Inverness off the Lovat family who had hit hard times and lost too many heirs, and a Bentley with the number plate, ANN 1, bought, according to the locals, from that other rather wealthy Ann(e), the Princess Royal. In the space of a generation, the siblings have gone from working-class to Scottish gentry.

This was nicely demonstrated on the train up to Perth, one evening, when in the dining car I sat opposite an aristocrat called Lord Palmer. He has a fabulous home himself, Manderston, near Berwick upon Tweed, which contains Britain's only silver staircase, and comes from the Huntley and Palmer biscuit family, though, he said sadly, the company is now owned by a French firm, BSN.

Hearing that I was off to visit Stagecoach, he said, 'Well, you could do me a favour.' The Right Honourable Lord Palmer got out his business cards and gave me two of them. 'I'm the chairman of the Historic Homes Association for Scotland and I wrote to Mrs Gloag about eighteen months ago asking if she wanted to join our association.' It was soon after she had bought Beaufort Castle, near Inverness.

'We need all the members we can get because it gives us more clout. We are effectively the trade union for stately-homes owners in Scotland. I wrote her a very chummy letter but I have never had the courtesy of a reply,' he said sadly.

I had to report back to him a couple of weeks later that she was not interested. The ex-nurse from the council estate in Perth had turned her nose up at the great Lord, not wanting to join his club.

In many ways, Souter has similarities with Richard Branson. Both are self-made men, who are eccentric, obsessed and eschew suits. But the contrast in their public image could not be greater. Branson is seen as the great saviour, the little man battling against entrenched interests, although the performance of Virgin Rail is tarnishing that image. Souter, however, has managed to get himself portrayed as the big bully pushing smaller operators off the road. Just as Branson's image does not bear up to closer scrutiny, neither does Souter's. What he is trying to do is just as 'customer-focused' as Branson and his ideas about how to achieve it are rather more sophisticated than those of the inarticulate hippy entrepreneur. Therefore it was hardly surprising that the two unconventional entrepreneurs should join together in June 1998 in a deal to secure the funding of Virgin Rail and which could be the first of several joint deals between Virgin and Stagecoach.

Souter might not believe in public-sector ownership, having worked himself as a bus conductor in both Perth and Glasgow when the industry was almost entirely publicly owned, but he does believe in public transport.

Souter strongly defends the performance and the record of his company even though some of its policies appear, at first glance, contradictory. He argues for low fares and yet demands an 18 per cent return on his bus companies. He believes in having as big a network as possible, but is fiercely critical of cross-subsidy. He has got where he is thanks to competition, but argues that most networks should be monopolies, except on busy routes. He feels that smaller operators have no right to come and cherry-pick off his profitable routes by providing 'copycat' services and yet his business started by taking on established operators. He admits that if a Stagecoach-type company tried to start up today, it would never reach the heights he has achieved. Stagecoach was in the right place at the right time to take advantage of the transformation in the bus industry created by deregulation and privatisation.

In analysing the success of Stagecoach, this book examines all these apparent contradictions and paradoxes. The story of Stagecoach is a microcosm of the way that Thatcher changed Britain. By being so innovative, Stagecoach played an important role in that revolution and strongly influenced the shape of both the bus and rail industries. And now it is such a big player in those industries that the Labour Government, whose White Paper on integrated transport was published in July 1998, badly needs the company as an ally in trying to change transport priorities away from the dominance of the car and towards better public transport. And Stagecoach is entering the world stage, having acquired toll roads in China as well as bus operations from Sweden to New Zealand. For all these reasons, as this book shows, the importance of the story of this remarkable company extends far beyond the industries in which it operates.

1
A Perth boy

The Stagecoach headquarters overlook a damp set of football fields lining the fast moving river Tay and look more like the offices of an unambitious estate agent than the nerve centre of a growing multinational company. The building is on a street corner of a terraced row of shops near the centre of Perth and the large display windows on the ground floor proudly advertise local bus tours and special offers for regular bus passengers.

Inside, two briskly efficient middle-aged receptionists, both with blonde permed hair, deal with a ratatatt of calls from around the £3 billion Stagecoach empire. They waste no time in chit-chat. 'Sandy Anderson for Keith,' says one putting a call through. Mr Anderson is the fattest cat of them all, the man who made over £33 million from the sale of the Porterbrook rolling stock company to Stagecoach and he wants a quick word with the group's finance director, Keith Cochrane.

'Keith's busy ... he's free ... sorry he's away again. You'll have to phone back. Oh, wait a minute, he's free, oh no sorry he's away again.' The calls seem to rain in faster than anyone could humanly cope with, but these ladies, with their soothing Scottish voices, are clearly expert at handling the oddest queries, which range from details of local bus services to concern over the latest share movement, without flapping or hint of exasperation. Monday mornings are particularly busy but the stream of calls seems to go on all day, throughout the week.

Despite the multimillion deals being conducted over these phones – 'We don't write each other many memos,' says Derek Scott the company secretary, 'we prefer to do it all over the phone' – the ground floor where the telephonists sit has the feel of a local bus station reception area. It is dominated by a display of local timetables and leaflets about the Bus Points scheme, the Stagecoach equivalent of Air Miles, in a spindly metal carousel. A poster advertises details of the local Megarider scheme which offers discounts on weekly tickets and another touts a Crieff lunch trip for just £4.50, including a two-course meal.

There is a little letter-weighing machine on a table behind the two hardworked women, who are joined by a third later in the day, and clearly their duties extend to ensuring the mail gets off. In the corner next to the stairs there are two tartan sofas and a matching armchair with a glass table. Only the pile of blue Stagecoach annual reports and a bunch of *Bus Focus* magazines whose entire issue features the company betray the fact that this is the headquarters of one of the UK's top 100 companies rather than the office of a local coaching firm, slightly on its uppers.

Gloag, tiny despite her heels, which barely get her beyond five foot, pops down to usher out a visitor, opening the door for him as he is carrying a box. 'Ann,' says one of the receptionists, 'here's a message for you.'

'Thank you,' she says, as she greets her next visitor and shows him up the windy little stairs. Only thirty people work at this head office, including the sterling receptionists, to run and oversee an empire with an annual turnover of £1.5 billion, which Souter hopes will reach £2 billion by 2002.

Upstairs, the offices are laid out higgledy-piggledy around a winding corridor, the sort of rabbit warren you expect in the offices of those high street solicitors who deal with the local crooks on legal aid. There is a modest boardroom, dominated by a stunning picture of a bus crossing a humpback bridge somewhere in the Highlands and a large office which Souter and Gloag used to share until she decided to withdraw from the day-to-day concerns of the company by going part-time. Mike Kinski, the chief executive appointed in 1998, now occupies that office as he is in Perth most of the time, and Gloag and Souter, who are in Perth only part of the week, are back sharing a much more modest little room. The other senior executives are housed in oddly shaped little rooms, broken up by partitions which add to the cramped feel of the offices. There are few secretaries or assistants, and Stagecoach executives often dial their own phone calls.

The modesty of the headquarters suits Brian Souter. Why, he would say, bother to have expensive offices which require extra overheads when there is no necessity. It is not parsimony but common sense, an example for all the subsidiaries to follow. Stagecoach does not need to impress anyone. Nor does it have to move nearer the financial centre of Scotland, let alone the UK. If people want to do business with Stagecoach, they can come to Perth, an hour or so drive through lovely hilly country away from either Glasgow or Edinburgh airport. Or they can see Souter on his weekly trips around the transport world, plastic bag in hand.

Certainly Souter is not going to move. He was born in this town of some fifty thousand souls and would not dream of foregoing it for some nasty metropolis. He was brought up on the Letham estate on the outskirts of Perth, an early post-war development of boxy and Spartan terraced houses. The local residents say that the standard has gone down, with the arrival of drugs and unruly teenagers, but it still looks like a respectable area of working-class housing, retaining a sense of community lost in so many other similar places.

Nowadays, Letham is serviced by a comprehensive but confusing array of Stagecoach buses criss-crossing the hilly estate on various small streets which seem too minor to accommodate a bus. Souter has indeed ensured that the estate of his childhood and the town where the company's headquarters are still located is well served by his company's buses, but, as elsewhere, it is not sentiment but commerce that has dictated the service pattern. Council house dwellers are big bus users and those on the Letham are no different. But whereas in the past when services were all state-run, the buses would all be double-deckers running solely along the main streets, nowadays smaller 'mini' and 'midi' buses tour round the estates taking the bus to the passenger rather than expecting her – the majority of users are women – to walk half a mile or so to the bus stop in the main road. Souter would argue that it is that type of responsiveness to demand that has been the bedrock of his company's success.

The Letham estate is a 65p bus ride away from Perth town centre, not cheap given that it's only a couple of miles. The pensioners, who predominate, pay just 15p if they show their card, and Souter is quick to point out that about half the rest of the passengers buy a weekly Megarider for £3.50, which allows unlimited travel for seven days.

That's not enough to satisfy many of the travellers. According to a middle-aged woman waiting at the bus stop in a huge mauve skirt, too young to qualify for a pensioners' pass, the services normally run on time but are very expensive. 'They still put the fares up,' says the woman, still waiting for her bus. 'It's thirteen shillings for a short ride. It's wicked.'

As in most areas served by Stagecoach, there is no competition, with all the services being run by the company, which, she says, is no better than its predecessor, Strathtay. The rival lost the local bus war to Stagecoach because, according to a former manager, the drivers refused to take a pay cut and work longer hours to enable Strathtay, then part of the still nationalised Scottish Bus Group, to compete with the new private operator.

In the row of shops in the centre of the estate, built largely in the fifties, few can remember the Souters and no one knows where the house is in which they used to live. There is a Co-op, a Chinese chippy, a pharmacy and a couple of other shops, neither particularly thriving nor on their uppers. The one empty premises has a sign up showing that its owner is applying for a licence to sell alcoholic drinks. Souter, a lifelong teetotaller, would not approve.

Only the man at the garage thinks he knows where the Souters used to live and even he gets it wrong, sending me up some steep steps to Appin Terrace when, in fact, the house is one block below, in Brahan Terrace. It is a three-bedroom flat in a small house, no different from any of those around it. The young man who lives below is apparently now a bus driver but he will not attain the riches of the previous occupants unless he wins the Lottery several times over. Outside the house, an old man is repairing his car and recalls the Souters as an unremarkable couple who worshipped at the Church of the Nazarene some distance away.

In 1954 when Brian was born (on 5 May), the Letham was a place of great pride for the inhabitants. Stuart Cosgrove, now a Channel 4 TV executive, who was also brought up on the estate, remembers it as a respectable working-class area: 'The estate was new. Quite a lot of people were rehoused from prefabricated houses built after the war and we were the first people in them.' It was before the days of mass unemployment: 'Most people had jobs. As well as farming, Perth had a lot of industry: whisky like Bell's and Famous Grouse, General Accident had their HQ there and there was a big glassworks.' Drugs were unknown, though there was quite a lot of drunkenness.

Brian and Ann were brought up in a small house on the estate, the little boy sharing a room for a while with his big sister who was eleven years older than he was, just as for many years they were to share an office together long after Stagecoach could have afforded to provide them with separate ones. The oldest child, David, who was later to become a missionary in Africa and then a Church of Scotland minister, had his own room and left when Brian was eight. Brian describes his childhood as 'blissful' and outlines a fifties ideal: 'Our home was full of laughter. There was no television. We had conversations, told jokes and played music.'

The Souters' parents are lifelong members of the Church of the Nazarene, which has also been a dominant influence on Brian throughout his life. The Church of the Nazarene is a small group of about four thousand Wesleyan Methodists, formed at the turn of the century and active in Scotland, mainly around Glasgow, and other parts of Northern Britain, who follow a puritan and strict regime. When Brian was growing up, the rules were incredibly strict with, as David put it, 'no drinking, no smoking, no entertainment not to the glory of God and no TV in the house. Dancing and the cinema, all that was out.' David, eight years older than Brian, found the austerity more difficult to cope with and left home to go to London when he was a teenager.

Members of the church are supposed to pay it a tithe 10 per cent of their income. Souter now makes up the tithe through large donations via his Souter Foundation, as does Gloag through her own charity, Balcraig, named after her house near Perth.

As ever with such puritanical religions, the credo has weakened somewhat and the rules on drinking have softened, but the Souters' parents still will not watch TV in their house, although the children gave them one a few years ago. Ann has long abandoned abstention but Brian has never drunk and neither has he ever smoked.

Brian doesn't want me to write about his religion. He sees it as a private matter and dislikes the inevitable media spin, but it is impossible to avoid some mention of it because clearly his credo informs his business practice. As a prominent Methodist said to me, 'Methodists are very good at making money because so many other pursuits are denied to them, what else can they do?' They are, too, he said, supposed to be 'timid in relationship to the world, the flesh and the devil', a term that well fits Brian's persona.

Money and its trappings have never been his motivation. He says he has always been careful with money, putting some away from his first earnings when he was berry picking at the age of ten.

'I was buying and selling cars at the age of fifteen,' and saving the money. He feels it is part of the Scottish character – not meanness, but a certain care and feeling of responsibility about money. 'Stewardship' is a word he uses a lot in relation to the fortune he has accumulated. Despite Souter's strong Calvinistic underpinning, it would be mistaken to characterise him as austere or severe. He is witty and charming, and laughs a lot. His after-dinner speeches have had people rolling between the tables with laughter. He has none of the closed-mindedness that many strongly religious people exhibit, and nor does he expect others to share his faith. There are no prayers preceding board meetings. He is an ideas man, seeking to work things through and to understand processes to ensure that he is best placed to second-guess the future. Nor does his timidity manage to disguise what everyone perceives when first meeting Souter: that he has a sharp brain and, moreover, he knows it and is confident of his abilities. Hardly anyone who has met Souter dislikes him, although some question whether his Christian ethic accords with his business practice.

Their father, Iain, a 'sturdy balding man' according to Stuart Cosgrove, was a bus driver, for Alexander's, which became part of the Scottish Bus Group while he was working for it. Iain had been a shepherd in his youth, working for £25 for half a year during the 1930s depression, a struggle that ensured he strived to save his family from a similar fate. David Souter says his father had a 'fierce' work ethic and a natural entrepreneurial bent: 'He drove buses, drove taxis at night, and sold cars, making far more money out of selling cars then he ever did out of driving buses. He was a dealer. He struggled his way up and he never wanted his wife to work, and she never did.' The long hours took their toll on family life: 'I would rather have seen more of him during my childhood, more of him as a person,' said David.

Derek Scott, who was Stagecoach's finance director between 1987 and 1996 and is now the company secretary, recalls how Iain made money out of second-hand cars: 'You could buy a car in rural areas and bring them down to Edinburgh or Glasgow and make a quick profit. Ann and Brian's dad used to club together with a group of friends, everyone putting in a fiver or tenner, and do that. Funnily enough, when my brother and I lived in Glasgow, we saw you could do the same sort of thing by taking cars south of the border and selling them in Carlisle where we were both born. We never did it but Brian's dad did. It's an entrepreneurial style which their family had and mine didn't.'

Brian Souter clearly learnt from his father's example, telling the *Sunday Telegraph* in 1996, 'My father taught Ann and I how to deal. He used to say that selling cars was easy if you bought them at the right price.'

Ann and Brian's mother, Catherine Souter, also showed a bit of entrepreneurial flair. She used to help out on the summer berry-picking trips, which were arranged to help the farmers gather in their crops for Smedley's and Robertson's and other big food companies. Described by one of the pickers as 'a busy little woman with a shock of grey hair', she was the 'gaffer', planning the trips and selecting who was to go on them, Iain would help by organising the transport. The pickers were paid threepence [about 1.25p] a pound, and those who resisted the temptation of eating too much could earn a tidy sum.

Brian always loved buses. He still has a collection of twenty or so different toy buses on the table next to his desk in his office in Perth, some of them models of the 12,000 buses which Stagecoach owns, and he remembers the first one he bought with his own money earned from berry picking: 'It was a Leyland Atlantean, a double-decker which was new at the time. I had seen it in the paper shop and really fancied buying it. I wanted to earn the money myself and I remember working as a wee boy all day to try to get the five shillings I needed to buy it. My mother wanted to help me but I didn't want to take help from her.'

Of course, he already had a garage full of buses which he had been given as presents and he made his first big financial error: 'I painted them all the same colour – a ghastly clash of red at the bottom and turquoise at the top – which was a shame because I knocked all the value off them by doing that.' It is a policy he has retained, as Stagecoach, unlike some of its rivals, right from the beginning painted all its buses in its livery of white with the three stripes: blue, red and orange.

At the age of five, he was already creating a putative bus company, mapping out roads on the carpet and running services: 'I was always short of buses. I was always planning where all the buses would go and my folks would get mad at me because they used to fall over them all the time, because I used to leave them in particular positions round the floor.' His father's conductress, who dropped in for tea, used to give him cardboard tickets to play with. Like many little boys, he said he wanted to be a bus conductor, and indeed, he did later work as one for several years.

At school, he says, he was not a very good pupil. He did 'OK' at primary school but got into trouble in his third year at the Perth Academy, the mixed secondary school where all the bright local children went: 'I flunked the third year and I wasn't getting leave to sit any O Grades [the Scottish equivalent of O Levels]. I either had to repeat a year or change my courses.' His father was not pleased and told Brian that he didn't mind whether he went back to school or not: 'I don't care what you do but you're not going back to school to mess about. If you go back you have to make a go of it, or otherwise go and get a job.'

Souter decided to return to school and change his subjects. He had two problems. First, he was the class joker: 'I was always making havoc in the class, making everybody laugh. I wasn't destructive or anything, just mischievous.'

Secondly, the man who is famous through the City for being able to assess a company's worth with a quick glance at its balance sheet is bad at maths: 'I dropped maths. I cannot do maths. I've a mental block about it. I can't understand algebra. All those xs and ys, don't make any sense to me and seem totally pointless. I just could never bring myself to learn it.' He also dropped physics and chemistry, which he was useless at, and took up economics and accounts. He became a model pupil, gaining the Dux award, for being top of the class in both subjects. He ended up with eight O Grades but none in maths.

Not having maths nearly proved his undoing. He had difficulty in finding a suitable course because of the lack of maths and eventually he went to Dundee College of Technology to do a Diploma in Commerce, a Scottish qualification which would have enabled him to teach economics and accounts in schools. It was a very practical and general course which included various types of accounting, shorthand and typing, 'which most of the boys hated'.

Part of the course involved a secondment for six months during which students were supposed to gain outside experience. It was the most enjoyable time of his studies, but led to a confrontation with the local mafia. Ever entrepreneurial, Souter decided that, rather than join a big organisation, he would get practical experience of running a business. Using his savings, he bought an ice cream van and, with a friend who is now a teacher, drove round the housing estates in Perth dispensing cones and lollies, calling themselves Jock's Ice Cream.

Although the project was really only meant to be a project for the course, they not only made money but became very popular round the estates because of the quality of the product. They bought it from a supplier in Dundee and Souter reckoned 'it was the best quality in the area. We developed strong brand loyalty as people would wait for our van rather than the others.' And there was a terrifically high profit margin, up to 150 per cent, because the ice cream cost only a few pence a gallon. Jock's sold only ice cream because Souter refused out of religious principle to sell tobacco or alcohol, and he realised that groceries such as bread and milk were not worthwhile as the margins were too low.

The success of the enterprise, however, attracted unwanted attention in the form of a local ice cream baron called Renato, 'who would curse and block our wee van in'. One night, Renato decided to apply stronger pressure and arrived with six vans who surrounded Souter and his mate. With some nifty driving, Souter managed to wriggle his way out, and continued in business, refusing to be intimidated by Renato's threats.

Souter not only ran the ice cream business but also, during his six-month secondment, worked full-time on the buses. He had started working for Alexander's in Perth, his dad's firm, as soon as he started at Dundee. It was better paid than his first job, as a shop assistant, and more fun and he had always wanted to be independent rather than a burden on his family. He was still living at home and at the time his father was ill, which meant money was short. With his older brother and sister gone, he was the only person in the house with a job.

Worried that the ice cream business would not make enough to support him, rather than giving up his part-time work on the buses during those six months, Souter did the opposite and went full-time. It meant horrendously long days, especially as his partner, despite being 'really hard-working', kept on failing his driving test. Souter would sign up for the earliest possible shift on the buses and during the lunch break, drive off to the cash-and-carry to buy the ice cream, and finish his shift in time to have the van ready for the children coming out of school. And he would keep driving it well into the night, even though he had to be up at dawn the next day.

He admits he was overstretched and sometimes had to ask Ann, or her husband Robin Gloag, to help out on the van: 'I was always coming up with these daft ideas in the family and then get everybody else to do all the work and get involved. I worked myself ragged.'

One of the myths around Souter is that he is a bus conductor who has climbed up the ranks. In truth he is an accountant who worked for a while as a bus conductor – in much the same way as many students work at McDonald's or in pubs – and then founded his own business. He had decided to train as an accountant when he finished the course, but, while he was at Dundee, the Institute of Chartered Accountants of Scotland changed its entry requirements, so that diplomas like his would no longer enable students to qualify to go on to an accountancy course. He was devastated, especially as he had done very well on the course.

'So when I was twenty-one, I had this diploma with distinction to be a teacher and that was the last thing in the universe I wanted to do because teaching bored me rigid and I had already decided I didn't want to do it.' After a lot of hassle, he managed to persuade Strathclyde University to take him as a mature student, without O-Grade maths, straight into the second year of the accountancy degree. But because he had already done a diploma, he received no grant and didn't even get the fees paid for him, though he eventually obtained a bursary from the Carnegie Trust to cover them.

So Souter went back to work on the buses, this time for the state-owned Central SMT Company in East Kilbride. His days were even more stretched, with a crazy schedule that few people could match, especially as he is not a particularly good early riser. He worked in the mornings on a shift that started at 4.49 a.m. To reach the depot on time, if his old Saab 96 was working, he would not have to wake up until 4 a.m. However, on the frequent occasions when the car was off the road, he would have to get up at 3 a.m., and walk for two miles through the East End of Glasgow to pick up the staff bus at 3.30 a.m. He would do a couple of those factory runs, and then take a bus into Glasgow in time for his lectures, which started at 9 or 10 a.m., turning up in his conductor's uniform. Sometimes he would leave the college at 2 p.m., then do the other half of the shift starting at 2.40 p.m. through till 7.30 p.m. Or he would do a later one which started around quarter to four, and, because he worked overtime, sometimes it would not finish till close to midnight, leaving him with, at best, four hours' sleep. On Saturdays, he would often work a double shift because it was paid at twice the normal hourly rate and one day he managed to do twenty hours in the day. Sundays, however, were sacrosanct and he never worked on the Sabbath. Indeed, he played music, his only hobby. Despite his work and his onerous studies, Souter had enough spare time to get involved with the gospel band called Bottom Line, in which he sang and sometimes played the piano for many years.

Even then, he found time to take on yet another commitment. He obtained a job at the College of Commerce, taking a three-hour night class on Wednesdays: 'I got three pounds per hour for that, which was incredible money as I only got around thirty bob (£1.50) an hour on the buses. So I had to fit all my shifts round my university lectures and my night class.' The week he did his term exams in his first year he remembers doing seventy-seven hours on the buses, as the company was short of staff, as well as sitting his exams and doing his night class. Unsurprisingly, he got lousy marks in those exams and had to really cram during his second – and final – year.

His phenomenal level of work was stimulated not only by the need to pay his way through university, but also by his strong sense of public duty: 'I always had a very strong sense of obligation. I hated the thought that we'd be cancelling buses because I wasn't available. Eventually, I wasn't really seeking the overtime but they would come and ask me if I could help them out and if I didn't do the work, they would cancel the service. I would say to the traffic controller, Rory, "I can only go up to nine-thirty today, because I've got a lecture," and he would say, "Just do what you can and we will just bring the bus off the road when you need to go to the university." '

His dedication was legendary. John Elliott, the depot manager who was Souter's boss at East Kilbride and who is now operations director of Strathclyde Buses, recalls an incident in which Souter was beaten up: 'He was on the 77 bus from East Kilbride to Hairmyres and as we'd had some trouble on that route on Saturday nights, we had some policemen and myself travelling on the bus. We thought the fighting would be upstairs but at a place called Westwood, one of these fellows got up and punched Brian in the face. The police were assaulted, too, and chased him off the bus. We continued, with Brian holding a tissue to his bloodied nose. We got to the terminus and I said that we would take the bus out of service. But Brian would have none of it, and insisted on remaining as the conductor on the return trip back to East Kilbride. Even as a twenty-one-year-old, he had this amazing sense of dedication.'

The attack prompted a protest strike the following week, despite Souter's efforts to prevent what was standard practice when there was a serious assault. Souter recalled, 'I spoke to Jimmy McClelland, the shop steward, and told him, "Jimmy, don't bring everybody out on account of me. I'm only here part-time, it's not fair to everybody else." '

McClelland would have none of it: 'You're a member of the union, same as everybody else.' So they all came out for the day. Despite his reservations about the strike action, Souter remembers the incident with some pride: 'Even though I was an accountant, they all went on strike. It's funny, but while I was at university, my bus workmates treated me as one of them, whereas they didn't treat the other students in the same way. I think it was because I was working-class, and friendly with everybody, and part and parcel of what was going on within the union.'

Indeed, Souter went on strike several times during his seven years on the buses between 1972 and 1979, the famous winter of discontent. He says, 'We were on strike all the time. Central had a terrible industrial record. Sometimes, the strikes went on for seven or eight weeks. It was a terrible situation and the trade union spent its time at war with the management. We took industrial action over wages, shift patterns, even things like heaters in buses.' Souter was in the union and followed the decision of the meetings: 'If the vote went, you went on strike. It was working-class solidarity and you stood by the strike.'

He remembers speaking against industrial action on one occasion. Mass meetings were held out in the cold in the yard and everyone made speeches. It was January and freezing, and Souter tried to warn his colleagues that they were playing into the hands of management. He got up and said, 'It's easy to go on strike, but the same ones that are voting for a strike, you'll be the first that'll be back when the electricity bills come in. If we are going to strike, then we should strike until we win, so don't vote unless you mean to stay out until you see the thing through.'

It was to no avail. The strike was called and they were out for several weeks: 'It was in 1976 and I was proved right. It seemed so daft. You hand it to management on a plate. It was patently obvious management wanted to precipitate a strike in January. We should have just worked to rule. All the hotheads make everybody have a strike, the electricity bills come in and two weeks later they start drifting back and what have you achieved? Nothing.'

The continuous bouts of industrial action had a disastrous effect on the bus service and many drivers left. Souter reckons the passenger base was destroyed: 'Folk on the country buses were lost for good. They found lifts and we never got them back. We went back to our jobs, but it was never the same again.'

Souter was critical of the management in other respects, too. Although the buses were heavily loaded and very profitable, the management wanted to convert them to one-person operation. This was prompted by a labour shortage which Souter said was created by the fact that negotiations were carried out nationally because Central SMT (later half of Kelvin Central) was part of the Scottish Bus Group: 'People were paid the same across the country, which was ridiculous. So while wages of crews in Perth were well above what anybody else in the town could make, in Glasgow it wasn't like that. It was a different labour market and this was the age of full employment. Women could earn as much in twenty hours on a twilight shift as we were making on the buses. In Glasgow, we needed overtime just to make ends meet, right?' As Chapter 10 shows, Souter has been adamantly opposed to having a national wage agreement for Stagecoach, although he has been prepared to negotiate nationally with the unions over various other aspects of their work, such as bus design and uniforms.

Souter also reckoned one-person operation was inappropriate: 'We used to have these big double-deckers and they were converting to one-man operation. The buses were taking 20–30 per cent longer and they had to put extra buses in the cycle. It made the bus service less attractive.' Interestingly, though, Stagecoach nowadays has very few two-person buses.

Above all, Souter was frustrated by the way that the company was run: 'It was all done very remotely. Many of the stoppages were because two people in Edinburgh couldn't agree with one another. It was nothing to do with local issues half the time. There were a lot of good people, a lot of good ideas, but the staff were not motivated and it was not a good way to run a company. I've always been fairly Left and I think in a way I wanted to make state capitalism work. But it didn't work.'

Despite all the problems, Souter could see the opportunities for profit. The services he worked on, mainly between East Kilbride, five miles outside the city, and Glasgow, were amazingly busy. He reckons that on a Monday morning, by the time he had done an early shift, he could have collected £230, whereas his basic wages for the twenty-hour week were just £30. Souter would make sure that everyone paid their fare. John Elliott says that when Souter was on the number 21, which was very heavily used, 'he would stop it at the bottom of a big hill and collect all the fares before letting the bus go on.' That way, no one was tempted to dodge the fare as they would not get off before the climb.

At the time, Souter had vague ambitions about becoming chairman of the Scottish Bus Group to transform it into an efficient operation. He liked the idea of taking over the company for which his dad worked, but in the event, because the group was broken up on privatisation, his dream was only partly realised. Twenty years later, Stagecoach, with Souter as chairman, would be the owner of three out of the SBG's ten companies.

Souter managed to concentrate on his studies more in the second year, taking five weeks off work, and he passed his exams with distinction. The university offered him the opportunity of staying for another year to get an honours degree, but he felt he had to get a job. He tried all the big accountancy firms and found that they were unwilling to take on this softly spoken and earnest son of a bus driver: 'I had a terrible time when I got interviewed by some of these accounting companies because they are terrible snobs. I didn't go to the right school, I didn't live in the right street and my father wasn't in the right occupation. They kept on asking me about my dad's occupation and I felt like telling them, "What's it got to do with you? You're not giving the job to him." So people like Coopers and Lybrand, Deloitte's and Touche never gave me a job because they were heavily into public school and the right sort of background.'

The rejections infuriated him, and he still feels strongly about his treatment: 'I did feel quite angry with it. I wasn't brought up with a big chip on my shoulder. The middle class teach their children that they're better than anybody else, but we weren't taught that. We were working-class. I was taught by my parents that we were as good as anybody else and could not be pushed about or bullied by anybody. I had never realised that all this class stuff really existed because I felt very confident, as we'd been brought up with a good set of values. We didn't feel disadvantaged, we felt we were advantaged. It was a good upbringing, really, secure, with a lot of good things and we felt really positive.'

Fortunately for him, one big accountancy firm was prepared to look at

Souter's undoubted ability rather than his background: Arthur Andersen, whose US origins may have meant the company was more of a meritocracy than its British counterparts. He started as a trainee accountant with Arthur Andersen in 1977, working around Scotland on auditing the books of its clients, but immediately fell foul of the firm's dress code because of his aversion to the cold: 'I got into trouble for wearing a jumper. They told me not to wear one. On the buses, when you are cold, you wear a jumper but at Andersen you weren't allowed to.'

Andersen also had to cope with his refusal to work on Sundays. Derek Scott, who was one of his bosses there, recalls, 'The induction course was very intensive because Arthur Andersen reckoned that we might be accountancy graduates, but that didn't mean we knew anything about accountancy. We were sent to France for three weeks and Brian said he would not be able to work on Sundays, as he wanted to go to church. Arthur Andersen had been established in Britain since 1957 and this was the first time that someone had stood up and said this.' Souter got his way.

However, Souter welcomed the discipline that working at Arthur Andersen gave him: 'It was a very important training ground for me because it gave me some professional discipline which I badly, badly needed. It taught me to put things on paper and how to be structured in my approach to things.'

Souter also found the time at Andersen valuable because he learnt about other companies' mistakes while auditing the books of firms involved in the Aberdeen oil boom: 'Some of these guys used to keep growing and growing, and they started to do things they knew nothing about, and all of a sudden they got big financial problems. So I was very privileged because I got to see all these mistakes that other people made and to study them in detail.'

The conventional way of doing an audit is to sit in the office with the accountant and go through the books, occasionally asking a question or two. Souter would do that, but went further, finding information from whatever sources he could, much to Scott's consternation: 'On a whisky distillery audit, I criticised Brian because we had three management accountants working with us in one big room. And I said, "Brian, you're going to spend a lot of time with these guys – you should be asking them a lot of questions." But I'd find Brian would be off down the canteen chatting to the canteen ladies, or walking round the plant.'

Souter always felt that talking to other staff and finding out the gossip was worth the effort. His unconventional approach occasionally bore fruit. On one audit, he discovered, through talking to the cleaners, that the management were actually closing the factory down and the auditors had not been told. Souter told the audit manager, who said that he must be mistaken. 'No, no,' replied Souter, 'they've seen the pink piece of paper in somebody's litter bin' – and, of course, he was proved right.

Souter had a reputation for doing thorough audits, but being a bit slow about them. He was once given a payroll check to do, which was supposed to take thirty hours, and he spent three times that on it. It was, though, according to Scott, 'the best payroll test ever written'.

While Andersen was pluralistic enough to take on someone like Souter, he still did not fit into the company's ethos. He remained an outsider, not least because he did not drink or smoke. He spent a lot of time in Aberdeen, but never went out in the evening with the other young accountants, who were drawn to the pubs and restaurants in the booming town. Souter told them that he lived in Parkhead, Glasgow, where many of his neighbours were alcoholics: 'How do you think it would look if one of my alcoholic Glasgow East End friends sees me going into the pub with my work colleagues? I can't do it.' He did gradually spend a bit more time with them, occasionally going for a meal and drinking orange juice or milk.

Souter was also unique in that he kept up his job on the buses for the first two years of his traineeship at Andersen. He still worked every Saturday as a bus conductor, unknown to the accountancy firm, whose permission should have been sought for moonlighting. The bus company was delighted to keep him on, even though he worked only on Saturdays, because it was always short of staff at the weekend. He even retained his membership of the union until finally he stopped working in 1979 under pressure from his then girlfriend, who wanted him to spend more time with her. Giving up moonlighting, though, did not save the relationship, and he split up with her just before the launch of Stagecoach in 1980.

Back in Perth, Brian's sister, Ann Gloag, had begun to spend some of her time building up a business which, though not a direct precursor to Stagecoach, provided valuable experience in running a small concern. Gloag had already bought and sold a few caravans and in 1976, with a bit of money from her father, she started a business renting them out to holidaymakers, operating out of her home in Glasgow Road, Perth. For Gloag, it was a sideline, as she continued to work as a theatre sister in the burns unit in the local Bridge of Earn hospital. She built up a stock of half a dozen caravans and four or five caravanettes, and her husband, Robin Gloag, who was a good mechanic, started spending most of his time on the business, which was called, with the same rather naff style that was to characterise Stagecoach's early days, Gloagtrotter.

The pair had met when Robin tore a cartilage in his knee while working on a farm and Ann was part of the nursing team in the Perth Royal Infirmary where he was treated. They married when she was in her early twenties, and went to live in Derbyshire for a while but returned to Perth. Robin, whose uncle, Matthew Gloag, was the founder of the Famous Grouse whisky firm, worked as an engineer, but had another accident and had to leave the job. The caravan business was set up partly to make use of his skills.

Their most famous clients were Paul McCartney and his wife, Linda (who died in April 1998), who, two years running, hired a couple of caravans. Robin drove them over to the McCartneys' home in the Mull of Kintyre, where they were used to house singers coming to the ex-Beatle's recording studios there. Robin remembers McCartney as 'very unassuming'. By then, Robin was working full-time on the business, which had begun to expand beyond the caravan and caravanette business, which was very seasonal. They purchased, in March 1980, a Ford Transit minibus for use on contract hire under the name GT Coaches. This was successful and they bought a couple more mainly for hiring out to Balfour Beatty, which was building a bypass locally. Souter, of course, did the books for the business but otherwise was not really involved.

In fact, Souter wanted to drop out for a year and had bought a bus, a forty-five seater Bristol (a former Bristol Omnibus Company ECW-bodied MW5G, according to the bus-spotters), to drive to China with some of his family and a group of friends from his local church youth group. The plan was to convert it into a motor caravan and spend a year going almost round the world.

Communist China, still a closed country following Mao's death three years previously, did British capitalism a big favour. The embassy turned down his request for permission to drive in the country, which meant that Souter, who had rather unwisely bought the bus before checking out the chances of getting into China, was stuck with it. If he had gone, he would have missed the first big opportunity that was to help the establishment of the company, the deregulation of coach travel. Souter, who had a taste for exotic low-budget travel, did eventually get to the Sahara in 1983.

And Souter turned the bus into the business opportunity that was to create Stagecoach. The price of the bus that was to become Stagecoach's first investment is a subject of dispute, being varyingly remembered as either £250 or £425. Either way, that demonstrates it was on its last legs. He lent it to GT Coaches, which, in turn, hired it out to Balfour Beatty. Robin remembers that there was a dispute with Brian over the price of the bus but the arrangement was lucrative for both sides and Brian quickly made his money back.

Souter had always been close to his sister and was keen to work with her. He said, 'I always was sparkling with ideas and Ann would encourage me with them. We've always been able to work well together.' He suggested to Ann and Robin that they make use of the bus that he had bought to start up in coaching, perhaps with a couple of school contracts. He did not see the caravan-hire business as having much potential: 'I said to them, "This is too seasonal." I never had a big vision for the caravan-hire business, although I told them that school buses were a sensible adjunct and they should try to get some.'

If there was one moment when the idea of Stagecoach was born, it was in June 1980, when Souter said to Ann, 'You know there's a change in the law, that you can run coach services. I think we should have a go.' He told me, 'I told her my ideas of the way we should run it and she thought it was a good idea. There was never any hesitation.'

Part of the motive in creating the hire company had been to give Robin a job. An affable former public school boy, Robin was happier working in the backroom, painting or fixing the buses, rather than running a business. He had had a chequered working career and had failed to find permanent employment. Ann had generally been the steadier breadwinner but creating the business offered the chance to give full-time employment to Robin. Expanding the business into a coaching operation ensured he would be able to work full-time and he was made a full partner along with the two siblings, even though, Souter says, Robin did not have a business brain: 'We always felt in our family a bit sorry for him. A lot of the problems he had were really down to the fact that he had been brought up in an environment and educated for high expectations, whereas he was a man who was very good with his hands and at practical things. We knew he wouldn't bring any business acumen to the situation, but he was Ann's husband and we thought making him a partner was a good thing to do.'

Brian left his job at Arthur Andersen in September 1980 to begin building up the business. Indeed, he had tried to leave a few months earlier but after giving his notice found that the Aberdeen-based firm he intended joining was involved in a fraud. Derek Scott reckons that Souter had worked as an auditor for just the right amount of time: 'He learnt a lot but he would have got bored if he had stayed any longer.'

Ann, too, went full-time, both of them paying themselves very little, around £3,000 per year. While the two siblings discussed strategy, Robin was, in his own words, 'underneath buses'.

The Bristol was quickly put into use taking road workers to remote sites and paid for itself within a few weeks. Another second-hand bus, a thirteen-year-old Leyland Leopard, was added to the fleet and the business began to expand, but only by relying on short-term contracts, which were not a sufficiently strong basis to build up a sizeable concern. But Margaret Thatcher had won the election in May 1979 and through deregulation of the bus and coach industries she was to give Souter and his sister the opportunity they needed to start a business whose potential turned out to be almost unlimited.

2
The first opportunity

The coach industry was one of the first to be deregulated by Margaret Thatcher's government soon after its election in 1979. It was an easy and obvious target. Coach services were closely regulated by the Traffic Commissioners, regional officials appointed by the government whose role was to oversee the industry at a detailed level. Operators had to apply for a licence for every service they ran and any alterations, however minor, had to be tabled with the Commissioners. Fares were strictly controlled, giving operators little financial independence and Commissioners normally turned down applications to run services from new operators on the basis that they would affect established ones.

At times the level of detail required by the bureaucracy was baffling and incomprehensible. Not only did the running of every scheduled service have to be lodged with the Commissioners, but tour operators who sold tickets individually to their customers had to register even, say, for a one-off trip to the Lake District or Blackpool. According to Peter White, professor of public transport systems at Westminster University, 'The Traffic Commissioners even demanded details of the mystery coach tours which were very popular at the time and operators had to get a licence for the exact route. They could be in trouble if they deviated from it by a few miles.'

The result, inevitably, was that there were few private operators of scheduled coach services and the industry was dominated by National Express, the coaching arm of the nationalised National Bus Company, which had nearly all of the market for local bus services in most suburban and shire areas in England and Wales. The coaches were provided to National Express by the local companies and the network was relatively undeveloped, as it was seen as a mere sideline of the main business, the provision of local bus services. The potential of coaches using the motorways had not really been exploited, and journeys were slowed by the fact that few vehicles were fitted with toilets. The journey times were not attractive to longer-distance travellers and coaches were, therefore, used only by those who could not afford the train, which was only marginally more expensive. Many routes on which there were regular trains had either an infrequent service or none at all.

Indeed, the tight regulation was partly rooted in the fact that successive governments had been keen to protect the nationalised – and heavily subsidised – railways against competition from what was, essentially, a rival state-owned company. The 1980 Transport Act changed all this. The thinking behind the new measure had been set out in the 1979 Conservative manifesto, which promised that deregulation would 'enable new bus and other services to develop, particularly in rural areas, and will encourage new private operators'.

Under the new Act, the Traffic Commissioners lost many of their powers in relation to coaches. Routes where the shortest journey was at least thirty miles were no longer subject to any controls, giving anyone the opportunity to run interurban express services. Fares control was abolished unless the Commissioners felt that there was 'abuse of monopoly power'.

The measure was controversial and opposed by both the unions and the established operators, but did not create the furore that greeted bus deregulation five years later, because express coaching was a relatively small industry, greatly overshadowed by the railways. Norman Fowler, the transport secretary, stressed that it was a prelude to full deregulation of the industry, which would include local bus services, but the new Government, still finding its feet on how to break up the entrenched interests of the corporate state, was, with hindsight, remarkably tentative.

Privatisation was but a vague notion touted by some right-wing think tanks and though the idea of selling back the shipbuilding and aerospace industries to the private sector was in the 1979 Tory manifesto, the concept of wholesale privatisation of nationalised industries was not on the Government's stated agenda. So the Tories started, rather hesitatingly, with deregulation.

Bus services were largely left alone, apart from in three mostly rural 'trial areas' where local operators were no longer required to apply for licences to run services. Elsewhere, they still had to obtain a licence, but established rivals no longer had what, under the old Road Traffic Act 1930 legislation, was in effect a right of veto. The Commissioners were supposed to view any new operator with a presumption in favour of the applicant, though in practice there were still many barriers to entry in the bus market.

The NBC was a bit concerned, but did not realise, as few did apart from Souter, that the change presaged a complete revolution in the industry. Things would never be the same. The 1979 NBC annual report warned that profitable interurban services would be subject to increased competition and this would result in cutting back less well-used services which were supported through cross-subsidy.

The situation in Scotland before the legislation had been particularly bad, with very few interurban coach routes, apart from a sketchy service linking Edinburgh and Glasgow run by the Scottish Bus Group, the equivalent of the National Bus Company south of the border. There were no express services from Aberdeen to Glasgow and Edinburgh, nor from Inverness to the central belt. People were expected to take the train or drive. The SBG also ran all the services between Scotland and London, a historical accident resulting from the fact that most passengers started their journeys north of the border, which meant that National Express did not operate in Scotland. There was, therefore, quite a market gap, which Brian Souter spotted.

The Act came into force on 6 October 1980 and Souter and Gloag were ready. Souter says, 'I always saw potential in that market. I could see that business getting bigger and bigger, with coaches full of people.'

GT Coaches had expanded in readiness for the deregulation, and now possessed four second-hand coaches, although the caravan and motor-van hire business was not disposed of until 1982, when the coach business began to look secure. The investment in the expansion had been funded thanks to a loan from Iain Souter, Ann and Brian's father, who put in £12,000. Of that, £3,000 came from his redundancy money, as he had lost his job with Alexander's that summer. The Inland Revenue later raised its collective eyebrow at Souter Senior's ability to provide this cash, given that it was four times the amount of his redundancy, and wondered if he had been moonlighting, but eventually accepted his explanation that he had merely hidden his savings. A friend called Kenneth MacRitchie also put in a couple of thousand. Neither of these early investors bought any equity in the firm, as their investment was simply a loan. If they had, they would be millionaires several times over by today. Fraser McColl, Catherine Souter's brother and therefore the siblings' uncle, who was a rich businessman in Canada, put in £16,000 the following year and did rather better. The Revenue refused to treat him as a partner but he was credited with 40 per cent of the Stage-Coach limited company and was bought out in the mid-eighties for £200,000, not a bad return.

Brian, with his phenomenal appetite for work and lack of interest in material goods, had also built up substantial savings through his moonlighting and had a £15,000 nest egg, which he lived on, meaning he made few demands on the business in its early days. Ann did not have any cash, but the bank took collateral on her home and invested the money in the business. This pile of cash, built up largely from family sources to invest in the new firm, was to prove vital, as so many small businesses fail in the early days through lack of working capital. Brian also supplemented his income with deals, having moved from buying and selling cars in his teens and early twenties, to buying and selling houses. The business was later based in one of these properties, in Marshall Place, Perth, after it grew too large to be run from Ann's kitchen. So Gloagtrotter was ready. Three days after the Act liberalised coach services, on 9 October, Gloagtrotter began a new overnight service from Dundee, running four nights a week to St Pancras coach station in North London.

The service was operated mostly by the two most recent acquisitions to the fleet, a Volvo, christened The Stage Coach, the first use of the name, and an AEC Reliance, neither of which boasted an onboard toilet or refreshment facilities. The single fare to London was £9.50 from Dundee or £6.75 from Glasgow, which was much cheaper than the £11.50 charged by the Scottish Bus Group for journeys between Scotland and London. The eleven-hour journey was via a rather circuitous route taking in Perth, Stirling, Cumbernauld and Glasgow in an effort to maximise potential revenue. On the first day, there were thirty-eight passengers – not just two as has often been claimed – who provided the company's first earnings.

At first, the new company was treated as a bit of a joke by others in the industry. Gavin Booth, then the marketing manager of the Scottish Bus Group and now a journalist covering the bus industry, recalls how his bosses would not take the fledgling rival seriously: 'They thought it was a joke. The sober-suited executives smiled at Gloagtrotter's presumption. Imagine this little Scottish company taking on the might of the establishment. And what a silly name – visions of cowboys and all that. They'll be out of business by Christmas. It will all end in tears. That was the prevailing view.' But, as another industry observer, Doug Jack, put it, 'They started by being dismissive, but soon became paranoid.'

And Souter's sartorial eccentricity had already attracted attention. As Booth put it, 'They thought, the boss doesn't even seem to own a suit. He wears casual clothes, allegedly *red* shoes and carries his business papers in a plastic bag. And good grief, the chap's still in his twenties.'

Other managers in the industry reacted more aggressively, possibly sensing that they faced a real challenge. Peter Huntley, who now runs TAS Partnership, which monitors the bus industry, recalls that opposition was fierce: 'When Brian started operating his first bus in 1980, I was a planning assistant with Tayside Transport. My managing director's instructions were to run him off the road. There was an establishment clique who regarded outsiders like him as cowboys to be eliminated.' The unions were also displeased and wanted to block the new company's access to municipally owned bus stations because, at first, Gloagtrotter employed non-union labour.

It was easy for established operators to dismiss the newcomer in those early days when no one knew how the new Act would affect the industry. Gloagtrotter was a small family concern with seemingly limited horizons. The company was still operating out of the Gloags' home in Glasgow Road, Perth, holding the first AGM in the kitchen, and the established operators thought it was doomed to fail. The rather Spartan service, though, began to attract passengers prepared to forego the relative luxury of the established operator for a cheap deal. While passenger loadings were tiny in the first week, the second was a 'Dundee Week' when many of the factories were on holiday and their workers turned to the new service. Traditionally coach travel between Scotland and London had been used by low-income groups – students, the unwaged and older people – and they, too, were attracted by the cheap fares.

Although Souter had originally planned to start off slowly, the success of the first route led to fairly rapid expansion. In January 1981, a twice-daily service was added from Aberdeen to Glasgow, one of which connected with the London-bound coach at Dundee. At the same time, the London service was expanded to operate on five days each week and, a month later, a new overnight service was inaugurated between Aberdeen and Newcastle upon Tyne. People were encouraged to use the service within Scotland by very low fares, such as only £1 between Aberdeen and Glasgow.

In February, the company, which was relatively capital-rich compared with other start-up enterprises, thanks to the borrowed money, bought its first brand-new vehicle, a fifty-seater Volvo complete with toilet.

By the spring of 1981, the overnight London service was being run every night of the week, and in July 1981, a third main service was introduced, just for the summer months, linking Aberdeen with Blackpool, to attract holidaymakers. The Blackpool service was successful right from the start, even though the fare, at £11.50, was much higher per mile than the London services. That winter, Stagecoach tried to run a service for skiers between Perth and Glenshee, operating only when there was snow, Souter having noticed the large number of vehicles heading for the slopes. However, this was one of Stagecoach's early failures and was quickly withdrawn. Another idea, Stagecoach Holidays, was not pursued beyond registering the name. Souter was beginning to exhibit the skills that were to lead to Stagecoach's transformation into a multinational. He was ducking and diving, sucking and seeing, and, on occasion, pushing at the edges of the legislation to test what was allowed. He would try out a route, and quickly assess whether it was profitable. He was not worried about admitting that he had made a mistake, being quite ready to abandon a scheme that proved to be a bad idea. He was ever ready to adapt quickly to changing circumstances. And crucially, Ann was there to bounce ideas off and to prevent his madder schemes from being pursued. As one Stagecoach executive put it, 'If Brian was the car, Ann was the brakes.'

Despite the expansion, Stagecoach remained throughout this period a family-run business firm with Brian doing the accounting and the traffic scheduling, Ann looking after administration and purchasing, Robin driving and helping on the mechanical side, and even brother David Souter occasionally driving. David had passed his test on the morning of the first service from Dundee to London and actually drove that inaugural coach down to London. Brian, too, sometimes did a bit of driving, having gained his Public Service Vehicle licence in July 1981. The parents, too, would help run the business, with both Iain and Catherine preparing the food, first sandwiches and other snacks, and later the hot meals which were provided on some services. The snacks were a real marketing innovation as it meant that passengers did not need to bring or buy their own, and Souter reckons it helped attract a lot of students and pensioners for whom the price of a meal made a difference.

The Stagecoach name was dreamt up by David, who had worked in marketing in London, after much discussion. He says, 'I made up the name. I had been involved in publicity in London and they came to me for ideas. We were talking about licences for stage carriage, and I was trying to get away from the bus image. We wanted to be coach, better than a bus, because we were offering more of a service, like feeding people, and showing videos.' Many suggestions were rejected, the funniest being Urbus which, in Glasgow, would have been pronounced 'Oorbus' and which appealed to Souter's socialist instincts. The new name was soon adopted on all the coaches, replacing Gloagtrotter or GT Coaches, although it took a while before the two words were united, albeit in hyphenated form for a while.

Souter revelled in the 'cowboy image' prompted by the use of the new name, turning up in a sheriff's outfit at the launch of new services, and producing publicity material on paper headed by a rough drawing of a Wild West Stagecoach being pulled by two overweight galloping horses. The marketing stressed both the family nature of the firm and its cowboy image. Under the heading THE STAGECOACH STORY, the 1982 timetable announcing a new Super Stage service had a page on the firm's history, which is remarkably revealing of the founders' self-image and the way they consciously promoted themselves as the small family firm battling it out against the big boys:

> So now to meet the people involved in running a STAGECOACH OUTFIT. First there's Brian THE SHERIFF who should keep the peace but sometimes causes a riot between being accountant, traffic manager and general fac totem (that's Indian language), there's sister Ann who runs THE BUNK-HOUSE; at least she says it often feels like that, while managing the office and everyone else at the same time. Brother-in-law Robin keeps THE LIVERY STABLES going, making sure that the horses are fit and rarin' to go. David, the RANCH FOREMAN actually has two calves on his farmstead but handles the publicity. The important thing is that we all have one job in common and that is driving the buses – we started that way and mean to go on that way.
>
> Granny and Paw (remember him – it's all his fault) provide THE VICTUALS, an ever-growing mountain of rolls, snacks and supplies required daily by the passengers. As the work grew, we had to hire in more RANCH HANDS, each one a character in his own right, but, at the wheel, a professional driver. Behind the scenes, there is a loyal little group of office staff, mechanics and cleaners who keep it all going – so that's THE STAGECOACH FAMILY.
>
> Now do you believe that we really are a family business?

It might have been naff in the extreme, but it worked. Stagecoach attracted lots of free publicity in the Scottish press thanks to these gimmicks and its name became almost synonymous with long-distance coach travel in Scotland. David Souter, who was in charge of publicity and marketing at the time, says, 'We lived on free publicity. It was absolute nonsense but we had a lot of fun and it worked.'

The Super Stage service mentioned in the leaflet was an early example of

Stagecoach's stress on market differentiation. The company had started running a new service between Aberdeen and London, stopping not only at Glasgow but also at Manchester and Birmingham, and costing £15, which included a hot meal. Using the double-decker coaches the operation was run side by side with the more Spartan and cheaper service, and both were well patronised.

Souter admitted later that the purchase of the two Neoplan Skyliners, costing around £100,000 each, for the upmarket London service was the biggest risk he ever took. The big advantage was that they took seventy-five passengers, compared with about fifty on a single-decker, for little extra cost per mile. They represented a big investment for such a small firm and if the new coaches had not quickly paid for themselves, the adventure could have ended there and then. He told a colleague that if the investment had gone pear-shaped, he would have had to go to Saudi Arabia for the rest of his life to pay off the debt. The notion of the strongly Christian Souter living under that authoritarian Muslim regime might, however, be slightly apocryphal.

In fact, there was no need for Souter to run off to Riyadh. The new acquisitions turned out to be particularly opportune, as within days of the purchase, a lengthy rail strike, prompted by ASLEF's rejection of 'flexible rostering', meant Stagecoach's services were massively oversubscribed. Indeed, several other coaches were hired from McLennan's, a small Perth-based company which ran some local services, complete with drivers. Another bit of good luck in the early days was the fact that the first two winters were mild, which reduced the number of breakdowns and stoppages, making Robin Gloag's task of keeping the vehicles on the road easier.

With the Neoplans came the Stagecoach livery. The German company provided them with the three stripes, blue, red and orange, according to a design suggested by Ann, and this was to become the physical expression of the company's spread throughout the UK. David Souter says, 'It was difficult to make a design for a double-decker because of the large amount of window space. The only thing you could do logically was put the stripes on the lower area, and spread them out around the back, and that's what the Germans did.' The new colours were soon universally adopted on the coaches and on publicity material such as timetables in a form that hardly differs from the current design used almost across the whole fleet.

David Souter recalls that the coaches were nearly banned from coming into the UK: 'They were the first anyone had imported into the country. We had a terrible time getting them through as the first one was one inch over forty feet [the maximum length allowable]. It was forty feet at the bottom, but had a slight swelling at the nose. The German authorities also disregarded the bumpers while the UK people counted them in. We spent a day waiting to see if they would let it through and in the end they just grumbled about it and passed it.'

However, the authorities had their tuppenceworth by forcing Stagecoach to lock up the back axle: 'The rear axle was a steering axle. British bus legislation said you could not measure overhangs to include steering axles, which would have pushed us well over the forty feet, and we had to lock up the axle.' That meant the ride was less comfortable and sometimes tyres were ripped off when the coaches went round tight corners. David Souter reckons, 'The coaches were too advanced for the legislation.'

South of the border, National Express managed to see off British Coachways, a consortium of independents, which was the main rival but did not venture into Scotland. North of the border, apart from Stagecoach, there were other smaller Scottish firms such as Cotter's and Park's of Hamilton, but for the first couple of years Souter and Gloag had a relatively clear run and managed to build up a sizeable business. Stagecoach quickly showed its readiness to crush the opposition from other fledgling companies. Tay Valley, a business with three relatively new buses, tried to take on Stagecoach on the Aberdeen–Dundee–Edinburgh route and became the first company to be defeated by Stagecoach's tough approach to competition as the Perth company cut its fares, a response that was to be characteristic of its approach to new rivals. It was also Stagecoach's first use of another tactic that was to become its hallmark: squeezing the opposition by running services immediately in front and behind.

By the end of the second year, Stagecoach's turnover had reached £1.3 million, and the profit margin was an amazing 28 per cent, even taking into account what Souter describes as 'an incredibly conservative depreciation policy'.

It could not last. Others were bound to notice and in a deregulated market there was nothing to stop them competing. The slumbering giant, the Scottish Bus Group, at last decided that there was a market for coaches both within Scotland and between Scotland and London, and began to imitate its small rival. As Souter put it, 'At first everybody thought we were daft, absolutely mental. And then they woke up to the fact that we were highly successful. So between 1982 and 1984, the Scottish Bus Group spent six million pounds on new coaches and marketing, competing on all our services and offering all the same fares.' Operating under the name

Citylink, the SBG simply copied its rival's timetable, a technique that Stagecoach was to employ later in the bus wars.

The fierceness of the competition and the size of its rival could have put Stagecoach out of business. But Souter believes his firm survived because Stagecoach's operation was 'extremely efficient, because we scheduled our coaches like aircraft', extracting much higher usage out of their rolling stock than their rivals, and had attracted considerable brand loyalty: 'People saw us as pioneers and we were extremely popular with them. They didn't switch to other companies.' All the efforts to establish the name had worked. People were 'taking the Stagecoach', rather than the bus.

Souter also realised, having learnt from the experience of the Aberdeen firms he once audited, that this was a time for consolidation and not 'overtrading' or expansion: 'I knew there was going to be discounting and we needed to pull back on some of the things that we did, tidy up and batten down the hatches.' He told his staff to oversell on the London service, to ensure full occupancy just as airlines overbook on heavily used services – sometimes selling the same 'hot' seat twice for different parts of the journey, even if they overlapped for part of it, forcing the passenger to stand for a while. Stagecoach withdrew, somewhat reluctantly, from the recently inaugurated Edinburgh–Glasgow service because Souter reckoned it was too difficult to make money on it.

Souter tried to join together with the other new operators to face off the competition. He spoke to Park's and Cotter's and suggested they form a joint business to combat the Scottish Bus Group: 'I told them that we are all going to get knocked out unless we get together. I suggested we create a triangle, Aberdeen–Glasgow–Edinburgh–Perth–Inverness, and all put buses into that service and make it work.' He warned them that within a couple of years, there would be only two operators, and he was going to make sure that Stagecoach was one of them. They turned him down, but by 1985, Souter's prediction had come true with only Stagecoach and the Scottish Bus Group surviving.

Souter reckons Citylink 'made enormous losses. If we'd known that there was such a thing as the Office of Fair Trading, we probably would have gone, but we didn't know such a thing existed.' Certainly in the decade that followed, Souter was to learn a lot about the OFT and its bedfellow, the Monopolies and Mergers Commission.

Stagecoach was not averse to playing hardball, either, and its capacity for ruthlessness was, later, to become almost its trademark. One of the early incidents showing that the siblings were not to be trifled with was over a dispute involving entry to Perth's Canal Street bus park. Stagecoach had negotiated with the council for access to the grounds and a coach from a rival company, Newton's of Dingwall, pulled in. Gloag went up to the driver to tell him to get out, but wasn't getting very far, so she went into the toilets, picked up a bucketful of water, and threw it over the hapless fellow.

Indeed, the mild-mannered Souter was often upstaged by his sister when it came to protecting the family concern. An executive of a rival firm described going into the Perth office. It was by then located near Perth Harbour, where the company had moved in 1981, and it sported a board proclaiming it to be 'Stagecoach Stables'. Ann Gloag was on the telephone bargaining over the purchase of the precious number plates which just had SC as the letters: 'She was on the phone to these people and I have never seen anyone be so tough over negotiations. She was extremely fierce in beating people down.' She was successful, too, as Stagecoach has many SC number plates, one of which is still on Souter's Jaguar. As Derek Scott explains, SC numbers had the extra advantage of not revealing, like conventional plates, the age of the coaches to the passengers, a real boon in Stagecoach's early days. Ann was always the negotiator, thrashing out deals and often terrifying those on the other side of the table. She was even once flown down in a helicopter from the Midlands to London by Robert Maxwell, who was keen on a property Stagecoach owned in Glasgow and came back beaming, having got the price she wanted. With suppliers who were too slow, she was wont to tell them that she had been a nurse 'and we never left a patient lying on the operating table waiting for parts'.

The tough side of the two siblings' character was certainly demonstrated in their dealings with Robin Gloag. On his own admission, Robin was happier underneath a bus than at the boardroom table, and played no part in the running of the business. But the two were beginning to be irritated by what they felt was Robin's tendency to undermine decisions they made by complaining to the staff. The marriage to Ann was, in any case, disintegrating, and Brian and Ann decided to break up the partnership.

In December 1982, Brian and Ann finally confronted Robin over what they felt was his continued moaning to the drivers, and asked, 'Do you want to go your own way?'

Robin said he did. As ever eschewing lawyers, Brian wrote out a deal on a sheet of Stagecoach headed paper, still sporting the cowboy and the chubby horses, a sad little document which Robin kept and later showed to the BBC television documentary producer, John Mair. Under the agreement, Robin received a Volvo coach, a Renault, £3,000 in cash and £5,000 in consultation fees to be paid that summer, and the siblings agreed to let him use Stagecoach's licence until he could set up his own. Robin's new firm, as a kind of dig at Ann and Brian, was called Highwayman. Robin even continued using the Stagecoach offices until the summer of 1984, concentrating on local coaching contracts, when he moved to Errol eight miles out of Perth.

Robin says he had no alternative when faced with Ann and Brian's offer: 'I couldn't say no, it was two to one. Things had been deteriorating for a while. Brian had been living with us for two years and the three of us would be in the room together and they would talk over me as if I wasn't there.'

He says he had wanted to be more involved, but was working too hard on the buses: 'My main complaint was that I was not privy to what was going on inside the office, and when I was trying to get brought up to date, they didn't have time to talk to me, so I was getting further and further behind on that side. I was being left in the dark about the progression.'

He admits, though, that it was always going to be difficult: 'I'm not as bright as they are, and found it harder to keep up with the speed that things were moving at.' Robin says that his main complaint about the way the business was being run was how hard Brian was on the staff, a feeling echoed by several others involved in the early days: 'Brian has a wonderful head on his shoulders but he was tough on the staff. He worked them very hard. I think he was the original zero-tolerance type.'

The partnership was dissolved and Stagecoach began operating as a limited company, which had already been set up a couple of years previously. In hindsight, the deal for Robin might look mean, given that a third of a company now worth around £3 billion was involved, but Souter reckons it was all they could afford, and even giving Robin that much put the business at some risk, because it represented virtually all the net assets apart from goodwill and the business was close to technical insolvency.

Ann and Brian were not, however, prepared to allow Robin to challenge them in any way. Robin Gloag continued to work for Stagecoach on a contract basis, painting and repairing coaches, but still had ambitions of his own to run bus services. In April 1984 he got into financial difficulties and Stagecoach repurchased the Volvo coach, but three months later Robin had managed to sort his business out and bought it back. However, the relationship was to sour in 1987 when Stagecoach was beginning to take off as a major player and was concentrating on its expansion south of the border. Robin decided to challenge his former partners on their own turf. For several years Stagecoach had run a local bus service – the first bus, as opposed to coach, service it had ever operated – between Perth and Errol and Robin, feeling they might have taken their eye off the local ball, thought this might be an opportunity to challenge Stagecoach.

Robin says, 'I had a lot of complaints about how they were running the service, and thought I could do a better job.' He started running against Stagecoach, offering cheaper fares, but Brian and Ann responded in kind by undercutting his fares. Robin first of all tried to outstay Stagecoach by responding with even lower fares, but Stagecoach started running free buses at high frequencies, and Robin was forced to withdraw, admitting later that he had 'made a mistake'. He says, 'Their response was surprising. They put on five buses, at the same timings as me, two at the front and three at the back, all running for free, all to put one bus off the road. It's a policy they have adopted elsewhere.'

Stagecoach insiders put the incident down to Robin misreading the signs about Stagecoach losing interest in its home patch and underestimating the attachment felt by the siblings to what was Stagecoach's first bus route. Clearly Robin had also felt aggrieved about what had happened in the separation of the business, now that Stagecoach was becoming a big concern.

Souter is not apologetic about what happened to Robin in the mini Errol bus war. He felt that Highwayman posed a real threat to a core part of the business and that they had done all they could to help Robin: 'We thought at the time that if we can create a business for him on his own, and give him some work, he could set his own rules and have his own people working for him. I guess when he started running against our local bus service, we felt that it was a breach of agreement and of faith with us. What sort of reaction did he expect? There was no way we were going to sit back and watch our business evaporate. Where's it to end up? Because here was a man who was driven by a pretty unhealthy chip on his shoulder. It wasn't a logical, commercial-driven idea and I said this to Robin at the time. He tended to surround himself with people who were disaffected employees from Stagecoach and they talked about Stagecoach seventy per cent of the time, which was pretty unhealthy. I told him there were some very frequent routes in Dundee where he could do exceedingly well, but on a country route it was crazy. But his whole business focus seemed to be against Stagecoach as opposed to where would be a good idea to get a commercial return.' Despite the spat, Stagecoach continued giving Highwayman occasional painting contracts, but the incident was later widely picked up in the media as an example of Stagecoach's refusal to allow sentiment to get in the way of its dealings with rivals.

Robin and Ann, who had two children together, Jonathan and Pamela, eventually divorced in 1988, and she remarried a couple of years later, to David McCleary, who ran a laundry equipment business in Perth. Robin also remarried and relations between him and his former wife and brother-in-law are not particularly cordial, although Robin says he bears no resentment. He is still running Highwayman in Errol, with five coaches for private hire and some minibuses used for school contracts: 'I've remarried and I'm happy. A few more bob would take a lot of the worry out of it but there you are.' He is, however, worried that Stagecoach will expand into his business: 'We do private hire and Stagecoach used not to do it, but are now creeping into it in Perth and Fife. I'm worried they will cross-subsidise and drive other people out of business. I feel they will not rest until they have a hundred per cent of the transport industry under their belt.'

As well as fighting battles against competitors, Stagecoach was ready to start pushing at the limits of the legislation in an effort to carve out new markets. Souter and Gloag hit upon the idea of running a service down to London, stopping at all the motorway service stations where it could pick up or set down passengers. They argued that the service would not only be useful for people stranded at service stations, but would offer a new facility for those living nearby. The bus company managed to gain permission from nearly all the relevant service station operators but had to get a licence from the Traffic Commissioners and the application became a test case, as it was stretching the existing law.

In fact, the idea seems to have been an attempt at a Trojan Horse because the market for such a slow service seemed tiny, and the number of people finding themselves stranded at service stations is even smaller. The importance of the case was that, while *coaches*, operating solely for journeys of more than thirty miles, were not subject to regulation, they were also not entitled to fuel-tax rebate. The rebate, given to all operators of *bus* services, defined as involving journeys of under thirty miles, meant they paid no tax on their fuel at all.

Stagecoach hired Menzies Campbell QC, now a Liberal Democrat frontbencher at Westminster, but the Metropolitan Traffic Commissioner saw through the plot, rejecting the application. According to Keith Jenkinson in *Stagecoach and its subsidiaries*, the Commissioner felt the benefits would be minimal and that the main beneficiary would be

Stagecoach, since it would enable the company to claim the tax rebate for the service. Indeed, Stagecoach argued that British Rail and the Scottish Bus Group enjoyed duty-free fuel which seemed unfair. Stagecoach did not see it as a total defeat, feeling that it helped influence the subsequent legislation freeing up the bus market.

While the company continued to flourish, there were a few hiccups on the way which again showed Souter's readiness to cut his losses, a characteristic throughout the history of Stagecoach. This toughness was demonstrated when a subsidiary, Adamson and Low, was put into liquidation. The Edinburgh-based company, with seventeen coaches, had been bought in November 1983 and had concentrated mainly on private hire and schools contracts. Some of its coaches were used on the Edinburgh–Glasgow run and, in common with other subsidiaries, the management, who had retained 10 per cent of the shares as an incentive to make a profit, were largely left alone to run the company. But the firm got into difficulties because it lost many of the schools contracts, which enabled it to keep ticking over through the winter. Souter decided quickly to stem the losses in the spring of 1985 by putting Adamson and Low into voluntary liquidation, even though the management thought the firm was likely to make a profit that summer. The creditors, principally The Royal Bank of Scotland, were paid off and Stagecoach bore the loss. But as Derek Scott put it, 'Had Stagecoach waited until the end of the summer, it would have made more of a loss. Lots of businesses make the mistake of going on too long when they are clearly losing out.'

Stagecoach was also, in 1985, in trouble in the courts, having two serious brushes with the law over its operating practices. First, one of the company's double-deckers running from Dundee to Perth was stopped by the police and found to be carrying ninety-seven passengers, fifteen of whom were standing on the two decks and five sitting on the stairs. Hauled in front of the Sheriff's Court, Souter eschewing his cowboy hat this time, Stagecoach argued that a relief single-decker which had been called up to take the overspill broke down on its way to Dundee from Perth. The conductress, reluctant to leave any passengers behind, had allowed them on, causing the overloading. The court was not impressed, imposing a fine of £500. Then, at another hearing, shortly afterwards, the company admitted fourteen counts of having allowed drivers to work longer than the legal working day.

Although Stagecoach argued that these events were untypical, clearly the young company, like many in the industry, regularly breached the law in its early days. Derek Scott admits that Souter and Gloag were 'a bit cavalier about the law in the first couple of years. It was a delegation problem, rather than they themselves encouraging employees to break the law. As a small company, you cut corners, skimp on overheads and skimp on all the things that big companies have. You tend to think that the law is for big companies, to stop them abusing the public.' He said, 'You are encouraged in this to some extent by the trade press, which tends to be ambivalent towards smaller companies. It's always a much bigger story if a large company gets caught.'

Stagecoach flourished partly out of luck and partly because of the sheer dedication of the two people running it. And the key was Souter's ability and his readiness to take on established competitors and seek out new opportunities. He was much more interested in buses than coaches. Souter had always felt that it was never possible to make very good margins out of coaches because of the seasonal nature of the demand. He says, 'Most coach users are leisure travellers, and peak demand is almost purely in the summer and the Easter and Christmas breaks. For the other six months of the year, it is very hard to make a profit, or even cover costs.' The first couple of years, before competitors piled in, and with the boost of the rail strikes, had been a one-off opportunity.

Souter felt that the coach market was a nightmare: 'I looked at buses and thought, This is a lot easier money than coaches. The only reason we went into the coaching market was that it was the only market open to us. With coaching, you made all your money in the holidays. It's a terrible business with coaches breaking down far from home and replacement coaches having to be chartered. Buses is a business that runs itself, once you've set it up.' The first five years, building up the coach business, were the hardest part of his business career: 'It was extremely tough work. I was working much harder then than I'm working now.'

Given Souter's feelings, it is hardly surprising that, once Stagecoach became established in buses, the coaching side was sold to National Express in 1989. Souter and Gloag felt it was becoming increasingly difficult, as a small company, to maintain their market share – they had a third and Citylink two-thirds – and that, with high interest and exchange rates, increasing motorway congestion and predictions of a tough recession, it was time to get out. Coaches by then represented only 5 per cent of the business, compared with 95 per cent in 1985. The coach operation was using a disproportionate amount of management time. The two businesses, buses and coaches, were very dissimilar, requiring different types of management and staff, and, of course, a completely separate fleet. National Express was preparing to compete as a third force in the market, so it was an obvious option to enter it as a purchaser. As ever, Souter and Gloag got a good deal, receiving £1.6 million from National Express for Stagecoach Express, which was £1 million more than the value of its assets because NE was prepared to pay for the goodwill on which Stagecoach's balance sheet placed no value. The Stagecoach head office was split up and many long-term staff were handed over to the new company. It was a decision that showed that sentiment had no place in the business. Derek Scott remembers that it had been a heartrending decision for Souter and Gloag: 'The workforce was cut in half. It was very emotional. There were tears that day.'

Deregulations are, by their very nature, unpredictable, because freeing up a market often leads to consequences that were not envisaged. The expectations of a sharp increase in coach travel did, in the short term, materialise. With fares going down, and the railways having sporadic strikes, ridership rose rapidly in the first couple of years of deregulation, with the number of National Express passengers going up from 9.2 million in 1980 to 14 million two years later. National Express retained around 70 to 80 per cent of the market, according to Peter White, but figures for the rest of the industry are not available. The industry did not, however, manage to retain its new passengers and usage fell sharply in the 1990s to reach a low of 9.8 million in 1993 as fares rose again and competition from trains heightened, which meant that deregulation managed to arrest the gradual decline in the industry but not to reverse it.

The most notable failure from the Tories' point of view was that the dominance of National Express – and of Scottish Bus Group north of the border – remained largely unchallenged, apart from the brief effort by British Coachways. In only a few corridors, such as London to Oxford where Stagecoach became a player in 1997 by taking over Harry Blundred's Transit Holdings, has long-term competition survived. North of the border, there was, for a time, a virtual National Express monopoly. Citylink was privatised through a management buyout in 1990, and, in May 1993, Citylink was acquired by National Express until 1998. However, in 1998, after winning the ScotRail franchise, National Express was ordered to divest itself of it, with Stagecoach emerging as a potential buyer, despite Souter's stated wariness of coaching.

By 1985, Stagecoach had grown to have a turnover of £2 million but Souter, who still drove the occasional shift, and Gloag were still paying themselves only £12,000 per year each, better than the £3,000 on which they had started five years previously but still a pittance compared with the salaries of managers of similar-sized companies. Nor were there any extras. Isabel Peters, a parsimonious Aberdonian, who ran the cheque-book, kept a tight rein on expenses, refusing even to pay Souter if he did not submit the right receipts. She was rewarded, in 1996 when she retired, with the gift of a new Peugeot 206, even though, according to Derek Scott, 'she was the one woman Brian was really scared of'.

At least Fraser McColl's and Iain Souter's loans had been repaid, but both Brian's and Ann's homes were still mortgaged to the business and Gloag was eager to start pulling some money out of Stagecoach by paying themselves decent wages. But Souter refused, knowing that every penny now would be worth pounds later.

The opportunities of the deregulation and privatisation of the bus industry were arriving and Souter wanted to be ready. After a long delay, Mrs Thatcher, pressed by her right-wing friend and Cabinet colleague, Nicholas Ridley, was finally turning her attention to that most unfashion-able of industries, buses. A White Paper on buses was published in 1984 and legislation was promised for the following year. Coaches had been a kind of trial run for Souter and Stagecoach. Buses were to be the real thing.

3
The market opens up

Brian Souter might be a strong Christian, but he has cause to be grateful for a bit of philandering. The reshuffle forced on Mrs Thatcher by the revelation of Cecil Parkinson's affair with his secretary during the 1983 Tory Party conference brought Nicholas Ridley to the Department of Transport in place of Tom King. Without the Parkinson affair, King, a much more consensus-type politican who was not a strong Thatcherite, would have brought about slower and less far-ranging changes in the bus industry.

Nicholas Ridley, on the other hand, had a vision. The old pal of Thatcher, who died in 1993, issued a White Paper in 1984 which proposed a radical reform of the bus industry. The paper was much in keeping with Ridley's right-wing ideology, removing most of the controls on the industry in an effort to create a free market. Unusually for such important legislation, there was no Green Paper to allow for consultation, possibly because the proposals were so radical. King would have consulted long and wide, but Ridley knew what he wanted: the total deregulation of the industry. As *Buses* magazine put it, 'Ridley could see no difference between bus operation and running a sweet shop. He was a male equivalent of Mrs Thatcher; bull-headed with a clear idea of what he wanted and little inclination to be swayed in his judgement ... the exact opposite of Tom King.' On Ridley's tours around the country, he was wont to ask local bus managers how many of their drivers owned their buses. Receiving the answer 'none', the minister would tell the hapless chap that he ought to consider the idea of selling off buses to the drivers.

This vision of countless tiny operators providing bus services was enshrined in the *Buses* White Paper. The paper went well beyond the Conservative manifesto for the 1983 Tory election landslide, showing that it took people like Ridley to persuade Mrs Thatcher to embark on the privatisation and deregulation revolution that was to be her most significant legacy. The manifesto had merely said that private capital should be introduced into the state-owned National Bus Company, but did not speak of the wholesale and concurrent deregulation and privatisation set out in the White Paper. Ridley's fervour had been stimulated by the relative failure of the opening up of the coach market. He realised that the 1980 Act's inability to attract many new entrants into the market was partly because of the dominant position of the state-owned National Express. He was determined to ensure that the same mistake was not made again by smashing the NBC into tiny pieces and selling them off.

Brian Souter, like Ridley, had a vision, but it was a rather different one. He simply wanted to become Britain's biggest bus operator, a rather grand idea for a small Perth-based coach company: 'My vision for the future in 1986 became much wider because I could see that there was an opportunity to become market leader in the UK, to pick up the right companies, and to put together a nice portfolio that would be difficult for others to attack because we would be spread across the country and would not be dependent on the geography or demography in any one area.' Souter's vision was largely to be fulfilled, while Ridley's did not materialise.

Most analysts of the bus industry feel that the two very radical changes envisaged in the White Paper and the subsequent Transport Act 1985 – the deregulation of the industry and the privatisation of the NBC – should have been undertaken separately. With hindsight, it is amazing that the NBC had not been an earlier target of the Tories' privatisation process. It was a lumbering, old-fashioned company presiding over the disintegration of its market, apparently making little effort to stem the decline and, as a consequence, costing more and more each year in subsidy. The figures were dramatic. The subsidy had gone up from £10 million in 1972 to £520 million ten years later, a thirteen-fold increase in real terms. Meanwhile, the number of passengers had gone down steadily since the peak in the early 1950s, falling at between 2 and 3 per cent almost every year. Between 1953 and 1983, the use of buses and coaches had gone down by half. Yet the structure of the industry had barely changed, a case of 'benign neglect' according to John Hibbs, a bus academic who was one of the architects of the 1985 legislation.

The industry was virtually entirely state-owned, either by central or local government. Apart from the NBC, and its Scottish equivalent, there were about forty-five council-owned fleets, many of which would later prove to be targets for Stagecoach. In the six English metropolitan areas and in Strathclyde, the buses were controlled by Passenger Transport Authorities, who all had dominant market positions. The private sector, therefore, was minimal, confined, apart from one regional company, to small independents, typically with a dozen or so vehicles and often providing a mix of local bus and coach services.

The NBC had been created by the Transport Act 1968 to take over the state-owned bus interests of the Transport Holding Company, itself the successor to the British Transport Commission. The Commission had, after the war, become the owner of the railways and a large part of the bus network, because in 1948 it had bought the Thomas Tilling company, who, along with BET, dominated the industry. BET refused to sell to the Commission but eventually its UK bus operations were nationalised just before the creation of the National Bus Company in 1968.

The NBC, therefore, was a huge concern with 84,000 staff in 1970 and 21,700 vehicles operating services in nearly all the country apart from London and towns where there were council-owned bus concerns. Like British Railways, it had a military ethos with lots of people in uniforms running the company and an army-style distinction between officers and men, which meant it was very good at providing the service but less able to respond to changing needs.

The White Paper stated baldly that 'there is no good reason why local bus services should be provided by a national corporation'. But, as with British Rail a decade later, the Government did not want to see the NBC sold *en bloc* to the private sector. In line with the purist economic theory underlying the *Buses* White Paper, the NBC was to be split up into a remarkable number of small companies – sixty-four bus operators and eight engineering subsidiaries – each of which was to be sold off separately. In order not to avoid creating any large companies, many of the fifty local subsidiaries of the NBC, like United Counties, were split up in preparation for sale in order to create new companies with fleets of around 200 to encourage both management buyouts and purchases by relatively small companies. The Scottish Bus Group was also to be broken up – but, in the event, later than the NBC – into ten operating companies.

The White Paper did not predict, or even discuss, the fact that companies would inevitably merge with each other, forming large and powerful groups such as Stagecoach, FirstGroup and Arriva. Ridley thought that not only would all these seventy-two companies continue in parallel, but also they would face a continuous challenge from tiny one-person operators who would ensure that fares levels were kept to a minimum. Ridley did not seem to realise that there were major economies of scale in the bus industry, and nor did he predict that the small operators would quickly fall prey to their larger rivals.

Outside companies were allowed to buy only three of the NBC subsidiaries initially, though there was nothing to stop secondary sales, an opportunity of which Stagecoach – and the other emerging big players – later took full advantage. Investment at the NBC dried up in the prelude to privatisation, which was to have dire consequences on the industry over the next decade, as many of the purchasers of the subsidiaries, particularly management and employee buyout teams, were undercapital-ised and unable or reluctant to buy new stock. This later made the management buyout teams much more ready to embrace the likes of Stagecoach.

The 1985 Act was to prove Souter's passport to a fortune. The Act's main aim was to reverse fifty years of regulation and to open the industry to market forces. The 1930 Road Traffic Act, which still largely governed the industry, specified that operators had to obtain a licence for every service they ran. The legislation was quite specifically aimed at avoiding competition, as operators had to demonstrate a need for their services. The 1930 Act also created the Traffic Commissioners, who had widespread powers to regulate the industry and used them very conservatively, ensuring that entrenched operators were virtually unchallengeable. While fares control had been abolished by the 1980 Act, the bus industry had largely been left under their control.

The Act not only resulted in the full privatisation and break-up of the National Bus Company, but also in a strong form of deregulation, which left the industry open to almost anyone who fancied running a bus service. Under the new legislation, for the first time, any operator would be able to challenge the existing bus companies, simply by registering a route six weeks in advance with the local Traffic Commissioners. Ridley also scrapped cross-subsidy – between profitable and loss-making routes – which he saw as inefficient. Blanket subsidies to whole networks were made illegal. Instead, local authorities would have the ability to subsidise loss-making routes through putting them out to competitive tender. So instead of supporting a whole network, local authorities were forced to identify the 'socially necessary' services – often called tendered services – that needed public subsidy to survive. As a corollary, though Ridley did not say it, subsidy was cut massively over the ensuing years, leading to sharp reductions in services in areas where local authorities decided they could no longer afford to support public transport.

In only one way did Ridley duck out of a confrontation with the entrenched interests of the industry. London was, for the time being, to be left alone. Deregulation there was considered to be too controversial and risky, and London Transport, still a huge monolith, was not ready for privatisation. Northern Ireland, where paramilitaries often force large taxi firms to pay protection money, was also left out, though Souter has long hankered after running buses there.

As with coach deregulation, Souter and Stagecoach were ready. Bus deregulation came before the sales of the NBC subsidiaries and therefore his first attack was on the established operators in Glasgow. As early as February 1986, the company had registered Magicbus (Scotland) Ltd with the intention of running services in Glasgow even though deregulation day was not until 26 October 1986. Freed by the Act to register services, Souter announced Stagecoach would run three routes linking Glasgow with East Kilbride, Easterhouse and Castlemilk. The Easterhouse route was innovative in that it was an express service making use of the M8 motorway, something the local company, run and owned by Strathclyde Regional Council, had never considered doing. On the first couple of days of deregulation, Stagecoach started operating with twenty-one buses in Glasgow under the Magicbus name. The company had built up the stock over the previous few months in Perth and, in another innovation, used old Routemasters bought from London Transport. As one slightly envious rival in the industry put it, 'It wasn't rocket science, but it was very clever to use buses from England's biggest city in Scotland's biggest city. No one had thought of it before.'

Souter undertook most of the preparation himself. 'I did all the market research, all the traffic stuff, like the schedules, as, at the time, I was the only person who could do it.' He knew the market from his days as a conductor and drove round the streets, working out a detailed route in Castlemilk where 'thousands of people lived with no bus services because some of the roads were too narrow. I worked out a wide loop to reach them.' Gloag was left in charge of the coaching services.

Stagecoach ran into heavy opposition on the streets of Glasgow. The company had intended to operate out of the bus station in Glasgow's St Enoch Square, entering it from a different route than the existing services, but the Routemasters were prevented from going into the station by a row of traffic cones and a posse of Strathclyde Buses inspectors. Souter, determined not to be thwarted, picked up a megaphone to attract passengers to his buses and also took direct action moving the cones away personally. A photograph in a bus magazine captured this moment, showing Souter with his jumper sticking out below his jacket. The result was a shouting match with a burly police inspector, but Souter lost because the ownership of the bus station was unclear and he had to park his buses by the side of it. The next day he tried a different ploy to create awareness of the new company, dressing as a 'magic bunny' dispensing pens, beakers and Magicbus lettered rock to passengers.

The Glasgow initiative met with mixed results. People liked the Routemasters because they had conductors and Magicbus built up some brand loyalty. However, the service to East Kilbride was withdrawn quite quickly, in January 1987, because of intense competition from the still state-owned Central SMT, Souter's former employer. The buses were transferred to double the frequency on the more successful service between Glasgow and Easterhouse. Stagecoach lost money for the first few months in Glasgow, but was in profit within a year.

Souter says that his attack in Glasgow was justified Stagecoach was providing a new type of service: 'Glasgow was all about innovation, providing express services and running on new routes. I have little patience with new entrants to the market who copy everything that everybody else has done and just run old buses and match existing services.'

Opening up a competitive front on Glasgow was part of a three-pronged strategy for Souter in response to the opportunities created by the 1985 Act. By not buying new buses, it meant a low-cost entry to the market with little capital risk.

Souter put Stagecoach on a war footing for other battles. To ensure that Stagecoach was ever ready to move into an area where the incumbent operator got into difficulties, the company bought a stock of thirty-five Leyland Leopards from Kelvin Scottish, part of the Scottish Bus Group, in the autumn of 1987, with no immediate plan to put them in service. The idea according to Scott was to create 'the pool to attack other companies, so that we were ready. If we saw an opportunity which everybody had missed we could put the buses in and recruit drivers locally, probably from other companies.'

But Souter was working at full stretch on his other ideas in what he reckons was one of the busiest times of his working life. The second part of the strategy was to ensure that the coaching service, Stagecoach Express, made money but that no risks were taken on expanding it: 'I wanted to consolidate a wee bit more to try to squeeze a very good year's performance out of the company, because I knew that year's accounts would be used as a point of reference for any bank that was going to lend us money for anything bigger. So it was the year to squeeze as good a profit as we could on Stagecoach Express. We didn't want to be taking a risk in the express market and a risk in the bus market at the same time.'

And the third part of the strategy was to look at the NBC companies, particularly the smaller ones, which Souter thought Stagecoach could afford. As Souter put it, 'The way forward was to make a glutton of ourselves and buy as many of these companies as we could.' At this stage, Souter also had designs on the whole of the Scottish Bus Group, but in the event it was, like the NBC, broken up and initially Stagecoach was able to buy only two of the ten companies.

To help Stagecoach begin this first major period of expansion through acquisition, Fraser McColl, the almost legendary Rich Uncle in Canada, was called in again to provide £400,000 in guarantees, to bolster Stagecoach's balance sheet.

At first there was very little interest in the sale of the NBC companies because, as the Public Accounts Committee later pointed out, 'there was no established market for bus companies'. There were few existing independent operators large enough to take on a company with a fleet of two hundred or so buses. Ridley had undermined the market further by pushing through deregulation and privatisation simultaneously, which meant no one could work out how much a bus company was worth. The management teams, thrown by the effects of deregulation, often put in very low bids, as the companies had no financial track record covering operations in a competitive market and their advisers and bankers, ignorant of the bus industry, were very conservative. Stagecoach benefited enormously from the fact that it was an early bidder and was prepared to risk that these companies were, at least, worth the value of their assets.

Souter put in a bid for the twelfth NBC bus company to be put up for sale, City of Oxford Motor Services. Most had, so far, gone uncontested to management buyout teams and again, in Oxford, the management team triumphed with a bid of £2.6 million.

Stagecoach tried again with Hampshire Bus, which was also contested only by the management team. Stagecoach had been given a steer by the team running NBC's privatisation unit that the management bid was a low one and that they were seeking a better price. This time, Stagecoach won easily with a bid of £2.2 million, becoming the first outsiders to gain control of one of the NBC bus companies, all eighteen predecessors having gone to management buyout teams. The Government was grateful for Stagecoach's early involvement, as, later in the process, the number of bidders increased dramatically and better prices were obtained.

Raising the money had been very hard for the small company. Souter said it was touch and go whether they could do it: 'We struggled to buy the company. Banks wouldn't lend us the money; we had to put all our houses up to the bank; we had to get money guarantees off Fraser; and we had to put up all of Stagecoach.' Nevertheless, on 2 April 1987, Stagecoach took control of Hampshire Bus, and its associated company Pilgrim Coaches, which, together, had 243 vehicles. The acquisition, therefore, more than doubled the size of Stagecoach's fleet, which was soon to expand again with the takeover of Cumberland Motor Services, the second NBC company, bought in July for £2.8 million. After several unsuccessful bids for other NBC companies – Stagecoach had investigated over twenty of them – in November 1987 Stagecoach finally bought its third NBC company, the last it was able to acquire under the rules – United Counties, based in Northants, Bedfordshire and Cambridgeshire, for which it paid £4.1 million. Souter had also been steered towards the two later acquisitions by the Privatisation Unit, which regularly pointed out to Stagecoach those management teams whose bids were likely to be too low.

For the time being, Stagecoach, at least, managed to keep clear of the regulatory authorities. Because the three separate NBC companies were in such widely different parts of Britain, the Office of Fair Trading, which did not want contiguous subsidiaries to be bought by the same company, played no part in these early acquisitions.

This was the fastest period of growth in the company's history, going from a £3 million to a £26 million turnover within a year. For Souter, the purchase of these geographically disparate companies began his life on the road with the famous plastic bags. He usually spent Mondays and Fridays in Perth, and the middle of the week travelling round Stagecoach's various businesses, a routine he has continued to this day. Souter was a hands-on chairman in the initial stages of taking on a company, but then left it in the control of the new management which often comprised existing senior staff who fitted into the Stagecoach mould.

The family nature of the business, which had already lost Robin Gloag, was to be further weakened with the departure, after seven years, of David Souter. He had never been employed by Stagecoach, always working as a consultant, as he also owned a local farm, which did not earn him enough to live on. He had done a lot of the early driving and all the publicity and marketing. Brian really admired his brother's abilities and wanted him to stay on: 'He used to do the night shift at the weekend and organise all the staff out on the road. He was a very good organiser and he did all the dealing with newspapers and printing of timetables. He had worked in publicity in London and used his skills to good effect.' Now that Stagecoach was expanding, Brian offered him 'a proper job which would have used his skills, looking after the marketing of the companies for which he had a real gift'.

David, who had always turned down the opportunity of having any equity in the business, decided to leave, having been offered a temporary post on a mission in Zambia: 'I had no desire to be in business. After seven years, things were going into megadrive and I was uncomfortable with the competitive side of things. I have my own particular view on fair play and why we run a business. I had no right to complain about things, because I never held a share, but I withdrew, saying I would rather do something else. It had been shifting towards a more cutthroat business. I was happy when we were the small boys and we were up against the giants: we were actually living up to our life story, that we were the little people and had come up from nothing and would try very hard to make it work.'

The Stagecoach team of Souter and Gloag was now strengthened by Souter's old friend at Arthur Andersen, Derek Scott, a quietly spoken and strongly nationalistic Scot, who really preferred to be an accountant for workers' cooperatives, but joined Stagecoach in June 1987 as finance director, attracted by the excitement of working for such an ambitious company. But the management was still very much in a learning process and mistakes were made. Hampshire Bus had been bought by Skipburn, a holding company, with Souter and Gloag as well as Fraser McColl and Dawson Williams, a personable Welshman, as directors. Williams, who had run the NBC Hampshire subsidiary, was allocated 7 per cent of Hampshire Bus, as Stagecoach wanted to provide incentives to management, but, as with the ill-fated Adamson and Low coach firm mentioned in Chapter 2, the arrangement did not work out and Williams left the company in November 1987, selling his share to Stagecoach. In doing so, the trade press proclaimed him as the first bus millionaire, something that angered Scott: 'He should have corrected them, as we only gave him a quarter of a million. The publicity fuelled people's expectations of the value of bus companies.'

Stagecoach escaped lightly. Williams went on to work for British Bus in the early 1990s, which embarked on an acquisition trail that bus watchers found bizarre because of its size and speed. It turned out that Williams had bribed an official of the Bank of Boston with £1 million to view the company's requests for loans favourably and was sent to prison in September 1997 for three years.

At Cumberland, though, Stagecoach found Barry Hinkley, a better managerial prospect than Williams. He was the chief engineer, and became the first in a long line of senior Stagecoach managers who were plucked from acquired subsidiaries to play an important role in the company's development. Hinkley, who has thinning ginger hair and a beard, is, like many of Souter's protégés, a self-made man. He started as an engineering trainee with Trent, an NBC subsidiary, and worked his way up through the ranks, with the help of evening classes, to realise a lifetime ambition to become a chief engineer. He is now an executive director on the main board, having become expert at restructuring companies, and he is the company's troubleshooter, with a reputation throughout the industry for toughness.

Hinkley, who was part of Cumberland's management buyout team, says they were badly advised, a feeling echoed by many managers in these sales, as the Manchester-based management consultants had no idea of the value of the business: 'They told us we would not be able to buy a new vehicle for seven years, which was total rubbish. They did not realise the power of the cash flow.' Souter, however, has always understood how the pennies rolling in every day from the passengers are an amazingly strong asset of any bus business.

The general manager, Mike Wadsworth, left within the first few hours of Stagecoach's takeover. Hinkley says: 'Mr Souter realised he was not going to be the person that would make the changes within the business that were needed.' Hinkley was made general manager, and then managing director in October 1987.

The way that Stagecoach began to transform the former NBC subsidiaries into efficient and profitable concerns was to be repeated many times over the years. While the circumstances and the measures taken were never exactly the same, a clear methodology was beginning to emerge. Ann Gloag outlined the approach in one of the first ever profiles of the company, in the *Sunday Express* in April 1988: 'Our success lies in breaking through the starchy, staid, class-based attitude which you find in nationalised companies. We introduce new working practices, break down the old barriers of management and workers and let the employees share in the profits. Our workforce accepts that we started with nothing, so they take to us in a way they didn't to the nationalised bus companies' managements.'

Ben Colson, who was United Counties' traffic manager at the time of the takeover, was part of its management buyout team, which lost out heavily and has first-hand experience of Souter's approach. Colson, who is now Stagecoach Manchester's commercial director, was surprised at Souter's initial concern about the managers: 'We had gone to Victoria coach station and waited for the result of our bid. The guy from NBC privatisation team said, "Sorry, lads, you haven't won it, but would you like to meet the preferred bidder? It's Brian Souter of Stagecoach." I was quite emotionally overcome by having lost and there was a feeling of emptiness, and tiredness. We were one of the last privatisations and it had been a long period, from the 1984 White Paper to September 1987, of uncertainty. Then, this guy walked in, wearing a pair of jeans, totally not the sort of person you expect to have as your boss and said, "Look, you guys have been through the mill; I feel for you. It's six weeks before we complete [the deal]. Have a good holiday to get your batteries recharged." And I did. That was all he said.'

But soon after the takeover, Colson recalls how swiftly Stagecoach set about transforming the company: 'The thing that hit me was that although at the time Brian Souter was managing director of all the subsidiary companies he would find time to visit United Counties once a week. Every morning he would phone Glasgow, where he had just started Magicbus, to find out how much money he was taking on each route. That was a completely different culture from the nationalised business.' Souter's concern about the managers getting a good holiday did not stop him ensuring that the managing director, John Tait, like his counterpart at Cumberland, left the company as soon as Stagecoach took over.

Souter quickly set about applying the same sort of financial discipline to his new business. Colson had to spend a day driving round the area with Souter in his car bombarding him with questions: 'He kept asking, "Why don't you run down there?" and I would say "Because the trees are too low," and he'd insist on having a look himself. We went round the whole of Corby, where there was a big problem with illegal taxis as unemployment was very high after the steelworks closed down. Everyone had got in the habit of using them and the council had even built a station for them next to the DHSS offices.'

Souter and Colson spent a couple of hours outside the DHSS offices, trying to check how quickly the taxis came and went to see how much money they made. But they all disappeared and didn't come back. Finally a local heavy got out of one of the taxis and came up to the two busmen, who thought they were about to be beaten up. But once they explained that they were only looking at the transport operations and were not from the DHSS, all the taxis quickly returned.

United Counties had been so badly hit by the taxis that it had considered closing its Corby depot but Souter, instead, decided to go on the attack.

'Why do you finish at six-thirty at night?' he asked. 'People then go out, and have to take a taxi, and get into a taxi culture. Why not run the buses till midnight?'

Colson protested that they would lose money.

'Doesn't matter, as it will break the taxi culture and repay you during the day.'

To Colson, this was a new world: 'With Stagecoach, it was a matter of Brian Souter saying, "I'm a businessman. I will put money into it." With the NBC, it was always taxpayers' money and we couldn't do it.'

There had been a few improvements to United Counties services after deregulation but Souter changed the network radically. Rather than ditching Corby, he invested in it, again using a fleet of old London double-deckers with conductors who were encouraged to help people on with their buggies and shopping. As Colson put it, 'The product changed. The buses went faster, and the passengers could sit down before they had to pay and the services ran until midnight.'

It worked, with usage increasing rapidly, but a couple of years later, Souter decided to change tack again, going to the other extreme by running minibuses, removing several seats for buggies and shopping and operating at intervals of as little as a minute.

They were called Magic Minis and still form the basis of the local service. Colson says: 'Fifteen years ago, before deregulation, the town network had about eight buses to serve fifty-two thousand people, with buses every half an hour. Now there are about twenty-five buses which operate at much higher frequencies.' Of course such increases are the exception, rather than the norm, but the story of Corby explains how Stagecoach's attention to the market and its readiness to make radical changes could reap dividends.

At Cumberland, there was an equally radical transformation. Hinkley recalls how headquarters staff were reduced by thirty-four and several depots were closed within the first four months, all without any cuts in the network. Cumberland was given the classic Stagecoach makeover, which, according to Hinkley, involves looking at the management structure, the administration, the engineering staff and, lastly, the network. (See Chapter 12 for a fuller analysis of this process.)

A year after acquiring Cumberland, Stagecoach embarked on a remarkable battle in the centre of Keswick over the fate of the bus station, showing the sheer ruthlessness and disregard for conventional ways of operating that has characterised the company's growth. Stagecoach had applied, with a developer, Conder Developments, for planning permission to create shops and a health centre, leaving enough space to operate the bus services. Instead of rejecting the Stagecoach-promoted scheme outright, the local council gave permission to an alternative project developed by a local company, Caterite, even though Stagecoach owned the land and made it clear that it wanted to deal only with Conder. Stagecoach appealed but Ann Gloag, who dealt with property matters, was furious and had the idea of trying to influence the planners. She told Derek Scott, 'Since the bus station is an eyesore, let's make it more of an eyesore so that the planners reconsider their decision.' So Stagecoach moved twenty of its old buses from the field in Spittalfield in Perthshire, where they were stored, some having to be towed by breakdown vehicles, into the centre of Keswick. The blockade started right in the middle of the summer, which increased pressure on the local planners as the town is heavily dependent on tourism. There was chaos in the town centre, with tourist coaches being forced to park three miles away from the town centre and local traders were incensed at the loss of business.

Dale Campbell-Savours, the MP for Workington, told *Scotland on Sunday*: 'Stagecoach is using this town like some sort of Wells Fargo stage dump. It is an appalling abuse of every planning consideration. It is like holding a gun to the town's head.'

Ann Gloag, tongue clearly in cheek, hit back: 'We have to have a reserve fleet somewhere. All these buses are runners. Keswick is convenient for the motorway.'

But Stagecoach won and made money out of it. As Scott put it, 'We created a bus graveyard in Keswick and it had the desired effect.' Stagecoach's chosen developer, Conder Developments, was given planning permission and the company made around £700,000 profit from the deal.

That was just a local row but it presaged a much more serious one a couple of years later over all the property which Stagecoach took over with the NBC acquisitions. It was to be one of the first times that the company hit the headlines, something to which Souter and Gloag were going to have to get accustomed. And it was the beginning of Stagecoach's reputation as a ruthless operator living at times on the margins of the law.

In order to help finance the United Counties acquisition, in the autumn of 1987 Stagecoach had sold the Southampton part of the Hampshire Bus company for £1 million. The sale, which involved eighty-two vehicles (40 per cent of the fleet), enabled Stagecoach to concentrate on the other, more profitable, operations. More important, at the same time, Stagecoach also sold the company's Southampton depot for redevelopment, gaining an impressive £3.4 million. In other words, Stagecoach sold bits of Hampshire Bus for a total of £4.4 million, twice the price it paid for the company, and kept 60 per cent of the operations, the part which Souter felt was the most profitable anyway. Derek Scott says, 'We had taken out a seven-year loan to buy Hampshire Bus but we were able to repay the bank after only six months. That's the kind of deal which really pleases one's bankers.'

It did not, however, please Stagecoach's enemies, particularly Labour politicians, who were to accuse the company of asset-stripping, particularly as Stagecoach was able to make a similar level of profit in Cumberland. This time Campbell-Savours, who was a vigilant member of the Commons Public Accounts Committee, took an interest in the story. A tenacious investigator and a good publicist, Campbell-Savours ensured the issue attracted widespread media coverage.

The property assets had undoubtedly been one of the big bonuses of the early Stagecoach deals: they were bought cheaply as an integral part of the companies and there were no clawback arrangements on most secondary sales. The National Audit Office report into the sale of the National Bus Company which, as normal, preceded the Public Accounts Committee's investigation, was anodyne, congratulating the government on a 'very creditable achievement' in obtaining some £165 million net for the NBC companies. It made no mention of the undervaluing of properties sold to the buyers. However, the PAC, prompted by Campbell-Savours, was aghast at the way the sale had been handled and was highly critical of the National Bus Company. Campbell-Savours found that, for example, Keswick had been valued at £55,000 by the National Bus Company, but was sold for £750,000, and in Whitehaven the figure rose from £165,000 to £1 million. Property bought by Stagecoach as part of the Cumberland concern, which included bus stations at Keswick, Workington, Whitehaven, Maryport and Carlisle, five bus garages and half a dozen sundry sites, had been valued at a total of £986,500, only a bit more than Stagecoach had received for Keswick alone after its bus blockade.

Sir Alan Bailey, the permanent secretary at the Department of Transport, was grilled by Campbell-Savours on why the valuations had been so low. He said that the NBC and the Department had taken advice from experts who said that 'none of the properties had a potential alternative-use value significantly beyond the book value'. The MPs also had to recognise, he said, 'that as going concerns, the alternative-use value for individual properties might have to be offset by the costs of relocating and the impact on the business of the bus company and the earnings of the bus company'. In fact, Stagecoach proved to be clever enough to sell the bus stations while maintaining the existing services. Sir Alan said there was no clawback because the estimated alternative-use value of the property was considered to be not much greater than if it continued to be used as bus stations.

Campbell-Savours accused Stagecoach of asset-stripping. He told Sir Alan that Stagecoach had effectively sold three bus stations and obtained almost the whole price that it had paid for the company. He reckoned the rest, which included 230 buses and other property, was effectively obtained for free: 'I think they have had the deal of the century and the taxpayer has lost out,' he told the committee.

The Tory-dominated Committee largely agreed with him. Noting that clawback on profits of properties sold on by buyers had been applied to only eighteen of the NBC's 1500 properties, the committee said that 'In the case of some of the properties formerly owned by Cumberland Motor Services, the new owner has realised much higher prices from selling properties into alternative use compared to the valuations put on them by the Company's property advisers ... we consider that more should have been done to identify operational and other properties that had an alternative use and to put a realistic valuation on it ... we do not feel that the taxpayers' interest has been fully protected.'

As ever with privatisations, the Tories had been so keen to offload the companies that details such as properties were not properly considered. It placed too much reliance on its London-based advisers and Stagecoach, benefited enormously from that mistake. In 1990, Stagecoach revalued the property acquired from the NBC by £3,686,000, but this was partly a result of the property boom as well as the fundamental undervaluation.

Both Scott and Souter, however, claim that the development gains from the acquisition of the Southampton and Cumberland properties were pure luck. They even deny that they were being clever in buying the companies because they knew so little about the property market. They argue that Stagecoach should bear no culpability for being the fortunate – unwitting, even – beneficiary of the Government's mistake.

Souter denies the suggestion that this early period of the growth of Stagecoach was founded on this cheap disposal of public assets: 'When we bought Hampshire Bus, we had no idea it was sitting on a really valuable property. When we discovered its value, the first thing we did was to flip it to reduce debt.' As for asset-stripping, he argues that Stagecoach always spent more on new buses and depot improvements than it received from sales. The proceeds from the sales were not pocketed but used to reinvest at a time when Stagecoach was highly geared with a debt-to-income ratio of 21.

Stagecoach created another furore in 1990 when it announced that it wanted to close down the bus station in Lewes for redevelopment as a shopping complex. The maintenance and overnight parking facilities would be relocated, while the terminal would be replaced with bus stops in several nearby streets in order to reduce costs. Local opposition and the end of the property boom put a stop to the scheme.

Actually, once Stagecoach had cashed in on the Hampshire Bus deal, Gloag, who concentrated on property matters, had expected the company to make much more on asset sales, but the market collapse of the early nineties restricted the opportunities to cash in. Overall, though, the sales of assets, mainly depots, garages in the centre of towns and engineering works, contributed £11 million to Stagecoach's coffers in the first couple of years of its acquisitions spree following the break-up of the NBC, a major factor in Stagecoach's ability to achieve its phenomenal rate of growth.

Brian Cox, who joined Stagecoach from the Scottish Bus Group just after the sale of the Southampton depot and was sent down to run Hampshire Bus, says, 'It was very controversial locally and it still comes up now, ten years later. We still get people saying, "Stagecoach, the asset-stripper that sold Southampton bus station", but the point is none of the money was ever taken out of the company. It was fed back in investment.' Bearded and quietly spoken, Cox has a rail and local authority background, and now runs South West Trains. Like Hinkley, he became an executive director on the main board in October 1992.

The sale of the bus depot at Southampton meant that for the first time since they started Stagecoach, Souter and Gloag were not in debt. At last, their houses were no longer under threat as they did not need to be used as collateral with the bank. This was important for Souter, who was about to get married. He had known his wife-to-be, Betty, for several years, having met her through the church in Parkhead, and they eventually married in 1988. They have three children – Amy, born in 1989, Scott (1991) and Fraser (1993) – with, at the time of writing, a fourth on the way. Betty was a social worker for Strathclyde and now works part-time for the Souter Foundation, the charitable trust which Souter has established that contributes to Christian and other welfare projects, as well as being involved in Stagecoach's contribution to the Labour Government's welfare-to-work programme.

Fraser McColl, too, was no longer needed, and was released from his obligations within three months of the purchase of Hampshire Bus. Uncle Fraser, through his McColl Investment Company, had made the quickest killing. He had put in £46,500 for Hampshire Bus, out of £100,000 equity with the rest (£2.1 million) coming from Standard Chartered Bank, and sold out within three months for £540,000.

The acquisition of the NBC companies had allowed Stagecoach to take off. Before the purchases, Souter and Gloag had spent over six years building the company up to own 110 vehicles and have a turnover of £4 million (in the year ending 30 April 1987). By the following year, turnover was £26 million and the company had an extra 700 vehicles. Profits rose tenfold, from £525,000 in 1986–7 to £5 million the following year. The pair boasted that Stagecoach was 'Western Europe's largest independent bus company' and were eager for further growth. 'We are ravenous for further acquisitions. We want to take on the really big boys. We have a David and Goliath mentality,' Souter told the *Sunday Express* in April 1988. But Stagecoach would soon be a Goliath.

While it had concentrated on acquisitions, Stagecoach had not neglected its Glasgow beachhead but had not embarked on any other major attacks. Indeed, Magicbus was involved in a savage three-way battle with Kelvin Scottish (part of the still nationalised Scottish Bus Company) and Strathclyde Buses (owned by the Regional Council) in Glasgow, which took up much management time. In early 1988, Souter decided to compete on fares with very cheap bargains such as 20p for travel within the satellites of Castlemilk and Easterhouse, and a maximum fare of 55p through to the city centre. In an innovation that illustrates Souter's political leanings, he also offered concessions to UB40 holders (the unemployed) who were offered 5p or 10p off their fares. The first weekly tickets, which would later become a widespread feature of Stagecoach's marketing approach, gave passengers a week's travel for £4 and any member of the family could use the ticket.

Pensioners, who paid just 10p, could also buy a Magicgran ticket, giving a week's travel for a mere 50p. This was very different from the traditional bus company approach which was to offer minimal discounts on the sale of such tickets and restrict their use to one person. In the public sector, such tickets were seen as revenue losers, whereas for Stagecoach they were envisaged as a way of attracting more people on to buses.

Stagecoach also found itself on the receiving end of a battle that was to lead to a counterattack and writs in the High Court. In the summer of 1988, Harry Blundred, who had led the management buyout team that gained control of Devon General, decided, through a subsidiary, Basingstoke Transit, to start minibus operations in Basingstoke, part of Stagecoach's Hampshire Bus territory. The service was due to start on 4 August but Stagecoach decided to counterattack. Linking up with City of Oxford Motor Services whom Blundred had attacked in Oxford and ironically the company Stagecoach had failed to buy the previous year, Stagecoach decided to retaliate, not in Basingstoke, but in Blundred's home territory, running a free service in Torbay between St Marychurch, Torquay and Paignton Zoo. Because fares were not charged, the service could be introduced without the delay of the usual forty-two-day registration period.

The route was one of Blundred's most profitable services, and Stagecoach went about the task of pinching as many as possible of his passengers meticulously. The eight buses were decked in a white livery marked FREEBUS and all the bus stops were fitted with timetable holders and FREEBUS STOP flags ready for the launch on 27 June. Brian Cox, the Hampshire Bus managing director, argued, rather lamely, that it was 'a classic fares experiment' to test the market.

Blundred was incensed and went to the courts, alleging that there had been a 'conspiracy [by Hampshire Bus and City of Oxford bus services] in that they combined with each other to operate a free bus service in the Torbay area, maliciously and/or with the real or predominant purpose of thereby injuring the plaintiff's business'. The writ also attempted to stop the former Devon General sales manager, Stuart Scott, from co-operating with Stagecoach in setting up the free service with the 'provision of information about Devon General's business'.

On 7 July Stagecoach and City of Oxford, realising they were in a legally indefensible position, retired unrepentant, agreeing just before the High Court case in London to a settlement with Blundred which involved withdrawal from the market and paying a proportion of Devon and General's legal costs. Cox maintained the experience had been invaluable, telling *Bus Business*: 'We have fallen foul of an obscure law. We have mounted a practical exercise instead of a survey using expensive desk-bound consultants. We have had such a fantastic response that we can already appraise our experiment and press on with our plans for the future.' He felt that the only reason that Stagecoach had lost the case was because it had teamed up with another operator, thereby creating a 'conspiracy', but the experiment had not tested the legality of running a free bus service against a conventional revenue-collecting service. Indeed, free services were a tactic that Stagecoach was to use several times in the bus wars, knowing that the company's greater size would ensure it could sustain temporary losses while its competitors would often be forced to withdraw. Most famously, the strategy would be used in Darlington (see Chapter 9) in 1994 in an affair that was to damage Stagecoach's reputation severely and attract the fierce condemnation of the regulatory authorities.

The Torbay Freebus service, along with all the bus stop timetables, disappeared overnight but the eleven-day war had, according to Blundred, cost Devon General £112,000 in lost revenue, theatening his business, and he decided to plough on with the attack in Basingstoke. Stagecoach, through Hampshire Bus, planned to retaliate again by introducing fifteen new minibuses in the town. But, through an error by the Traffic Commissioner, Blundred's service was delayed for a month, and Stagecoach entered negotiations with him. Realising they would both lose a fortune, Stagecoach agreed to buy the nascent Basingstoke Transit operation before it started running and the bus war was averted.

Interestingly, Blundred, an innovative busman credited with first introducing minibuses to the UK, ended up friends with Stagecoach and there were several business dealings between the two over the next few years, including sales of companies in both directions, and Blundred, who emigrated after selling up to Stagecoach and FirstGroup in 1997, was involved in seeking opportunities for Stagecoach to expand in the Australian market in 1998.

Although Stagecoach had been buying new coaches since 1981, the company had relied on second-hand buses to use in its bus wars. But now, with three sizeable local bus companies, the strategy changed and the first order for full-sized buses was placed: thirty Leyland Olympians with bodies built by the Falkirk-based Walter Alexander, which was to become a long-term supplier to Stagecoach. The bus order was part of another innovatory strategy of the company. Whereas most of the new players used old and cheap buses and rarely bought any new ones when making acquisitions, Stagecoach realised that there were large cost savings to be made by buying new stock, which were also popular with passengers.

The *Buses* White Paper and its subsequent revolution had served Stagecoach well, but it had not fulfilled the expectations of the politicians. In particular, the White Paper completely failed to forecast the bus wars that were to have a highly damaging effect on the bus industry over the next decade. The White Paper had said, 'There are few reasons in principle for fearing that competition will lead to frequent and unsettling changes in the supply of services.' As we shall see in the following chapter, bus wars, with frequent changes of service and timetables, broke out in many parts of the country, usually providing short-term benefits to the consumer but long-term deterioration. Most damagingly, many bus users, confused by the array of services and the constant timetable changes, never set foot on one ever again.

The fundamental problem with the 1985 Act and the subsequent changes is that three very important policy changes were mixed up and implemented rapidly: deregulation, privatisation and reduction of subsidy. The loss of many services was a result of the third, but the public blamed deregulation. Subsidising the whole network – as opposed to individual routes – was made illegal by the new legislation. In some places, like Sheffield, where the South Yorkshire Passenger Transport Executive had a policy of very cheap fares – 10p for most journeys – the cost went up three- or fourfold overnight. Inevitably, bus usage plummeted.

Ben Colson reckons that it was this move that has created the enduring controversy over the bus revolution: 'Local authorities could still subsidise roadbuilding and car parking but not bus networks. Taking away that subsidy overnight was a gross political interference in the marketplace. They shouldn't have ended the cheap fares straightaway. It was done to shaft Labour politicians and led to a lot of politicians saying deregulation was wrong.'

The manifesto had also said, 'Merely to replace state monopolies by private ones would be to waste an historic opportunity.' In fact, private monopolies were precisely the final result in many areas. That was an inevitable result of the new structure of the industry. Perhaps Ridley could not have guessed that there were companies like Stagecoach who were to ensure that the monopolies emerged quickly after relatively short bus wars. But he should have known what would happen by opening up the market. The notion that thousands of small operators could flourish was always destined to be a nonsense. Anyone with the slightest knowledge of economic history could have told him that local monopolies and large-scale consolidations would be the inevitable result. Bus deregulation was, in many ways, a textbook case for students of economics on the behaviour of markets and the lack of understanding of the process by politicians.

Souter was better than the politicians at reading the runes. Much better. He had read the market, predicted the way it would go and helped it along. He was ready for more. After the NBC acquisitions, 1988 was mostly a year of consolidation with a few minor purchases. But Souter had a vision of creating a much bigger company and, for the first time, needed some serious outside capital. He knew he had to go beyond Perthshire and his immediate family to get it. Souter and Gloag talked to a few London institutions until they hit upon Noble Grossart, an Edinburgh-based merchant bank, where the reception was particularly warm.

It was to be the beginning of a long and fruitful relationship.

4
Wars here, there and everywhere

The offices of Noble Grossart in Queen Street, Edinburgh, reek of old money. The downstairs reception room has the feel of a gentlemen's club with its fusty decor, ornate fireplace and luxurious but hopelessly uncomfortable sofas. It was on one of these that Souter and Gloag sat in 1988 when they came seeking capital to expand their business.

Actually, Noble Grossart's image is a bit misleading since the company was only formed in 1969 as part of Scotland's then fledgling independent merchant banking industry and therefore the money is newer than it looks. So the bank is a bit of an upstart, like Stagecoach, but the pair of bus driver's children from Perth, perched uncomfortably on the edge of the sofa, knees on elbows, and very much outsiders in Scottish business circles, were not to know that. They were clearly ill at ease in these surroundings but, if their body language may have seemed tentative, their approach certainly was not. Nor had Souter tried to disguise his unconventionality by putting on a suit and tie.

They need not have worried. Ewan Brown, a director at Noble Grossart, was immediately impressed when Souter and Gloag made that first visit to his offices in 1988: 'Brian and Ann were not comfortable at all about working with people they had not known before. Previously, they had used local insurance brokers, local solicitors and, of course, Arthur Andersen. So even looking at someone from Edinburgh was a significant move.'

Brown says he had never quite met business people like them before: 'They were extremely open. They were absolutely clear about the business they wanted to be in. They wanted to stay within a transport remit, led by buses. No deviation, to be a travel agent or whatever.'

Brown was most impressed that they had mapped out the following four years: 'Even then they were precise about when they wanted to go public. We never have people coming to us with that degree of clarity. They said that flotation should be at the end of 1992, and they wanted me to come up with something that helped them through until then because they saw a lot of opportunities in that period. It was a complete contrast to most people who come to us and say, "We would quite like to sell out." We were pleased they wanted to keep so much equity. The more commitment they had to the company, the more it was likely to be successful. The placing was all to raise new money into the company, and there was no suggestion they wanted to take out big dividends or big salaries.' By then, Souter and Gloag were paying themselves £36,000 per year, which rose to £54,000 in 1989.

Indeed, Souter and Gloag were anxious to keep as much equity as possible and did not seek to cash in their chips at all at this stage. While they were clear on the date of a possible flotation, they wanted to keep their options open. They wanted to retain the choice of remaining as a private, family-run firm if, in four years' time, that seemed to offer the best prospects for the company. Therefore, they wanted a financing deal that enabled them to retain 100 per cent of the ordinary shares if they decided not to float. The London institutions wanted Stagecoach to float on the Unlisted Securities Market, but Souter and Scott felt it would have just meant lots of fees for the advisers and no advantage for Stagecoach.

Brown was struck by the way that dealing with Stagecoach involved so little haggling and detailed negotiation: 'It was straightforward. They felt that it met their requirements, and, moreover, the company's bankers agreed that there would be more money available for acquisitions.'

Noble Grossart came up with a financing structure that suited Souter and Gloag, providing them with £5 million to invest, doubling their capital base. It consisted of a mix of £3 million in 8 per cent redeemable preference £1 shares which would be converted into a minimum of 16 per cent and a maximum of 25 per cent of the share capital upon flotation, and the other £2 million in preference shares of £1, also giving 8 per cent, which, at the shareholders' option, were redeemable at £1.20 from 1993. But Souter and Gloag were so confident of the company's future success that they ensured the ratchet of conversion of the newly issued shares was dependent on the value achieved at flotation. The higher the value of the shares at flotation, the lower the percentage of shares could be converted into ordinary shares. In the event, because of the good performance, the investors got only 16 per cent of the equity when they converted.

Not all the companies whom Brown approached were interested in this small company in an industry that had been a habitual poor performer. However, seven major Scottish institutions signed up, including Murray Johnstone (which took 30 per cent), Standard Life (which took 20 per cent), and the Government's Scottish Development Agency. The involvement of the SDA provoked anger among Labour politicians, and the issue was raised again when Muir Russell, a senior Scottish civil servant, joined the board of Stagecoach as a non-executive member in December 1992 as part of the scheme to encourage links between business and government. The SDA, though, did well, selling its £500,000 stake for a profit of £2 million four years later.

Brown, a solid and cautious banker, who is both a qualified accountant and the holder of a law degree, was the perfect man to take an active part in Stagecoach's development, and Souter invited him to join the board as the company's first non-executive director. He is considered the doyen of the Scottish non-executives, extremely knowledgeable and always ready to protect the shareholders' interests. He knew about transport because he had been on the board of the Scottish Transport Group, the parent company of the Scottish Bus Company, and he remembered the dismissive comments about Stagecoach in 1983 during the Scottish coach wars: 'The board members of the Scottish Transport Group would say, "There is this long-distance bus company, Stagecoach, but they are not going to be a problem because they are in trouble. Indeed, we understand they are not going to be able to pay their wages next week." '

Brown also came from Perth, and later discovered that, by coincidence, he knew Iain, Souter and Gloag's father. As a child, Brown's best friend had been the son of a Perth funeral director and one of Iain Souter's moonlighting jobs had been to drive the hearse, earning some of the money that would later help the start-up of Stagecoach. Brown remembers Iain as 'a perfect gentleman in all ways' and this shared background helped him understand how Souter and Gloag worked: 'You knew immediately where they were coming from.'

Brown's role has been far more than that of many conventional non-executive directors who wander in to a meeting every quarter and pick up an unearned fee. Souter has used Brown as a sounding board for all his ideas, talking to him every day at crucial moments, and this close relationship has continued throughout Stagecoach's growth. In particular, Souter would phone Brown on his return to Scotland on a Thursday night or Friday morning, after following his routine of being in Perth on Monday and then spending three days on the road around Britain, Europe or the world. There is almost as close a relationship between the two as there is between Souter and his sister. Brown and Souter would discuss every idea that Souter suggested. Brown says, 'Brian is the person I would speak to most regularly. Brian would say, "I'm thinking of this," and I would say, "Have you thought of A, B and C?" '

According to Brown, Souter has never had to force anything through a board meeting before or since flotation. 'Ideas would be discussed over time. Then the thing comes back in a form that everyone lives with. He will have already won a consensus.'

Nor does Souter suddenly bounce decisions on his fellow directors: 'There are never any surprises. Right through the financing, the flotation, he never sprang anything on us. The communication is such that you are never surprised. He is a very good communicator and makes sure everyone is informed.'

Armed with the £5 million equity injection and a promised £50 million bank facility, early in 1989 Gloag and Souter set about spending their war chest. There was a lot happening and, in a strategy that was to become typical, they were interested in everything going. First, there were the NBC companies. Stagecoach might have been able to buy only three NBC companies at privatisation, but nothing in the rules specified how many could be bought second-hand.

Of the seventy-two subsidiaries sold by the NBC between 1987 and 1989, forty went to management and employee buyouts, who were given a 5 per cent advantage in the tendering process. By the mid-1990s, only a couple of these management buyouts had survived as independent operators. Stagecoach had bought eight from management teams, and, along with three purchased directly, eventually owned eleven out of the seventy-two NBC companies put up for sale in 1986.

There was the prospect, too, of the ten Scottish Bus Group companies coming on to the market. There were about fifty major municipal concerns in England and Scotland, which ministers were pushing local authorities to sell, by offering incentives such as the right to use the receipts for other council investment as long as they were sold by a given date. London, too, was slated to be privatised, but in the event the sale was postponed until 1994. There was also the potential of expanding abroad, which Souter and Gloag were actively considering.

And there was still the opportunity of taking advantage of deregulation. Souter knew that by setting up an operation in an area that had hitherto been a monopoly, like Glasgow, the incumbent could be weakened. Stagecoach would try to grab between 15 and 35 per cent of the market. He could then either buy the rival at a much reduced price, or try to drive it off some routes through fierce competition if it was weak enough in the first place. It was a win-win situation, provided Stagecoach chose the right battlegrounds.

In preparation for the spending spree, Stagecoach created what became known as the BAD team – Brian, Ann and Derek (Scott), the finance director – to comb the UK and abroad for opportunities.

Stagecoach started its expansion with more NBC companies acquired from management teams. First it bought East Midland Motor Services with a fleet of 300 buses, based in Chesterfield, in April 1989 for £4.5 million and then, two weeks later, Ribble, based in Preston, Lancashire, with a fleet of 830 buses, for £6.2 million. The prices paid looked on the surface less than the amount the managements had paid for them two years previously but they came with more debt. Stagecoach also made its first venture abroad, by buying UTM, the major bus operator in Malawi, on 30 March 1989 from BET. Stagecoach held 51 per cent, with the rest being in the hands of the government of Malawi. Stagecoach had already cut its teeth on foreign operations by setting up an odd deal in China which involved giving buses away in return for the right to advertise on them (Malawi and China are discussed in Chapter 6), but Malawi was the first time the company actually ran foreign bus services. Therefore, within three weeks in April 1989, Stagecoach had doubled in size, but the acquisition blitz did not stop. Southdown, a company based in Lewes, Sussex with 300 buses, and according to Souter, in a poor state, was bought in August 1989 for £6.2 million. This also was lower than the management buyout price of £7 million attained in 1987 but again landed the company with extra liabilities. There were a few minor purchases during this period, too, including a couple of small Cumbrian independents, purchased by Barry Hinkley at Cumberland, and a few minibus services from Southern Vectis, as well as Basingstoke Transit following the battle with Harry Blundred. The BAD team were in overdrive. Souter managed to buy all this without any further raising of capital, helped by the controversial sale of the properties and a few sundry disposals such as the chunk of Hampshire Bus (both outlined in the previous chapter) and, in August 1989, the Scottish coach operations (covered in Chapter 2). Stagecoach was always quick to sell off any parts of acquired companies that it did not feel were part of its core business, particularly coaching and engineering activities. The bankers, too, were ready to pour money into the company. Borrowings increased from £10 million in 1988 to £33 million the following year. Indeed, Stagecoach had bank facilities of up to £50 million under the terms of the private placing.

But trouble lay ahead. The Southdown purchase prompted a string of rationalisations along the south coast out of which Stagecoach South was eventually created. These reorganisations led Brian Cox to realise that the company needed to acquire some of the municipal undertakings that served towns along the coast and had never been part of the NBC, though now faced competition from either ex-NBC companies or new entrants. Cox says, 'The old NBC cronies had bought Brighton, Hove and District and carved it up nicely for themselves, leaving Southdown like a Polo without a centre. The management had been poor, with half of them in Lewes, and half in Chichester, and they never talked to each other. So it was a distress sale, but Brian was always willing to buy anything at the right price. It wasn't a very good company, but it had the potential with some additions and changes to become one. In particular, it needed Portsmouth at one end, to give it a substantial network, and Hastings at the other, to prevent it being infiltrated from that end.'

Therefore Stagecoach purchased Portsmouth Citybus in October 1989 for £550,000 and Hastings & District (owned by a holding company, Formia) for £1.2 million two months later. Inevitably, these acquisitions attracted the attention of the regulatory authorities because they operated in the same area as Stagecoach-owned Southdown.

Neither company was in a good shape. Hastings & District had made heavy losses in 1987–8 and there had been recruitment problems that led to a loss of reliability. Stagecoach had originally attempted to buy Portsmouth CityBus at privatisation in January 1988, but, after protracted negotiations, it was eventually sold to a company in which Southampton City Transport owned three-quarters of the shares and the workers the rest. Portsmouth remained loss-making and its owners were now happy for Stagecoach to rescue them since they could not afford to invest in new buses.

Nevertheless, the purchases prompted the first two of the eight Monopolies and Mergers Commission reports over the next decade into Stagecoach's activities – which were to result in seven defeats for Stagecoach and one victory. Until then, Stagecoach had avoided any such problems. However, another growing bus company, Badgerline, had already fallen foul of the regulatory authorities over its activities in the Bristol area, the first of the dozens of reports and enquiries into the bus industry which almost single-handedly kept the regulators in work over the next decade (see Chapter 9). The skirmishes between Stagecoach and the OFT, the MMC and ministers were to occupy a phenomenal amount of management time and energy over the next few years, particularly for

Brian Cox, who based himself in Lewes, and would create swathes of bad publicity for the company.

These initial references were over concerns that in the two areas, Stagecoach's takeover would result in a reduction of competition and the establishment of a monopoly. In Hastings there had been two operators: Topline, run by Stagecoach, as it had been acquired as part of the Southdown purchase; and the incumbent Hastings & District. Topline offered cheap fares which had originated with the previous owners. After the purchase of Hastings & District, Stagecoach merged the two operations very quickly, causing thirty redundancies, and within two weeks brought the fares of the combined operation into line with the higher ones charged by Hastings & District. Stagecoach told the MMC that it regarded the existence of two operators in a town the size of Hastings as unviable. Topline, it said, was an aberration and had only been in the market since May 1988.

There had been four operators in Portsmouth prior to Stagecoach's takeover of Portsmouth Citybus but Stagecoach was now responsible for 90 per cent of bus provision in Portsmouth and Havant. Stagecoach again argued that competition between Portsmouth Citybus and Southdown was unsustainable as both had incurred losses on their Portsmouth operations over the previous four to five years. There was scope for competition on some routes but the geography of the area, with the concentration of routes along a main corridor, made it impossible for network-wide competition. The MMC reports, as usual, were published nearly a year after the referrals, restricting the scope for action without further disruption to the local bus markets. Both Portsmouth and the Formia (Hastings & District) reports expressed concern about possible abuses by Stagecoach of its monopoly position and came to similar conclusions. They both recommended that Stagecoach should give undertakings not to increase fares on routes if the company were to lower them in response to competition. In other words, if a future competitor came in, and Stagecoach responded by slashing its fares, the company would have to retain those fare levels even after the competition disappeared. It was all fairly theoretical stuff because the recommendations were about undertakings on future events that might never happen.

But the minister, Nicholas Ridley, adjudicating on the Portsmouth MMC report in July 1990, did not feel that the Commission had gone far enough. In his last act before resigning over his famous *Spectator* article in which he likened the current German government to Adolf Hitler's regime, he insisted that the Office of Fair Trading should ensure the divestment of Portsmouth Citybus by Stagecoach. Ridley had clearly been dismayed that his model of dozens of small regional bus companies, harried by hundreds of tiny one-man operations, was being rapidly dismembered by Stagecoach, and two other emerging groups, Badgerline (now part of First Group) and Drawlane (now part of Arriva), who between them had bought twenty-five companies by 1990.

And then Peter Lilley, the Trade Secretary, did the same with Formia at the end of 1990. The MMC suggested the same sort of undertakings on fares from Stagecoach and did not recommend divestment, not least because the panel realised that the long-suffering passengers needed stability, but Lilley did not listen. The new Trade Secretary said that he was not convinced that these undertakings would be 'sufficient to deal with the consequences of the loss of competition caused by the merger'. Again, the Director General of the OFT was asked to 'explore with Stagecoach the possibility' of finding a buyer for part of the merged business. Souter and Gloag were infuriated by these decisions. Ann Gloag coolly dismissed it at the time by telling the *FT*: 'In the past year, we spent over £27 million on acquisitions. Formia and Portsmouth Citybus amount to less than £2 million. I would describe this as an irritation, not a major problem.' Souter feels that it was no coincidence that the two ministers who tried to force Stagecoach to divest were ideologues: 'Both these characters were coming from an extremely right-wing dogmatic view of the market. These are the people who wanted to see everyone having a minibus start at their front door and have "perfect" competition. Our assessment of the market in the early eighties was that long-distance coaches would end up with an oligopoly. And candidly, our review of provincial bus markets was that it would also end up as an oligopoly.' Souter feels that the process of consolidation of the seventy-two NBC companies was inevitable but that Ridley and Lilley did not understand this and were taking out their anger at the failure of their plans on Stagecoach. There is still, to this day, a feeling in Stagecoach that the company is hard done by, especially in comparison with other large bus companies. Scott points out that FirstGroup, in 1997, 'was not only allowed to acquire the Portsmouth Transit company, which we were forced to divest in 1991, but also the main competitor, People's Provincial, as well as Southampton City Transport. Yet we got pilloried by Lilley for trying to put together one piece, Southdown-Portsmouth, of that three-piece jigsaw in two of England's larger cities on the south coast.'

As well as calling into question Stagecoach's acquisition strategy, the ministerial decisions caused immediate practical problems for Stagecoach:

'If you have a tuppence-halfpenny business in the middle of nowhere, it's totally and completely impractical to divest it. We were in the middle of a recession and selling bus companies wasn't ever that easy.' There was a clash between the Department of Transport, which saw nothing wrong with Stagecoach's deals, and the DTI, which had, according to Souter, 'very dogmatic views of the bus market'.

In the event, Stagecoach sold Portsmouth Citybus six months after Lilley's decision. The buyer, ironically, was none other than Stagecoach's old High Court opponent Harry Blundred, who had defeated Souter and Gloag in the High Court over the putative bus war in Basingstoke and Torbay only two and a half years previously. The sale did not do Blundred any favours. According to TAS, the bus industry monitors, he lost £2.5 million in his bus operations in Portsmouth over the next five years.

But Hastings was to remain permanently in Stagecoach's ownership. Stagecoach had managed to stall the divestment while awaiting the result of a House of Lords court case over South Yorkshire's principal bus company on what constituted 'a substantial part of the UK'. This was because the legislation was concerned with monopolies only if they applied to a sufficiently large area and the definition was part of a legal challenge currently going through the courts. In the event, by the time the South Yorkshire court decision came through two years later, Michael Heseltine, a less ideological minister, was at the DTI (or Board of Trade, as he preferred to call it) and he was happy to reverse his predecessor's decision.

Stagecoach found itself involved in a third spat with a right-wing minister, Michael Portillo, over the proposed sale of West Midlands by the local passenger transport authority, which prevented Stagecoach from gaining control of its first large municipal concern. The West Midlands company, with 1,400 buses and a turnover of £150 million had been valued at £60 million by KPMG Peat Marwick, but Stagecoach considered it to be worth much more and approached West Midlands Passenger Transport Authority suggesting a price of £85 million. However, the PTA wanted to sell it to the 6,000 employees and refused to discuss the proposed sale with any other bidders. Souter protested to the Office of Fair Trading and to the local district auditor, arguing that the sale was a fundamental breach of the ethics of public bodies who were legally bound to obtain the best possible price when selling assets. Malcolm Rifkind, the Transport Secretary, handed over jurisdiction to his number two, Portillo, who not only rejected Souter's plea but showed just how unpopular the Perth company had become on the right of the Tory party. Portillo said that it was not a matter for the OFT, and the PTA could decide to sell it to whom it wanted. The sale was voluntary and Portillo was more concerned that it took place, ensuring privatisation, and was less bothered about the details of the price and the identity of the buyer. Souter's protests did, however, manage to help the residents of the West Midlands, as his intervention led to an increase in the valuation from £60 million to £70.7 million after pressure from the district auditor.

Stagecoach's valuation of £85 million proved to be rather closer to the correct one when, three years later, immediately after the clawback period had ended, West Midlands was sold to National Express for £240 million.

Stagecoach had a better reception from the Tory politicians over a legal battle concerning the purchase of Fife Scottish, one of the Scottish Bus Group subsidiaries, but fell foul of the Labour opposition, which was to be a source of yet more bad publicity for Stagecoach. The Scottish Bus Group had been brought into the fold of a nationalised structure in the same way as the NBC in 1968, but its sale required separate legislation, the Transport (Scotland) Act 1989. The sale had been delayed because the Tories had been reluctant to bring in the Act, since there was so much political opposition in a country dominated by Labour, and the people still felt bitter about the hated poll tax, which had been introduced in Scotland before England.

Again, rather than sell the company, which had a fleet of 3,000 buses and 11,000 employees, as a single entity, which would have enabled Brian Souter to realise his long-cherished dream of taking over the SBG, the Tory government decided to break it up into ten companies. Ministers argued that SBG's market position was too dominant, as it ran over 50 per cent of the route mileage north of the border and owned over 40 per cent of the country's buses. As with the NBC sale, there was a restriction on the number of companies that could go to the same bidder – only two non-contiguous subsidiaries could be bought by the same group. Management teams were successful in five of the bids and of the other five Stagecoach obtained Northern Scottish, in March 1991, and Fife Scottish a couple of months later, which precipitated a legal tussle and a major Parliamentary row.

Fife Scottish was the best and most profitable of the SBG subsidiaries and the 850 employees had been particularly keen on buying the company. Disappointed that their bid had failed, they lobbied their local MPs, who included the future Chancellor, Gordon Brown, and campaigned to stop Stagecoach from buying the company. Their bid was around £1 million less than Stagecoach's £9.1 million, well outside the 5 per cent leeway that was given to management and employee buyout teams. However, the workers managed to get a planned announcement of Stagecoach's selection as preferred bidder, scheduled for 29 May, cancelled at the last moment. The workers were allowed to file a second bid, for £9.2 million, even though, according to Stagecoach, 'this was against the rules'. Lord James Douglas-Hamilton, the Junior Scottish Office Minister responsible, decided to review the position but two weeks later confirmed Stagecoach as the preferred bidder.

Still the workers, backed most vociferously by Henry McLeish, MP for Central Fife and Labour's employment spokesman, did not give up and launched a legal challenge, seeking a judicial review of the ministerial decision because there was doubt over whether the second bid had been properly considered. However, in July, the judge in the Court of Session rejected the worker-manager team's attempt to review the decision and the Stagecoach takeover went ahead.

The affair led to a fierce attack by McLeish in the House of Commons a few days later when he said that Fife Scottish management had pulled out of the judicial review at the last minute because of fears that 'Stagecoach would come into Fife and destroy the newly fledged MEBO operation' if the company lost the court case. At that point, the Bank of Boston, McLeish said, which had promised the extra money for the second bid, pulled out as a result of 'the first signs of intimidation by Stagecoach'. The workers, he said, 'had been treated with contempt' and now they find themselves 'dealing with a predator who would stop at nothing to secure the bid and who was prepared to threaten to come in and destroy their company'.

Attacks on Stagecoach by Labour were to become a recurring feature over the next five years, with McLeish and Brian Wilson, another Scottish MP, who were both for a time frontbench transport spokesmen, usually in the forefront of the criticism.

Labour's attack on Stagecoach was helped by an own goal, the appointment of Bill Walker, the Tory MP for Tayside North, as a director of two of the company's overseas subsidiaries. With the Tories forever pulling up Stagecoach by going beyond the recommendations of the regulatory authorities in forcing the company to divest, and with Labour now, more predictably, joining in the attacks, having a few friends in high places seemed like a good idea. Walker was a local MP and had been a bus driver in Dundee; the thinking was that it would help not only in lobbying but also in Stagecoach's forays abroad. Walker was made a board member of Stagecoach Malawi, which meant he flew out there every quarter for a meeting, and of Stagecoach International, for which he was paid a small retainer.

Scott says, 'At first it went well as he got a VIP reception in Malawi, whereas we didn't. But as the Malawi government got to know us, they preferred to talk to Brian and Ann. Bill's ability to pull strings didn't count any longer.'

In fact, Walker became a liability. In the Commons attack on the role of the Scottish Office and Stagecoach in the Fife takeover in July 1991, McLeish also singled out Walker's role.

McLeish said in the Commons, 'I had a meeting with Brian Souter, the chairman of Stagecoach Holdings, in Westminster Hall cafeteria. Mr Souter may be a good businessman, but he has an awfully slack tongue. He said to me, "Mr McLeish, don't be silly. Mr Walker has been doing the same as yourself and Mr Brown. He has been lobbying intensively on our behalf [as he is] not only a director of Stagecoach (Malawi) Ltd and Stagecoach International Ltd but he is a paid consultant." '

Wilson, speaking in the same debate, accused Walker of acting as Stagecoach's bagman. He said, 'On one occasion [during the debate on the Transport Bill, Walker] nipped out of the door to telephone the Stagecoach management. He then came back to refer to the interests of Stagecoach. Every time we drew attention to the Hon. Gentleman's behaviour, he said, reasonably, that he was acting in his role as a constituency Member. Although Stagecoach is not in his constituency, he pointed out that some of his constituents worked for it. The Committee stage ended on 14 February 1989 and imagine our surprise a few weeks later when we read a reference to the Hon. Member for Tayside North as a director of Stagecoach.'

Walker denied any wrongdoing – indeed, during the passage of the Scottish Transport Bill, Walker was not connected with Stagecoach and only joined as a director after the Bill had gone through. He had become a director of Stagecoach after the committee stage, but despite the embarrassment of the debate, he continued to represent Stagecoach. Scott admits now, 'We kept him on too long. People thought he was on the main board, which he wasn't. And the message we got increasingly from the trade unions was that we are happy to work with you, but having a Tory MP doesn't help.' As late as December 1995, Walker, who was by then no longer a director, was still batting for Stagecoach, surprisingly defending the company after it had produced a poster blaming the Tory Budget for fare rises. The poster angered the Scottish Conservative Party, who pointed out that Stagecoach had benefited from Tory policies of privatisation and deregulation, but Walker said, 'Stagecoach have not been the beneficiaries of Conservative policy. It has simply made use of the market.' Wilson and McLeish both became Scottish Office ministers in the government formed by Tony Blair in May 1997.

The Fife Scottish story also illustrates how Stagecoach bears no grudges in its battles, as with Harry Blundred. The manager who was the mainstay of the Fife workers' challenge, Jim Moffat, was the only one who stayed right through to the final court case. The others thought they would get jobs with Stagecoach if they dissociated themselves. In fact, Moffat is the only survivor and is currently managing director of Fife Scottish. Derek Scott explains, 'He had the balls to take us to court, and see it through. He probably thought he would be the first to be sacked by Stagecoach. No hard feelings. If the roles had been reversed, we would have done the same.'

In England, Stagecoach made two final major UK acquisitions before going to the Stock Exchange. In March 1992, the company bought a controlling stake in National Transport Tokens, for £2.1 million. NTT is an alternative to the bus pass for concessionary fares schemes and is operated by many local authorities. They give the tokens to eligible people, such as pensioners, students or people with disabilities, who then use them on the buses, trains or taxis. The company makes its profit in a curious way, relying on interest earned on the money paid by local authorities to buy the tokens at the beginning of their financial year. There are also, inevitably, some tokens that are lost and never redeemed. Then, in October 1992, Stagecoach bought part of another former NBC company, Alder Valley, for £1.3 million from the Q Drive group and instantly renamed it Hants & Surrey. After that, the BAD team took a rest while considering whether to go for flotation.

The years between the private placing in 1988 and the flotation in 1993 represented the peak of the bus wars as deregulation took effect and new entrants sought opportunities. Even as early as this, Souter was telling the MMC – which seemed reluctant to listen – that seven or eight groups would emerge as the industry matured, although he accepted there would be room for some medium-sized and lots of small operators. Souter and Gloag realised that there would be only one opportunity to build up an empire in the bus business because the price of new companies would go up once the industry matured. Therefore Stagecoach went on the attack in so many parts of the country that it seems almost unimaginable that the effort could be co-ordinated by a very small number of executives – the

BAD team, with help from Brian Cox and Barry Hinkley – mostly based in Perth. This was possible thanks only to Souter's ability both to think strategically and to know the minutiae of every market in which he was a player.

One of the fiercest and longest wars took place in Stagecoach's home town of Perth. The attack by Stagecoach on a Scottish Bus Group subsidiary, Strathtay Scottish, then still in the public sector, had been carefully planned for several weeks. It was launched in June 1989 on two of Strathtay's most lucrative routes, including one to Letham, the Souters' old council estate, and the service was free for the first week. Strathtay responded with new buses and a new service to Letham, and the pattern was set for a lengthy battle.

Souter, however, was never going to lose this fight on his home patch and simply continued pouring in buses. Giving forty-two days' notice as required by the Traffic Commissioners, Stagecoach simply notified a new bus service in the area every week over the next two months, always on routes already served by Strathtay. The Stagecoach services also used the same route numbers as its rival, fooling many passengers unwittingly into using its services. The copying of route numbers was a common tactic by Stagecoach when trying to take business off incumbents. It was the sort of attack that Souter later deprecated, in that Stagecoach was doing little new other than duplicating its rivals, though its fares were usually lower. But Perth was his home town and, as Derek Scott puts it, 'Perth was one of the few occasions where Brian let matters other than commercial considerations influence his decisions. He wouldn't really like to have seen someone else's buses running past the office window all the time.'

Cleverly, Stagecoach at first ran only Monday to Saturdays, leaving Strathtay to pick up the tab for the city's loss-making Sunday services. In August, Stagecoach started running in Dundee, Strathtay's base, to keep on harrying its rival.

In October, Souter rationalised the whole Perth network, retiming all the Stagecoach services so they ran a few minutes ahead of Strathtay's buses. Strathtay responded with price cuts of up to 50 per cent but clearly, with both companies pouring in huge resources, losses were mounting and it finally caved in to Stagecoach's onslaught. In February 1990, Strathtay agreed to share all its operations in Perth with Stagecoach on a 50–50 basis and to co-ordinate timings with its rivals. In other words, after seven months of battles, Stagecoach had gained half the Perth bus market and was able to scale down the operation. The bonanza for the Perth people had ended. Stagecoach's win was not complete, however. In

Dundee, where Stagecoach's attack had been half-hearted, merely intended to keep Strathtay on its toes, customers remained loyal to the established company and Stagecoach withdrew.

It was to be another three years before Strathtay was finally seen off in Perth. Souter had dearly wanted to buy the company as one of the two SBG subsidiaries Stagecoach would be allowed to buy. But the Office of Fair Trading said that it would object to a Stagecoach purchase because it already operated in the area. Souter was incensed, but concentrated on ensuring he bought two of the other SBG companies. Strathtay was sold to Yorkshire Traction, which showed little interest in remaining in Perth & Kinross, closing first its Crieff depot and then the Perth one, selling the sites to developers. Finally, in August 1993, Strathtay abandoned the joint agreement and left Perth to Stagecoach. A former executive of Strathtay said that his company had wanted to keep on the fight but 'our workforce was intransigent. We were paying 30 per cent more, taking into account pension schemes and so on. We told them it was a matter of reducing wages by 10 per cent or making them redundant, and the drivers chose redundancy. Most of the good ones got jobs with Stagecoach anyway.'

The local battles normally followed a similar pattern, with a period of fare cutting, rear-mirror scheduling (waiting for the rival bus behind to turn up and then leaving the stop), buses leaping in front of each other between stops and massive overprovision. Typically, both operators would lose money and eventually, after a few months, one would withdraw bloodied and beaten. And it was rarely Stagecoach, given its superior resources and its readiness to keep harrying its opponents. Later, when Stagecoach's reputation spread, operators facing an attack would simply withdraw at the mere hint that the Perth-based company was coming to town or threatening an attack.

Glasgow was an exception to Stagecoach's run of victories. The battle there between Magicbus and Strathclyde Buses was to last five years until April 1992 when finally Stagecoach gave up, selling its underperforming Magicbus operation to Kelvin Central Buses. The sale, in fact, was a clearing of the decks so that there would not be any competition issues if Stagecoach bid for the huge Strathclyde Buses, then being mooted for sale. In the event, the attempt to buy Strathclyde Buses from the Regional Council failed when the council, after much delay, decided to sell it to a management-and-employee buyout team in February 1993. As with the West Midlands, Souter had complained that his company had not been given a fair chance to bid and that the local poll-tax-payers of Strathclyde were being cheated out of between £6 and £10 each because the company was being sold on the cheap to its managers and employees. However, Ian Lang, the Scottish Secretary, had refused to intervene, saying he did not have the powers to do so, and merely sought advice from a merchant bank that the sale price was correct. He rejected Strathclyde's original price of £28 million, but eventually let the deal through at £30.6 million in February 1993, a price described as 'ludicrously low' in the *Glasgow Herald* in May 1996, anticipating FirstGroup's £110 million takeover bid the following month.

The Magicbus operation, Souter's initial exploitation of the deregulation legislation, was to be the first of three attempts by Souter to gain a foothold in Glasgow, and the third war, between Stagecoach and FirstGroup, was still raging during 1999 (see Chapter 11).

There was another type of battle, too: the dawn raid organised with all the precise planning and logistics of a military operation. Describing them today, the Stagecoach executives betray an almost wistful tone in recounting how rolling stock was rustled up around the country and driven overnight to the chosen target. For a moment as they recollect these battles, they are old soldiers who have fought and won the war, the frontiersmen who conquered the West. The name 'Stagecoach' was no accident.

The first of these confrontations was in Inverness, where Stagecoach had arrived as something of a white knight in November 1989. There had been a fierce battle between the incumbent, Highland Scottish Omni-buses, at the time still part of the Scottish Bus Group, and a new company, a workers' co-op called Inverness Traction, which started in May 1988. Highland Scottish, whose core business was providing urban bus services in the Highland towns, reacted fiercely, duplicating its services and effectively ran the fledgling firm off the roads, forcing it into bankruptcy a year later. The routes were eventually taken on by Stagecoach's Magicbus subsidiary. The lumbering old MMC, as ever, reported in July 1990, long after the demise of Inverness Traction, heavily criticising Highland Scottish. Stagecoach, for once, was praised by the MMC, as it provided the competition that the publicly owned Highland Scottish had wiped out. Brian Souter told the MMC that Stagecoach was planning to stay in town and reckoned that Inverness Traction would soon be profitable. He was doubtful, though, that Highland Scottish could make money 'unless it adopted major economies, particularly in the engineering workshop'.

Souter was right. The new owners of Highland Scottish, Rapson and Clansman Travel, could not cope with the competition from Stagecoach-owned Inverness Traction, and, within two weeks of the privatisation in

August 1991, told its 250 staff of plans to make ninety of them redundant unless they agreed to a cut of 60p an hour in pay and a reduction of holiday time. The managers, used to the non-unionised coach business, were not adept at dealing with organised labour and threatened to make the staff redundant within a month, ignoring the normal ninety-day period for a company of that size. The union, the TGWU, was incensed, and the drivers were threatening to walk out. The union's Scottish national transport organiser, Archie Wilson, contacted Souter at 6 p.m. that evening to tell him about the problem in Inverness and enquire whether Stagecoach would be willing to help out. Souter, never one to lose an opportunity, saw this was the chance of gaining control in Inverness and told Wilson, 'If your drivers walk across the road, they will find a job.' The two depots were opposite each other. Moreover, Highland had been fool enough to try to undercut Inverness Traction's wage rates and therefore the drivers had little to lose. Souter, an old trade union hand, was quick to exploit this and to point out the legal situation over the redundancy period to Wilson. Fifty drivers went across straight away and Stagecoach knew that, without sufficient drivers, Highland would be unable to run many of its services.

Stagecoach, meanwhile, called up all its spare buses in Scotland and northern England. The company no longer had a reserve fleet of old buses rusting in fields around the country because the company now considered itself too respectable to run old bangers; but fortunately it had a few new ones awaiting collection at Walter Alexander's in Falkirk, and most of its nearby subsidiaries could spare some stock for a few days. Stagecoach managed to move forty of them overnight up to Inverness, including several from Cumberland, in time for the 6 a.m. start of services. With another twenty-seven on the way, some from as far as Hampshire, it promised to establish near-normal services within a couple of days.

Because there had not been time to comply with the forty-two-day notice period required by the Traffic Commissioner, Inverness Traction had to run the services for free. The Traffic Commissioner, sensing that the change was likely to be permanent, issued emergency licences within a couple of days, allowing fares to be collected. Inverness Traction also picked up many of the school bus duties which Highland had been unable to carry out – 350 pupils had missed classes on the day Highland's services collapsed – and its victory was almost complete by the following week when Highland conceded defeat by withdrawing entirely from Inverness and Easter Ross. Derek Scott later said, 'Inverness had not been so much a bus war, as a bloodless coup.' Stagecoach retains control of the town to this day, running some 95 per cent of local services, while Rapson's, which had been half of the consortium that bought Highland Scottish, remains as a successful operator in more rural parts of the Highlands. Stagecoach emerged well out of the Inverness fiasco, gaining a new territory while appearing to be the hero ready to provide a public service for free, and Souter had passed his test with the unions who had, so far, been wary of Stagecoach, which had helped break the Scottish Bus Group (and Citylink) strike in 1987. However, there was a downside. The success in Inverness may have influenced Souter's actions when a similar situation arose in Darlington three years later, with disastrous consequences for the company's image (see Chapter 9).

There was, in the meantime, another damaging episode, arising out of a different form of bus war, the David-versus-Goliath. Only now, Stagecoach was the Goliath and the company was accused of squeezing out a small operator in Bognor Regis, part of its south coast empire. It was an accusation made in various parts of the country as Stagecoach consolidated its local position, but the Southdown episode over the fate of a few minibuses, was to provoke a full report by the MMC, via a tussle in the High Court which Stagecoach, amazingly, won.

The complaint to the Office of Fair Trading was filed by Ian Hunter, who operated four minibuses under the name Easy Rider. The service had started in January 1987, three months after deregulation, and ran broadly along two existing Southdown routes though his service extended a bit further into a couple of housing estates where they went off the main roads to save people having to make long walks to the bus stop. The Southdown management left Hunter alone, and, so at first, did Stagecoach who bought Southdown in August 1989. However, in July 1990, Southdown attacked Easy Rider, running services shortly ahead of its tiny rival. Although this service was withdrawn in December, a few months later, Southdown attacked again, running just ahead of Easy Rider's services. Hunter resisted for eighteen months but eventually succumbed, selling out his business to Stagecoach.

The OFT went wild, saying Stagecoach had operated 'against the public interest' and referred the matter to the MMC, which as usual reported a year after Hunter had retired from the fray. In the meantime, however, Stagecoach won a victory in court which limited any collateral damage from the case. The OFT had tried to extend the remit of the MMC enquiry to cover all bus services in the Southdown area but Stagecoach went to the High Court seeking to overturn this decision.

The judge ruled in favour of Stagecoach, saying it was not open to Sir

Bryan Carsberg, the Director General of the Office of Fair Trading, to vary the terms of the enquiry. Had the MMC been able to investigate the whole of Southdown, there could have been other complaints and Stagecoach might have faced more widespread punishment than the feeble telling-off it eventually received. It was the first successful challenge by a company against a decision by the UK competition authorities, and certainly did nothing to endear Stagecoach to the regulators.

The Bognor case attracted widespread attention when it was used as the basis for a BBC regional TV programme, *Battle of the Buses*. Hunter told the BBC of aggressive tactics by Southdown in the Battle of Bognor: 'The worst tactic was blocking our buses in. The double-deckers came in on the main bus stops in town, which meant ours were held back and squeezed in. Sometimes we couldn't get out until twenty minutes after our departure time.' Some of the Stagecoach drivers were aggressive, he claimed, and 'tore timetables down off the bus stops'. The Battle of Bognor even spread to the punters. Hunter recounted tales of rows between passengers over which bus they took as his customers showed remarkable loyalty: 'There was a lot of animosity between my passengers and their passengers. There would be arguments at the bus stop. If one of their buses pulled up, people would say "Oh, no, don't get on that bus, wait for the Easy Rider, they'll be along in a minute." '

Hunter even found that a 'spy' had been sent in to work for his company for a month to gather information: 'He worked for exactly a month and he had previously been at Southdown and he returned there.' Inevitably, he complained at the slowness of the action taken by the regulatory authorities, suggesting that if the OFT had come in earlier, he would have been able to maintain his business. Eventually he sold out to Stagecoach, who paid him around £3,000 for each bus, about £1,000 more than they were worth, but nothing for the goodwill.

Stagecoach was unmoved and unrepentant, denying both the claims over its drivers' aggression and the allegation of anticompetitiveness. Easy Rider had competed with Southdown, posing a threat to its business, and therefore it was Stagecoach's right to retaliate. Indeed, it would have been anticompetitive not to have done so. Southdown accepted that it had run the rival services at a loss, collecting so little revenue that it did not even cover the drivers' wages, but claimed they were part of a network. Easy Rider, it said, 'was a classic creaming operation' abstracting revenue from Southdown and therefore the company was forced to defend itself.

None of that washed with the MMC. The fact that the MMC was powerless to take any meaningful action, since Easy Rider had long since been gobbled up by Stagecoach, did not stop it from berating Stagecoach in its report, saying the company's actions were 'anticompetitive' and 'against the public interest'. However, its only recommended punishment amounted to less than a slap on the wrists. Stagecoach was supposed to maintain the services for two years at the same level and not increase fares by more than RPI.

Hunter remains angry to this day: 'I never got an apology for all the hassle. They behaved appallingly and the routes which they took over from me are still being run today, which proves I had identified a new market.'

Stagecoach argues that this row over two routes in a small seaside town was a disproportionate use of resources and a waste of time for all concerned. But actually the Bognor incident illustrates, in microcosm, the main criticism of Stagecoach's behaviour, its readiness to drive smaller opponents off the roads if they are perceived as presenting a threat (see Chapter 9 for a fuller discussion of the issues raised by the OFT and MMC enquiries into Stagecoach).

As 1992 ended, Stagecoach was now among the big boys. In the year to April 1992, it had a turnover of £140.7 million and profits of £8.2 million. It employed 11,000 people and was operating in New Zealand, Malawi and Kenya although it had pulled out of Canada (all described in Chapter 6). It had tested the market in rail (described in Chapter 7) and, although that experiment was failing, Souter and Gloag were confident that rail privatisation had enormous potential. They were not, however, entirely convinced they needed the City. There were downsides, like dealing with the City types and consultants whom Souter views with scorn. Moreover, Stagecoach's reporting and accounting standards, and their procedures over such matters as directors' remuneration and presentation of annual reports, were already in line with those required of listed companies. The pair from Perth had come this far thanks to a relatively small private placement and a large bank borrowings facility which they had never used up entirely, taking at most two-thirds of the £50 million available to Stagecoach. Almost everything had gone to plan, although property sales had not brought in as much as hoped for, but bus operations had performed better. As the performance had been so good, why not stay private? Souter had, by then, begun talking about having a £1 billion company by the year 2000. They approached the Bank of Scotland to see if it was prepared to fund another bout of acquisitions, which might need facilities of up to £150 million or £200 million. No chance, said the bank.

There was, therefore, no alternative. Stagecoach had to go public in

1993 and Souter was eager to press forward to ensure Stagecoach got there first, before any other bus company and, in particular, Badgerline, which was close to being ready. That was a few months later than Souter had promised Ewan Brown in 1988 but the delay was a result of the late privatisation of the Scottish Bus Group. Otherwise, Brown is certain, Souter would have met his deadline.

5
Hitting the Stock Exchange

Brian Souter was persuaded to wear a suit and tie and black shoes for the month that he, Ann Gloag and Derek Scott trailed round the City trying to convince the institutions that this funny little bus company from Perth was going places. Souter describes suits as 'the most uncomfortable clothes ever invented' and certainly he looked distinctly ill at ease in his off-the-shelf number, which did not quite hide his red cardigan, posing in photographs for the accompanying publicity. One picture showed him standing rather perilously on top of a single-decker, presumably unbeknown to his insurers, its destination board proud proclaiming STOCK EXCHANGE 1.

On the City tour, Souter talked the most, Gloag focused on property and overseas, while Scott summarised the financial history. Reluctantly, Stagecoach took on expensive PR advisers, choosing Lowe Bell principally because William Clutterbuck, who fronted the presentation, 'turned up in a crumpled suit', according to Scott. He was also straightforward, unlike 'the other firms who had talked down to us', says Scott. Sir Tim Bell, Mrs Thatcher's favourite PR man, who owned the firm, was so impressed with the unassuming pair from Perth that he agreed to waive his normal £100,000-plus fee and charged them only £30,000.

The strategy was to give the company a homespun image of a little family firm which 'had growed and growed', and it worked a treat. The 'children of a bus driver' and the 'brother-and-sister' relationship were both stressed throughout: 'We have never fallen out in 12 years. We get on extremely well and we can substitute for one another,' Souter told The Scotsman. Much of the publicity in the run-up to flotation centred on Ann Gloag, since women in business remain a tiny minority. She had, after all, won the Businesswoman of the Year award in 1990 and was selected as one of three European Women of Achievement in 1992. The tale of running Robin, her former husband, off the road attracted much interest. 'It makes me sound awful,' she told the *Daily Telegraph*, 'but I can't deny it is the truth', stressing that she and Robin had made their peace afterwards. Putting Gloag forward had been a deliberate strategy by the pair in an effort to soften the company's image, and led to the widespread misconception that she, rather than Souter, was the main powerhouse behind the company. Both Souter and Gloag, however, were wary of too much coverage of their personal lives and were troubled by the fact that the Scottish papers, in particular, focused on how much money they were worth.

Stagecoach's offices were almost *literally* floated in late January 1993, a few days after the announcement that the company would hit the Stock Exchange in April. The river Tay, which is wide and fast because it takes the mountain melt through Perth, burst its banks and the Charlotte Street offices, beside the river in the flood plain, were inundated, shorting out the power and wrecking the ground floor. Souter helped clear the office, and ran operations from his house for two days while the flood abated. Richard Hannah, the analyst from UBS Phillips & Drew, which had been appointed as Stagecoach's brokers for the flotation, recalls his first visit to Perth with amusement: 'We met him in the front of his house and he came out wearing his wellington boots.'

The plans for the flotation were received generally well in the press and the City. The performance of the company to a large extent spoke for itself, given the phenomenal growth since 1987, and in interviews Souter stressed how Stagecoach had got the basics right, particularly increasing margins and revenue growth. Souter set out his vision for the future, citing four main 'areas of opportunity': the privatisation of London buses, the thirty-five bus businesses still in municipal hands, rail franchises, and expansion overseas. Indeed, the whole basis of the flotation was that Stagecoach had to concentrate its expansion principally outside the deregulated UK bus industry, which did not really present enough opportunities for Souter to achieve his aim of a £1 billion company.

Souter says that the company was floated 'for the right reasons: we did it to get access to capital and we didn't do it to cash in our chips'. Having started out in a council house and been 'a student in a flat with no toilet', he said 'my needs are pretty basic'. Souter stresses that the principal objective was to raise capital and to increase the pace at which the company developed. Of course, both Souter and Gloag used the opportunity to take a considerable amount of money out of the company – a total of £8 million – which they used largely for their individual charitable foundations and for *inter vivos* family trusts for their children. However, they retained a remarkably high proportion of the equity, 55 per cent of the votes at flotation if the charitable and family trusts are included. They felt this controlling interest was still important to them while they found out how listed companies operated in practice. As acquisitions were made over the ensuing years and shares were issued to pay for them, their holding went down gradually, going below 30 per cent when Porterbrook was bought in the summer of 1996. Souter felt that if he took too much money out at flotation, he would spend all his time trying to manage his own fortune, rather than looking after the needs of Stagecoach.

The City began to take an interest in Stagecoach, even though it had no experience of the bus industry. An analysis by UBS Phillips & Drew in February 1993 highlighted the company's underlying strengths. The figures, the first time the wider public had an opportunity to examine the company's performance, looked good. They showed not only the sharp rise in turnover, from £37 million in 1989 to £140 million in 1992, but how Stagecoach's cost-cutting was managing to push up margins in an industry that had traditionally relied heavily on subsidy. Apart from a blip in 1990 when loss-making companies were bought and interest rates were high, the operating margin had increased annually, doubling from 6.2 per cent in 1988 to 12.9 per cent for the first 36 weeks of the 1992–3 financial year. Pre-tax profits were not so impressive, partly because of interest paid on hire purchase to finance Stagecoach's heavy investment programme in new buses, but nevertheless went up from £4.3 million in 1988 to £8.2 million in 1992, with the same amount being earned in the first thirty-six weeks of 1993.

What the analysts rather missed out was the clever way in which Stagecoach had been careful to limit the damage from poor-performing areas in time for the float. The Gray Coach Lines acquisition in Canada had been disposed of in December 1992 with limited losses of £929,000 (see Chapter 6) and the experiment with overnight rail services between Aberdeen and London had been 'rationalised' in October 1992. What was, in fact, a contraction of the company's rail involvement was cleverly presented as an expansion, allowing the company to put sufficient gloss on its rail performance for the City not to notice that the scheme was a total flop and, indeed, was scrapped soon after the float, in the summer of 1993. Most important, the failure of the rail initiative was not allowed to undermine the City's confidence that Stagecoach would be a leading player in rail privatisation, which had been a major plank of the Tories'

1992 election manifesto. Just how big, no one at the time conceivably guessed, although Souter was already looking very carefully at where the real money could be made.

There were a few other little deterrents to investors. There was, for instance, no comparable company with which to benchmark Stagecoach's performance, as it was the first bus company to come to the market. National Express, which had successfully floated a few months previously, was a coaching operation, providing most of its services on a franchise basis, contracting in coaches from local bus operators, and therefore a very different proposition.

Secondly, there was a little late hiccup which was causing concern in Perth over a potential industrial dispute with the staff at the Chesterfield-based East Midlands company, where the unions claimed they were being asked to accept a £20 pay cut (10 per cent) and the implementation of a profit-related pay scheme which gave Stagecoach tax advantages. The union threatened an overtime ban but Souter sent down a squad of Scottish drivers by plane and the union recommended acceptance of a compromise deal with Stagecoach, claiming that overall the drivers would receive an increase.

There was, too, the much more awesome spectre of the Office of Fair Trading overhanging Stagecoach's expansion plans. The Bognor Regis affair was pending, although, as we have seen, Stagecoach had managed to limit the scope of the enquiry. Soon after the announcement of the flotation, there was a further complaint to the OFT by a small operator, Moffat & Williamson in Fife, about alleged anticompetitive practices: Stagecoach was competing on its subsidised routes and cutting fares below an economic level. In Lancaster, there was a nascent bus war, with Ribble attacking the local municipally owned firm after the council announced it was for sale. Even the latest acquisition, Alder Valley, could have faced a referral by the time of flotation, although in the event Stagecoach escaped one. The battles with the regulatory authorities were viewed in the City quite equivocally. On the one hand, they were a source of bad publicity and attacks from politicians, but on the other they showed a buccaneering spirit which was attractive to some analysts and investors.

With these possible downsides, several commentators were sceptical about Stagecoach's potential. *The Times* was distinctly cool, saying that 'the shares may go to a small premium when trading begins, but they are unlikely to achieve the substantial stagging gains of some previous issues'. The *Daily Telegraph* pitched it the other way: 'The shares are likely to perform well in the short-term, but over the longer run the appeal is more debatable.' Souter was skilful at making the right noises to give the float a bit of pizzazz and at dodging the potential problems adeptly. He made it clear that Stagecoach would be at the forefront of bidding for the rail franchises and when John MacGregor, the Transport Secretary, announced in February 1993 which lines were likely to go private first, Souter indicated that his company would be most interested in ScotRail and the London commuter routes. Souter stressed the experience Stagecoach had in running rail services and emphasised that the company wanted to create integrated transport opportunities for people using bus and rail together.

Souter was unfazed by the City. The company's stockbroker, UBS Phillips & Drew, had told him at the outset that it would be, in Souter's words, 'the most stressful time in my life'. Souter had replied that 'Anyone like me who had done time on the Glasgow buses knew everything there was to know about stress, thank you very much.'

The brother-and-sister duo from Perth certainly created a powerful impression in the City. Richard Hannah was amazed at how Souter belied his appearance: 'If you had an identity parade to see which person was worth three hundred million pounds, you wouldn't choose Brian Souter. Yet, his grip on business issues is unbelievable. He will cut through the crap in any conversation and get to the point very quickly.' Hannah recalls how, when he was pitching for UBS to be the brokers for the flotation, 'Brian Souter was telling us how wonderful the company was, rather than the other way around, which is what normally happens at pitches.'

Another broker, who bid unsuccessfully for the contract to underwrite the deal, described Gloag as quite the most terrifying person he had met during the course of his job: 'While we made our presentation, she sat glaring at us and was fierce in her questioning. We came out feeling that we had just sat through a bad exam paper. I don't think it was personal, as the other teams said they had also been given a bad time.'

Noble Grossart placed 21.8 million shares with institutions and sold 11.7 million to the public at 112p, valuing the company at £134 million. In the event, Souter needn't have bothered putting on a suit. The public responded with enthusiasm, forcing Noble Grossart, the merchant bankers, to print a further 30,000 mini prospectuses after the first run of 60,000 had been sent out. The offer was oversubscribed 6.9 times, with 45,094 private investors applying for shares despite a postal strike in Edinburgh. With hindsight, placing so many shares with institutions had been overcautious but a necessary part of playing the flotation game. The applications had to be scaled down in much the same way as the utility privatisations, with smaller investors being favoured and those trying to get 10,000 shares or more receiving none. No one got more than 1000 shares.

Both sets of pessimists – those who said that Stagecoach was worth buying only as a short-term investment and the others who said only the long term was worthwhile – were proved wrong. On the first day of trading, dealing closed at 124p, a premium of 12p or 10 per cent, and the price never looked back. Now there was to be a tangible measure of the Perth-based company's success – its share price. By the time of the announcement of the annual figures, in July, the price had gone up to 140p, even though almost half the small investors had cashed in their profits. They were to miss out. Within less than five years, the price would increase over tenfold and by Autumn 1998 topped £15.

On 27 April, the night that Souter and Gloag became paper millionaires, worth £36 million and £29 million respectively, the City boys and girls who had helped them held a party, but the pair, and Scott, all sent their excuses, returning to Scotland, where both Souter and Scott had new babies born within the past month. UBS's corporate entertainment budget for Stagecoach was always to remain greatly underspent.

As a side benefit of the flotation, Stagecoach recruited Keith Cochrane, the accountant who had been audit manager for Arthur Andersen's during the process. Cochrane had worked well on the preparations for the flotation and Souter and Gloag had taken a liking to the young man from Dunblane. Realising that they now needed a number two to Derek Scott, the finance director, they took him on in the Stagecoach tradition of hiring people with whom they had already worked or done deals. Cochrane, an obvious high-flyer, was only twenty-eight when he joined Stagecoach in October 1993 as group financial controller. He also became company secretary, replacing Scott, who was keen to reduce his workload and begin withdrawing from the front line. Cochrane eventually took over as finance director from Scott, who had long wanted to ease off his work commitments to Stagecoach for family reasons, in early 1996, aged thirty-one, and he is now a key player in Stagecoach's acquisition programme.

In preparation for the float, Souter and Gloag had already strengthened the board and the management team, largely with people who had been picked up from acquired subsidiaries. Two non-execs were appointed, Barry Sealey, a millionaire who, like Ewan Brown is a very experienced non-executive on the board of Scottish companies, and Muir Russell, the civil servant from the Scottish Office. Two new executive directors were also appointed: Barry Hinkley, who had been chief engineer at Cumberland when it was bought, and was swiftly promoted, becoming chairman of Cumberland, Ribble, East Midland and United Counties; and Brian Cox, the chairman of Stagecoach South and Stagecoach Rail. Their pay was modest by the standards of executive directors of quoted companies, receiving £65,000 and £60,000 respectively, while Souter and Gloag were now paying themselves £95,000 and £85,000, also relatively little compared with their equivalents elsewhere. With all its UK bank debt having being cleared with the capital of £20 million from the float, Stagecoach's lower gearing now meant it could set about growing again through acquisitions. Gloag had laid out the strategy in an interview during the flotation: 'Our growth in the next two to three years will be in the UK. Beyond that, the Pacific Rim; Australia is also planning to privatise.' Indeed, Souter reckoned there was only a limited amount of time to cash in on British bus acquisitions before they became too expensive. There were, now, other serious players in the market such as Badgerline and GRT (who later merged) and British Bus (later acquired by Cowie, now Anniva) and Go-Ahead, who would not leave Stagecoach with such a free hand when bidding for ex-NBC and municipal companies.

The first post-flotation acquisition was East Kent, another former NBC company, which had been the subject of a successful management buyout. In July 1993, Stagecoach bought the company for £4.9 million, and, for the first time, used shares – worth £1.5 million – to pay part of the cost. East Kent, with 250 buses and six depots, including Canterbury, Dover and Folkestone, was a natural extension to the company's south coast empire. In November, there was another of those little buying sprees that were becoming a hallmark of the company, with the acquisition of Grimsby-Cleethorpes Transport, for £4.4 million, and Western Travel – the parent company of Midland Red South, Cheltenham & Gloucester, and Red & White, which operate principally in a swathe of the Midlands, Gloucestershire and South Wales – for £9.25 million. It was hastily renamed Stagecoach West. The Grimsby deal was something of an exception, as Stagecoach was becoming much more adept at purchasing from management buyout teams like Western Travel than winning competitive tenders from privatisations of municipals. Souter, indeed, admitted this at the announcement of the interims in 1993 – which showed a 47 per cent rise in profits – when he said, 'We've been very successful at buying companies that were privatised through management buyouts but less successful with new privatisations, which have tended to represent not such good value.' This ability to find bargains was partly a reflection of Souter's knack of keeping up with events in the incredibly decentralised bus industry. If he noticed an ex-NBC company in a bit of trouble, or which offered a good deal, he would spend a day in the area and then approach the management. According to people who have been on the other side of the negotiating table, it was this personal touch that won him many of these deals.

The Western Travel and Grimsby deals did not attract the wrath of the OFT but it was soon back to business as usual with the regulatory authorities. The longstanding affair over the acquisition of Hastings & District (Formia) was finally resolved (outlined in Chapter 4) after the related decision on the South Yorkshire court case was issued. Michael Heseltine, now at the DTI, merely confirmed that Stagecoach should give a few pretty meaningless undertakings about potentially predatory activities.

Both the Fife and the Lancaster bus wars turned nasty and led to more trouble with the OFT and more adverse publicity. In Fife, Stagecoach, through its Fife Scottish subsidiary, had started running commercial services on tendered routes covered by its main local rival, Moffat & Williamson, a long-established local coach firm which had branched out into buses after deregulation. Fife is excellent bus territory, helped by a local council that, unusually, provides free travel to pensioners during the off-peak hours, thus underpinning a comprehensive network. Stagecoach not only attacked its rival on the normal commercial services provided by Moffat & Williamson, but also on the tendered (subsidised) services let out on contract by the local Fife Regional Council. This was highly unusual, given that the tendered routes were, by definition, unprofitable and therefore attracted subsidy from the local council, which felt they were socially necessary. Gradually, Fife Scottish attacked a significant part of Moffat & Williamson's business, duplicating services on thirteen routes where the smaller company had won council contracts, often against competition from Fife Scottish. Stagecoach argued that it had duplicated services only on those tendered routes where passenger surveys indicated that they were commercially viable and that its lower cost base allowed it to turn unprofitable routes into commercially viable ones.

Then, in January 1994, claiming that it was undertaking a series of fares experiments across its companies. Stagecoach offered return fares for just 10p more than the single journey. This was originally supposed to be a 'January Sale' but in fact stretched into the spring. Twice, Stagecoach attempted to buy out its rival but could not agree a price with the owners of Moffat & Williamson.

Moffat & Williamson complained to the OFT, which, reporting in March 1994, used the most critical language to date about Stagecoach's behaviour. Finding that Stagecoach's antics had been anticompetitive and predatory, Sir Bryan Carsberg, the director general of the OFT, said, 'The services operated by Fife Scottish were not commercially viable and were operated with the intention of removing Moffat & Williamson from the market.'

Stagecoach responded in kind. Jim Moffat, the man who had fought Stagecoach when it was buying Fife Scottish from the Scottish Bus Group and who was now managing director of the Fife Stagecoach subsidiary, was vociferous in his new loyalty, saying he was shocked that 'a supposedly impartial body could come up with such a mishmash of inaccuracies, half-truths and outright misrepresentation of the facts of this case'. He denied strongly that Stagecoach had tried to run its rival off the road.

Stagecoach, seeking to avoid yet another reference to the MMC, agreed to comply with the OFT's ruling, by giving a series of undertakings, including not raising the fares on the routes in question by more than the Retail Price Index, not reducing the frequencies on these routes and not registering new commercial services against other operators' tendered services. The OFT report did not, however, save the services provided by Moffat & Williamson, which soon withdrew from competing head-on with Stagecoach, apart from in St Andrews, simply letting the larger rival take over any routes where it staked a claim. Moffat & Williamson reduced its fleet from ninety-four buses to fifty-four.

Fife remains to this day virtually a total monopoly for Stagecoach, and Fife Scottish is one of the jewels in the company's crown, a highly profitable bus service which faces little outside challenge, apart from a recent attack by FirstGroup on some services in south Fife in retaliation for Stagecoach's launch of the Glasgow bus war.

In Lancaster, the criticism was equally fierce. In late February 1993, Lancaster City Transport, the 'arm's-length' municipally owned bus company, was put up for sale by the council, which was encouraged by the Government's decision to give incentives to local councils selling their bus companies by the end of the year. There had also been increasing pressure from Stagecoach, which had begun to compete with the Lancaster municipal company's services. Yet, surprisingly, Stagecoach did not bid. Stagecoach claimed that this was because it owned Ribble, which operated in the area, and fears of yet another reference to the MMC precluded a bid. So, instead, Stagecoach announced in a press release on 21 April that the company was registering a series of additional services starting two months later, adding that there were likely to be fares cuts. In other words, another bus war. Stagecoach argued that this was not an attack but that it was defending its interests in the area against a potentially aggressive buyer of Lancaster City Transport.

Brian Souter and Barry Hinkley went to see the Lancaster Town Clerk to argue for an alternative proposal, explaining that they would be interested in buying the Heysham Road depot and twenty of the council's buses (subsequently reduced to twelve). The council was in an impossible position. If it resisted the bid for the assets, Stagecoach's newly registered services would quickly have driven the local firm, with no subsidies available to allow it to operate at a loss for a long period, out of business, while the value of other bids was falling, given Stagecoach's declaration of war.

The council, in a panic, brought forward the deadline for bids from 22 May to 12 May, as Stagecoach had said its offer to buy the assets of LCT was on the table only until 21 May. There were five offers to buy the company and the highest, from Blackpool Transport Services, was initially £900,000 but was later reduced to £809,000. On 17 May, the council bowed to the inevitable and accepted the Stagecoach bid, which brought in a net total of £1.4 million for the depot, the buses and sundry other bits and pieces. Stagecoach took over the town's bus services from the now essentially defunct company on 23 August.

The MMC report into Lancaster, which came out in December 1993, was a rerun of the previous ones, finding that Stagecoach's move had reduced competition in the town (although the MMC admitted this had been 'limited' beforehand), which was 'against the public interest'. Again, the Commission shied away from forcing divestment, recommending instead, as in other reports, that Stagecoach give undertakings on its behaviour in dealing with new entrants. Stagecoach had to pledge to maintain any reductions in fares for at least three years and keep up the frequency of services for the same time after the withdrawal of any competitor against whom these measures had been introduced.

Despite the bad publicity and the criticism from Neil Hamilton, the Corporate Affairs Minister who was to become even more infamous than Stagecoach itself, Souter and Hinkley had got away with it, although publicly they expressed 'disappointment'. Lancaster became another Stagecoach town, with little prospect of challenge, and there was nothing that the regulatory authorities could do about the situation. However, just as with the Inverness takeover, Stagecoach's success in Lancaster may have contributed to the hubris which resulted in the damaging Darlington fiasco (outlined in Chapter 9).

There did not seem to be any losers, even though the council's pride took a dent. The council had, in fact, received over half a million pounds more for its assets than the other bidders had offered for the whole company, and the level of bus services had, according to the MMC report, not deteriorated, as 'there is no evidence of adverse effects to date'. Some staff did, however, suffer, because Stagecoach took on only twenty of Lancaster's drivers, leaving eighteen other applicants to find other work in an area of very high unemployment.

But, while the Fife and Lancaster enquiries attracted considerable media attention, they left the stock market completely unmoved with the share price barely suffering a blip each time the regulatory authorities reported. As Derek Scott told the *Financial Times* at the time of the Fife OFT report, which principally criticised Stagecoach over just six routes, 'the issue is not of material importance either to Stagecoach or Fife Scottish which has a turnover of £17 million'.

However, there were three other clashes during the period 1994–5, the height of Stagecoach's regulatory battles with the OFT and MMC, which were to be of greater significance. The one that attracted most media attention was Darlington, but its outcome did not prevent the company from continuing on its planned acquisitions trail. The other two, both over 20 per cent holdings of ex-municipal concerns in Sheffield and Glasgow, were more significant because they affected Stagecoach materially. They stymied its expansion in two potentially lucrative metropolitan areas and, again, in one of the cases, it was the politicians who took a harder line than the OFT and MMC.

In Sheffield, Stagecoach agreed to buy a 20 per cent stake in Mainline, an employee-owned firm which had previously belonged to the three local councils. Mainline was badly undercapitalised and was keen to merge with a bigger partner to allow it to compete against a bunch of cowboy operators who had made Sheffield infamous as the most overbussed city in England (along with Darlington). A myriad small operators had piled in partly as a result of Mainline's weakness, and the tie-up was designed to afford the company better protection against these competitors.

Stagecoach bought its minority interest in September 1994, for £1 million worth of new shares, and Souter became a director of the Sheffield company. Not only did the deal give Stagecoach a key stake in the firm, but it also put Stagecoach in the position of being able to take over the whole company at a later stage. Any offer by an outside bidder could be matched by Stagecoach.

The OFT was concerned that competition would be restricted by the fact that Stagecoach's East Midland subsidiary operated in an adjoining area, although its nearest depots were at Chesterfield and Worksop, thirteen and eighteen miles away respectively, and it ran very few buses into South Yorkshire. The merger situation therefore 'extinguishes or sharply reduces the possibility of competition developing between Stagecoach and Mainline'. It was not so much the fact of the reduction of competition that was the problem, but the perception that the merger would mean that Sheffield became 'Stagecoach country' and therefore unchallengeable by other operators because of the company's 'reputation for aggressive competition'. Therefore, the MMC sought to 'alter this perception and expectation'. Rather than suggesting divestment, which the Commission felt would be a 'disproportionate' response, it recommended that Stagecoach be banned from increasing its shareholding in Mainline above 20 per cent.

The Government, however, went further. When the report was issued in March 1995, Jonathan Evans, who had replaced the now disgraced Neil Hamilton in the Corporate Affairs job, decided that Stagecoach had to sell its 20 per cent. Souter was furious, but said that the setback would not alter the company's strategy. Nevertheless, Stagecoach's share price, which had just reached double the flotation price, dropped 28p to 209p as some analysts suggested that the company's acquisitions bonanza would have to end.

Stagecoach applied for a judicial review and ten months later sold its share to its large rival, FirstBus, for £1.7 million, a profit of 70 per cent. The judicial review, which combined both the Sheffield and Glasgow decisions, resulted in a partial victory, in that Stagecoach was not prevented from going back into those markets, a restriction the OFT had originally tried to impose. In fact, in the spring of 1998, FirstGroup acquired the rest of Mainline for £54. Derek Scott comments, with pique, that it 'is funny how FirstGroup, despite being the biggest company in West Yorkshire, can acquire the biggest company in South Yorkshire, when Stagecoach wasn't allowed a meaningful presence in either market because of contiguity with little old Chesterfield.'

In Glasgow, Stagecoach acquired a 20 per cent stake in return for abandoning a planned bus war. The initial Magicbus operation, Stage-coach's first bus war, had eventually been sold to Kelvin Central, a neighbouring bus company, in 1992 to clear the decks for a bid for Strathclyde Buses. However, as we saw in Chapter 4, Stagecoach had complained about the sale of Strathclyde Buses to a management employee buyout team with no open market tenders, but was unable to prevent the deal going through for £30.6 million in February 1993. Still keen to get into the Glasgow market, Stagecoach had tried to buy Kelvin Central but was beaten by Strathclyde Buses in October 1994. Stagecoach had, in the meantime, snaffled up Western Scottish, based in Kilmarnock, for £6 million in June 1994, making Stagecoach, briefly, the biggest operator in Scotland, but Souter had a personal interest in taking over in Glasgow, where he had worked on the buses. So, having failed to get Kelvin, he registered a lot of routes, using a depot over which Western Scottish fortuitously had an option, and gathered up spare rolling stock to mount an assault with sixty buses planned for early 1995. The thinking, Souter insists, was not vindictive but 'we simply believed there was room for two operators in the market'. However, the attack never materialised. Instead, Peter Shaw, the chairman of Strathclyde Buses, made Souter an offer he felt he couldn't refuse. Souter recalls, 'He said, "I'll give you twenty per cent of the company for eight million pounds." So I did the deal, knowing there was a very, very big regulatory risk involved.'

Indeed there was. This time the MMC did not wait for a minister to step in and force a divestment, but recommended it directly by forbidding Stagecoach from entering into an agreement that would inhibit it from competing with Strathclyde. Souter felt the decision was incomprehensible since, in a report published almost simultaneously, the MMC waved through Strathclyde Buses' acquisition of Kelvin, a company that had enormous competitive potential within the Glasgow area, as it ran contiguous services on both the north-west and south of the City.

Souter wanted to turn the defeat into victory by holding on to the stake long enough for Strathclyde to be sold, ensuring that Stagecoach was in a prime position to mount a successful bid. But one of Souter's business touchstones is never to pay more for a company than he thinks it is worth, however desperate he may be to make a successful purchase. Souter had reached a deal with Shaw, whom he considers as a friend, agreeing that £95 million was a reasonable price for the whole of Strathclyde Buses. This meant he would have had to pay only £75 million, since Stagecoach already owned slightly above 20 per cent. But FirstBus came in with an offer valuing the company at £110 million, which Souter felt was much too much. The personal antagonism between Souter and FirstBus (now FirstGroup) occasionally slips through: 'They were very late in the deal,' he says, 'which is very typical of FirstBus. It was overvalued, nearly thirty million pounds higher than our bid, but that was their problem.' Shaw insisted that the deal had to go through before any MMC enquiry, which meant that Stagecoach's biggest rival had to hand over £23.9 million for Stagecoach's stake bought only eighteen months previously for just £8.3 million. And by 1997, Stagecoach was back in Glasgow waging a war against FirstGroup (see Chapter 11), which had, in turn, also fallen foul of the MMC, who, in January 1997, ordered it to sell one of its Glasgow depots as well as its Midland Bluebird subsidiary.

The fact that Stagecoach was able to make good out of the SB and the Mainline divestments, selling both 20 per cent stakes at a healthy profit, demonstrates Souter's skill as a deal maker. The company was adept at holding on to the stakes for as long as possible, having learnt from the Hastings experience that circumstances can change.

Those profits did not, however, mollify Souter, who was bemused and angry at what he saw as the inconsistency of the regulatory authorities. Souter feels that both the regulators and the Government were specifically targeting Stagecoach, as it had in the Hastings and Portsmouth acquisitions: 'Stagecoach was on a run of acquisitions and the press coverage of it was such that it seemed like Stagecoach was taking over the world. They thought that to stop consolidation in the market, they had to stop Stagecoach. And if they couldn't stop Stagecoach, they felt they couldn't stop anyone else.'

The regular trips down to the MMC did not deter Souter from continuing to look everywhere for further acquisitions, and both Manchester and London were in his sights for 1994. The Government had forced the old municipally owned Greater Manchester Buses to be split into two for sale. Manchester had always been of interest to Souter, as the company's Ribble subsidiary already ran services nearby, and Stagecoach bid for the southern Manchester company when the two were put on the market in October 1993. Stagecoach was so keen to buy the company that it took out local newspaper advertisements trying to woo the staff away from their buyout bid. That was not enough to stop Stagecoach being beaten by the management buyout team after a bit of late shenanigans similar to the row over the Fife Scottish privatisation with the roles reversed. Stagecoach put in a late bid of £20 million after being beaten in the initial round by the management-employee team that was planning to pay £15 million. However, Stagecoach was rebuffed but was to come back two years later to buy the company and make a lot of the drivers comfortably well off (see Chapter 11 for a discussion of Stagecoach in Manchester).

London had always been a target for Souter, even though he disliked the framework that had been created by the Government. London's buses became a battleground within the Tory party as many MPs were worried about the effects of unfettered competition on the capital. Ironically, the buses had been nationalised in 1933 by a Conservative-influenced National Government worried about 'wasteful competition' and keen to integrate the transport system.

The privatisation of London's bus companies had been announced as far back as December 1992, but the political wrangles over deregulation had delayed the sale. The initial idea had been to deregulate and then sell the companies, the lessons of the chaos engendered by the simultaneous deregulation and sale of the National Bus Companies having been learnt.

However, Steve Norris, the Minister for Transport in London, realised the dangers of deregulating after the sale. With the support of Norman Fowler, the former transport secretary who had started the deregulation of the industry back in 1980 and was now the party chairman, Norris announced that the sale of the bus companies would precede deregulation. Later, he managed to get deregulation postponed until the next Parliament, which effectively meant the policy was shelved indefinitely. Norris says, 'I had Fowler's support. He was getting badgered by senior people in local London parties who were worried about the bus wars outside London.' There were fears that Oxford Street would become so clogged with buses that there would be no room for shoppers and that gridlock would result in places like Trafalgar Square and Regent Street. Without Fowler's intervention, London would have been deregulated and Stagecoach may have been a much bigger player in the capital.

Souter would have loved a deregulated London. He even claimed to Norris that the London bus companies would have been worth more had there been deregulation before their sale. Souter knew that with deregulation, he would have been able to buy a foothold in the capital and gradually taken over other companies. Stagecoach could have become, in effect, London Buses. Norris recalls that Souter told him at the time that if he had been allowed to operate in a deregulated environment, 'within a couple of years, he would have been running three-quarters of London'. Souter would, too, have wanted to bid for the whole of London Buses, but was not allowed to under the rules, which restricted any company to two of the ten London subsidiaries.

Souter's ambitions were, in this instance, stymied. Instead, London remains tightly regulated with London Transport letting out franchises for each route which are retendered every five years or so. The privatised companies inherited the bus fleets and a bundle of contracts which were then progressively put out to tender. Souter dislikes the system because he says it gives him no incentive to use his flair and skills at growing the business. The fares are fixed by London Transport and, in a way that harks back to the old pre-1986 regulated environment outside London, every route change, however minor, has to be approved by London Transport. Frustratingly for Souter, decisions are made very slowly, and it is impossible even, say, to run a service an extra 500 yards into a council estate without going through the bureaucracy to obtain permission. Initially, the London routes were franchised out on the basis that all the revenue went to London Transport, but now the system is being changed to a 'net cost' basis, which means that operators keep the income and receive (or pay) a set amount from (or to) LT to run the operation.

Despite these constraints, Souter made sure that Stagecoach won the bids for two of the ten businesses. Indeed, in a canny move, he bid for one of the best companies, East London, in combination with a real dud, Selkent, which had long been a poor performer for LT. In September 1994, Stagecoach paid a total of £38.2 million for the two companies, adding around a thousand buses to its fleet. In recognition of the particular circumstances in the capital, Souter lowered his normal requirement of an 18 per cent margin on acquisitions to 15 per cent. As Souter pointed out at the time, while the system constrained his freedom, it also guaranteed that there was no competition, apart from the five-yearly tendering process.

Roger Bowker, a gentlemanly Lancastrian much admired within the industry for being a successful bus operator, had headed the East London team and was frustrated at not winning the bid with his management buyout team. Indeed, his disappointment was compounded when he discovered that he had been outwitted by Souter's canniness, as Stagecoach's bid for East London on its own would have lost, but London Transport was so eager to get rid of Selkent at a reasonable price that the two were taken together. Souter, never one to miss an opportunity to turn a good busman into a loyal Stagecoach manager, not only initially kept Bowker in London as chairman of both companies, but later gave him the chairmanship of Stagecoach Portugal and transferred him to Swebus as the number two, with the task of reorganising the company. Stagecoach, meanwhile, had begun to provide the soap *EastEnders'* local bus route, with one of its Routemasters featuring regularly on the programme.

With London in the bag, Souter was paying increasing attention to rail as the next source of expansion, making sure that he kept abreast with every twist and turn of the long, drawn-out and controversial privatisation saga.

The acquisitions had continued apace throughout 1994. Apart from those mentioned above, in July 1994 Stagecoach had also bought Busways of Newcastle, which had been a management-employee buyout, for £27.5 million, the company's biggest acquisition to date with 600 buses, again largely funded through a share issue. The 1,750 employees who had bought the company received between £4,000 and £13,000 each. It was Busways that was to become involved in the Darlington row and the establishment of Stagecoach Darlington. The Busways and London acquisitions demonstrated Stagecoach's ability to move into the big metropolitan areas which Souter now saw as the best opportunity for rapid expansion, despite the setbacks in Birmingham, Glasgow and Manchester. There were other smaller purchases later in 1994, such as Cleveland Transit, Kingston-upon-Hull City Transport and Hartlepool Transport, but the pace cooled. The bus market was maturing and the opportunities for good deals were diminishing because of increased competition from the other emerging groups.

Souter not only likes being the ground breaker when an opportunity arises, but also tries to make sure he is the first to realise that a particular area is no longer fertile ground.

In the media, some of the coverage was not just critical about the battles with the regulatory authorities, but also expressed City fears that Stagecoach was biting off more than it could chew. Commentators had noticed that profits were being kept down as a result of Stagecoach's large investment programme in new buses and its fares policies. A *Guardian* profile of the company in July 1994, following the announcement of its profits of £19 million on turnover of £191 million, was particularly doom-laden. The company had net debt of £55 million and a gearing of 111 per cent, enough to 'give sleepless nights to most finance directors. But Mr Souter and Mr Scott appear to have no qualms,' the paper said. 'This is all very worrying. Thoughts of Sock Shop, Coloroll, Spring Ram and the other over ambitious companies are impossible to banish. Can Mr Souter and his team cope with the pace of acquisitions? ... Confidence might be easier to come by if the top two roles were not occupied by the founding brother and sister,' the writer suggested.

The criticism misread the business. Buses are an amazingly cash-rich industry. As Barry Hinkley says, 'If I ever get depressed, I just go down and watch the drivers putting the cash into the counting machines.' The revenue from bus operations is very steady. Despite the undercapitalisation of the management buyouts from the NBC and the other shaky businesses that emerged from deregulation, fewer than a handful of significant bus firms ever went bust. Stagecoach is no Polly Peck and Souter no Asil Nadir. The company was also showing healthy organic growth, with profits from the older subsidiaries rising sharply as margins increased as a result of restructuring.

Indeed, the share price did not reflect the doubts of these commentators. The shares stood at 190p in July 1994 and, a year later, 236p.

Accepting that the pace needed to slow down, Souter ensured that 1995 was a period of consolidation, during which rail and overseas markets were investigated. Apart from the £3 million Chesterfield company, Stagecoach acquired nothing significant that year in the British bus industry until the purchase of Cambus for £12.6 million in December. Indeed, Stagecoach was establishing a pattern with a period of feeding frenzy, followed by digestion. Souter focused much of his attention on seeking organic growth for the firm, creating special offers for passengers. By then, he had decided to ease off launching attacks on existing smaller operators, seeking to avoid further references to the MMC.

There was also rail, which was the natural next step. The start of the franchising process for the railways was to mark the end of the period in which British bus services dominated Stagecoach's activities. The next couple of years would see the company expanding overseas and becoming a major player in rail, the subject of the next two chapters.

6
Foreign affairs

In the early days of Stagecoach before he was married, Souter, who likes travelling to exotic places, used to go on holiday to places like the Caribbean and Hong Kong with his sister. The pair would always take the opportunity to investigate the potential of the local bus market. Expanding overseas was on the Stagecoach agenda right from the beginning, much earlier in the company's existence than would normally be expected of a small start-up business. Even when he was operating just a few coaches in Scotland, Souter always saw beyond the UK, because he did not want to be constrained by the size of a relatively small home market.

As with many British companies expanding overseas, Stagecoach's record has been patchy, with some notably bad experiences as well as successes. One of the failures, Canada, could have threatened the whole future of the company, as it got into difficulties shortly before the planned float, but, on the other hand, the operations in Africa were, at one time, an unlikely contributor of substantial profits to the business for a very small outlay.

The first attempt at an overseas venture was in Sri Lanka in 1988 with a plan to import forty Routemasters which were being sold off by London Transport. London Transport had suggested to a Sri Lankan transport minister who was visiting Britain that Stagecoach, which had been a long-standing customer for second-hand Routemasters, might be interested in such an arrangement. Stagecoach even appointed a project director for the scheme, but the minister was removed from his post and the connection was lost before the project could be seen through.

A bizarre venture involving Hong Kong and China was therefore to become Stagecoach's first overseas operation. The scheme arose from a link with a local engineer, Clement Lau Ming-Chuen, whom Souter and

Gloag had met on a fact-finding trip to the colony in the spring of 1988, when they studied the operation of the massive Kowloon Motor Bus company. When the pair came back to Perth, they kept in correspondence but found themselves receiving letters in Chinese, which they took to local Chinese restaurant workers to translate.

Lau had set up a company called Speedybus to supply various municipal operators across China with former Kowloon double-deckers. Stagecoach became a 50 per cent partner in this venture, which started in November 1988 and involved giving the buses to the municipalities free in return for putting advertising, principally from Korean and Japanese companies, on the outside. To check that the buses were still sporting the advertisements, every few months they were filmed outside the relevant railway stations on date-stamped photographs. Because the buses were second-hand and the advertising relatively expensive, the payback period was only two years. At its peak, Lau and Stagecoach had over a hundred buses operating in various parts of China with advertisements for products such as Panasonic and Mild Seven cigarettes – this was before Stagecoach's cigarette and alcohol advertising ban – but the Chinese began to go off the idea as they replaced their old petrol-driven buses with modern diesels. Therefore, soon after flotation, Stagecoach sold its half to Lau, who had also lost interest because he was concentrating on his other businesses. However, the foothold that Souter had gained in the colony through this connection had almost brought about a major coup just before the float. In 1992, the Hong Kong colonial authorities decided to remove twenty-six routes from China Motor Bus, which was the second-biggest company there, but banned Kowloon, the largest, from bidding, because they were seeking to make the market more competitive. The contract was large, involving two hundred buses. Stagecoach bid on the basis of new rolling stock, which would have cost £20 million, and only just lost out to Citybus, which was going to use second-hand buses bought in from Singapore. Stagecoach bid deliberately high on the basis that the flotation was coming up and the company did not want to take any risks, especially as Canada had gone pear-shaped.

The Hong Kong authorities said they liked the Stagecoach bid and wanted the company to remain as a resident operator because they preferred to deal with locally based outfits. Setting up in January 1994, on its own this time, Stagecoach began bidding for routes coming up for retendering, but in the next couple of years the company managed to obtain licences to run only a paltry eleven buses, which made the project unviable. Stagecoach found that the three companies, Kowloon, China

Motor Bus and Citybus, which dominated the local market, were being given extensions without open competition and eventually decided to pull out in October 1996.

Souter still remains deeply interested in the now united China, seeing it as the world's largest bus market, but suffered another setback in the spring of 1998 when Stagecoach tried and failed again to get into the market. It bid in conjunction with the Ngan family, which owned China Motor Bus, for a 570-bus concession, but was defeated by FirstGroup, which teamed up with a Hong Kong Chinese company, New World. However, in the spring of 1998, Stagecoach bought a stake in Road King, a company which operates toll roads in China and, in March 1999, Souter was more than adequately compensated by Stagecoach's acquisition of Hong Kong Citybus which operates 1,200 buses (see chapter 11).

The first successful venture abroad, therefore, was in the unlikely setting of Malawi in southern Africa. Souter had heard on the grapevine that BET – the same company whose British operations were merged into the NBC in the late sixties – wanted to dispose of its businesses. With the growing unrest in South Africa, Souter realised the price was bound to be cheap. He travelled to Malawi and thought the company had considerable potential: 'I went out and loved it. It seemed like a really good company. BET were downsizing it all the time, but I could see there were a lot of new opportunities for extra routes and for double-deckers, which were unknown in Africa outside of South Africa at the time.'

BET ran its bus firms as if Victoria still ruled over Africa. Scott described the BET management as 'having a patrician attitude that dates from the great days of the Empire. It was the sort of company we love to deal with because they don't drive a hard bargain. The typical BET manager would fly in for a day for a board meeting, have a ceremonial tour around the company and then go off on a safari for a week, being treated throughout like a VIP. They certainly never sat in a bus.'

BET's only reluctance in selling the operation was that these young upstarts from Perth might make a hash of it and BET would get the blame. BET were not particularly bothered about the price of the deal, selling the company for £800,000 in March 1989. As Scott says, 'Three hundred buses for eight hundred thousand pounds, compared with Britain, where you would get eight buses for that.' Stagecoach thus obtained a 51 per cent stake in United Transport Malawi (UTM), which was the country's principal bus operator, while the Government retained the remainder. The company suited Souter because, wary perhaps of relying too much on Chinese takeaway staff, he had been looking for opportunities where the locals spoke English, drove on the left and where there were some UK expats.

Malawi, formerly Nyasaland, is a very poor, small, landlocked country with a population of nine million, principally scattered in rural areas, heavily dependent on bus transport. Hastings Banda had been in power since independence in 1964, ruling through his Malawi Congress Party. The President's party occasionally commandeered Stagecoach's buses for political rallies – paying for the 'hire' but not for the disruption – but Scott insists that, apart from these occasional incidents, Stagecoach did not pay bribes to a regime that, unusually in Africa, did not have a corrupt civil service.

Although ridership had been declining, Souter was impressed with the company that BET left him. UTM ran virtually everything with little competition, which meant Stagecoach had around 90 per cent of the market. There were long-distance coach services, principally between Blantyre in the south, the capital Lilongwe and Mzuzu in the north, as well as an express to Harare in neighbouring Zimbabwe. There were rural services split into three divisions, most of which were on dirt roads that were frequently flooded in the wet season. Thirdly, there were city services running within the two main conurbations, Lilongwe and Blantyre.

The driving conditions were typical Third World, with unlit and overloaded lorries speeding through the night, and the bad weather occasionally created elephant traps for buses. One former East London bus manager, dispatched to help out in Malawi, described how a bus disappeared into a thirty-foot-wide crater after the rain had washed the road away and it took three days to dig a slope and haul it out. The massively overcrowded *matatus*, unlicensed small buses, were Stagecoach's only significant rival, and another Stagecoach manager said he was shocked to count 119 people on a single-decker.

Despite Stagecoach's virtual monopoly, Malawi was problematic from a business point of view, too. Stagecoach first left in an expat manager from BET but he failed to rationalise the business in the way Souter felt was necessary. There was a need for flexible approach, with fewer services being run in November to March, the rainy season, since most of the rural people, dependent on their crops, had no money for transport during that period and the roads were difficult. Non-productive miles were expensive because fuel made up 30 per cent of the operational costs (seven times the proportion in Britain at that time) and spares another 20 per cent, while fares, controlled by the government, were low, necessitating high loadings. Souter and Gloag had to go to Africa every month, alternating with each other, to ensure the business was turned round. The number of buses was increased from 260 to 330 over the first three years and services were restructured.

Stagecoach imported sixty second-hand Daimler double-deckers from Hong Kong, which at first were greeted with concern by some passengers, who refused to go upstairs because they could not see the driver. Nevertheless, they became very popular and Stagecoach also ordered ten Dennis Dragons in kit form from the UK for assembly in Malawi and therefore boasted, with a bit of licence, that these were the first double-deckers to be built in Africa outside South Africa. By 1994, over 200 new vehicles had been introduced by Stagecoach, mostly through local bank borrowing and some finance from the Commonwealth Development Corporation, which lends money at a favourable interest rate to investors in Commonwealth countries. The fleet size had increased by nearly 50 per cent to 360 buses and the number of miles had risen by 20 per cent. Souter and his managers had, too, given the company the usual Stagecoach makeover, improving productivity – not so vital when drivers were paid £70 per month – but, more important, squeezing costs through better purchasing. Souter was desperate to promote local people on to the board, seeking to promote 'an enterprise culture', but largely failed because most of the suitably qualified people, with experience of the West, preferred to work for government rather than a local bus company. An employee share-ownership scheme was created, though, involving 15 per cent of the local company's shareholding.

A tragic incident had already signalled the difficulties of working in such an alien environment. In November 1993, fire had swept through the accounts section of the Stagecoach Malawi head office at Chichiri in Blantyre. Two people, the chief personnel officer, Simon Siula, and Smart Liwonde, an accounts clerk, perished in the fire, which managers first thought was just a tragic mishap. However, Siula's presence in the office late at night had been considered odd and, on investigation, arson was discovered. Petrol had been poured on to company records and set alight because the two men had been cheating their employer and had feared they would be discovered, as an audit was due to begin. Souter stresses that his involvement in Malawi was a business opportunity, even though he recognises that providing an efficient bus service was a vital social service: 'If a bus doesn't operate in the UK, there is social hardship incurred by some people, but if a bus doesn't operate in Malawi, the quantum of the social hardship is greatly heightened and the health of the economy threatened. You would go into a bus station and see a hundred people waiting for a bus, which was in the workshop, and you would wonder how these poor folk would get home tonight. It really was a social service, and we provided a comprehensive network which ran on dirt roads, which were loss-making and cross-subsidised by very profitable intercity services.'

Stagecoach's investment was repaid within two years of the takeover, and, by flotation, Malawi was contributing an annual £1.66 million of operating profit, over 10 per cent of the group's overall profits. Although Souter called Malawi 'his hobby', the subsidiary's contribution was impressive for an operation in the fifth poorest country in the world, bought for half the amount of that year's profits. The Malawi operation was badly hit by rampant inflation in 1994 after the overthrow of Banda and Stagecoach lobbied the Government, successfully, to be allowed to put fares up.

Stagecoach achieved legendary status in Malawi, with even its livery, considered banal in the UK, being fêted for its bright colours, unheard of on African buses since they get so dirty on the dust roads. As Ben Colson, then the group's network analyst, put it, 'You could do almost no wrong if you worked for Stagecoach. You were on a pedestal.' Stagecoach became part of the very fabric of the country. The 11 a.m. from Blantyre up to the North took twenty-four hours and had a trailer on the back. On Mondays, Wednesdays and Fridays, it carried the soap for the area and on the other days it had the post.

Initially, Stagecoach used the Tory MP Bill Walker (see Chapter 4) to try to forge links with the Malawi Government, but Gloag soon established close relations with ministers and, in particular, Hastings Banda, the ageless long-standing president who was only finally ousted in May 1994 and died in November 1997. However, the freeing up of the market that Stagecoach had lobbied for rather rebounded on the company, as there was increased competition from the unregulated *matatus*, which are supposed to carry around twenty-five people but often have twice as many aboard. The lack of any control of these vehicles led to Stagecoach's abandonment of its Malawian subsidiary in September 1997, and its handover to the Government.

Keith Cochrane, Stagecoach's finance director, says that operating conditions just became too difficult: 'The market has just become too deregulated. Every pick-up truck will stop and pick people up, and there's been the importation of a lot of illegal minibuses which haven't paid duties or taxes, so it became impossible to run a professional operation in that environment.'

Africa proved to be a learning experience, and was consciously used as a training ground for managers by Souter. Colson, who spent a couple of months out there to train staff, was amazed at how much he learnt: 'There was amazing market segmentation which was far more sophisticated than anything in the UK. On the long-distance routes, you had basic coaches going every hour or two, night and day, with no advance booking and called Inter City. Then, next stage up, there was the Express, running four or five times per day, which was prebooked and you were charged a bit more. And then there was the Rapide, the luxury service, with hostess service and was nonstop between Blantyre and Lilongwe. And amazingly, though the coaches had to dodge gunfire at times from the Mozambique border next to where the road ran, they did a journey which was the same as London–Manchester in less time. This was a really sophisticated market differentiation through price and quality of product, which we have in the UK on trains but not on buses.' It was a lesson that Colson was to apply in Manchester a few years later (see Chapter 11).

Gloag was particularly taken with Malawi and devoted considerable amounts of energy to charitable work there. As a former nursing sister in a Perth burns unit, she was concerned that there were no such facilities in Malawi. She organised for Stagecoach and her own Balcraig Foundation to fund a burns unit at the Queen Elizabeth hospital in Blantyre; Stagecoach paid the wages of three of the unit's thirteen nurses and for a plastic surgeon to visit from Britain. The original cost was estimated at £40,000 but eventually about £100,000 more than that was spent. Stagecoach was also involved in much other charitable work in the country. Buses due for export to Malawi were stuffed with clothing, old spectacles and medicines, while Stagecoach adapted ten buses to help distribute maize and rice food aid in 1992–3 following a severe drought. A link, for the donation of medicines and equipment, was created between the Scottish town of Blantyre, birthplace of the explorer, David Livingstone, and the Malawian city of the same name.

Gloag's diligence in her charitable work is shown by her continued interest in the hospital. Colson recalls dropping into Perth on his way to Malawi and ending up being Gloag's bag man for the Christmas presents in 1996 just before the company was sold: 'We've got lots of Christmas presents for the children,' she told Colson, 'every one in the hospital. Could you please take them out there with you?' Colson agreed, though he was terrified that the customs and airport security would not believe that the contents of the packages were innocent. Even when Stagecoach left Malawi, Ann Gloag retained an interest in the running of the hospital and just gave her house away to the people living there.

Given the success of Malawi, Souter had begun trawling round the world for other ventures abroad and a Canadian merchant bank, Royal Dominion Securities, approached the company, as it was desperately seeking buyers for Gray Coach Lines, owned by the Toronto Transit Commission. Souter went to Toronto with Derek Scott and thought there was potential for a profitable operation even though it was making only a small margin at the time. There was certainly scope for extra revenue, as he personally discovered. When Souter and Scott took the Gray Coach bus from Pearson International Airport, the ticket they were issued with showed March 1990 – and they were in May 1990. Scott recalls how Souter pulled out the ticket at the business presentation and there were blushes all round.

In October 1990, after a lengthy delay following the conclusion of the bidding in May, Stagecoach took over most of the assets of Gray Coach Lines, including eighty-five coaches, from the Toronto Transit Commission for $13.5 million Canadian (£6 million) with money the company borrowed locally from ScotiaBank. Gray Coach Lines ran principally high-frequency intercity operations in Ontario, and a few to the US, and the airport bus from Pearson to downtown Toronto.

The deal was to be nothing but trouble. There were inherent problems, such as high wage rates and restrictive working practices, which had deterred Canadian bidders because, under local employment legislation, they would have had to pay the same rates throughout their companies. Secondly, and uniquely among the Stagecoach group, Gray Coach did not carry out its own maintenance. Instead, as part of the deal, this was contracted to TTC, an arrangement that was to be the source of an ongoing row, which attracted a lot of local criticism of Stagecoach.

Stagecoach could probably have overridden all this, except for two fatal pieces of bad luck. First, the recession began to bite in Ontario almost as soon as the ink was drying on the deal and the expected growth in passenger numbers did not materialise. Secondly, and worse, the Gulf War and the preparations for it terrified North America and the people stopped travelling through fears – unfounded – of terrorist action. As Souter puts it, 'Passenger numbers began to plummet through the floorboards.' The airport bus, one of the steady earners, started to run virtually empty. Under the contract with the airport, Stagecoach had to run a bus every ten minutes when one an hour would have been sufficient at the time of the Gulf crisis and subsequent war. The Niagara Falls part of the business also collapsed and the small profit of Gray Coach turned into a big loss.

Souter recalls without hesitation the precise figures, and the way that

Stagecoach had done its best in turning the company round, showing just how painful the failure remains to this day: 'We bought Gray Coach for sixty-six per cent of asset value, which seemed a great deal, and in the first year we took twenty-three per cent out of our costs. But our revenue fell twenty-five per cent. It was bad luck. Just as getting the Southampton bus garage was providential, so was this.' If it had been a British company, Souter says he would have bought out some of the other people and used the tax losses, but with the bank on his back and no way of exporting Canadian tax losses, he could not do that here. Stagecoach had managed to sort out a labour deal, reducing the restrictive practices and staff overheads but maintaining the hourly wage rate, which made the company more saleable, but it was still leeching money, especially as Stagecoach had borrowed c$16 million to buy the company and pay for the restructuring. Souter, desperate to get the company off his balance sheet before the flotation, went in search of a purchaser. He started spending every other week in Canada, having left Malawi and the newer acquisition, Kenya, entirely in Gloag's hands, and eventually he managed to wangle his way out of trouble. Barry Hinkley and Brian Cox were left in charge of the UK businesses while Souter sorted out the disaster.

The rescue was three-pronged. First, Souter sold the thirty northern routes to Ontario Northland Transportation Commission at a substantial profit because of the new labour agreements, which Souter reckons was 'amazing' given he had bought off one public body and sold to another. Secondly, Souter went to Calgary with Scott and negotiated a deal with Dick Huisman of Greyhound Canada for the rest of the business.

To do so, however, as the third part of the rescue strategy, Stagecoach had to seek protection under the Companies Creditors Arrangements Act (CCAA), the Canadian equivalent of the USA's Chapter 11, which enables companies to trade while legally insolvent. According to Souter, the reason for seeking this refuge was that the dispute with the TTC seemed unresolvable. Stagecoach claimed that once the Commission had decided to sell in 1989, it had stopped carrying out major maintenance and there was a huge backlog when Stagecoach took over. Scott maintains that 'we had engineering records to prove it'. The TTC had an ace up its sleeve. Much of the revenue from the services was still collected by the Commission, as it sold many of the tickets in Toronto outlets. It stopped handing over the ticket money in response to Stagecoach's refusal to pay for the maintenance or to hand over the $500,000 of the purchase price that Stagecoach was withholding, claiming that the buses had not been maintained properly in the presale period. By using the CCAA, the debts were frozen but the business remained a going concern, new creditors being paid in full, and Greyhound Canada took over the remaining routes. The judge who presided over the CCAA hearing thrashed out a deal through which the creditors – principally the TTC – received 15 cents in the dollar. Souter reckons that the arrangement was fair, as only Stagecoach and the TTC really lost out: 'If I had sold to Greyhound and they had wanted only an asset buy, the liabilities would have gone into a receivership-type situation. And the TTC would have got next to nothing.'

Under the deal, the Commission received $800,000 of the c$2.3 million claim for maintenance and the remainder of the purchase price. Incredibly, Souter made a healthy profit on the sales of the assets, receiving £18.5 million, a profit of c$5 million, but the massive trading losses and interest payments meant overall there was a deficit of nearly £1 million.

The Canada episode had cost Stagecoach dear and caused Souter a lot of headaches, but ultimately the saga did not look too bad in the flotation prospectus, which said only that 'the loss of £929,000 incurred by the Group in connection with this investment has been fully provided for'. The most important point was that Souter had got rid of a potential millstone, as it would have been much more difficult to float Stagecoach with a subsidiary in CCAA. Souter had learnt a lesson, too, which was that companies could lose a fortune in a regulated market: 'Every tiny change of service needed six months to negotiate with the regulatory authorities and the problem was that we were outpaced by the recession. It was like moving sands underneath us.' He also realised that a problem in an overseas subsidiary can eat up an enormous amount of management time, which, in a business like Stagecoach – where so much responsibility is vested in a few hands – can be very damaging.

Fortunately for the company, Souter had been cautious from the start by ringfencing the debt, ensuring that a failure overseas would not put the whole Group in danger. 'In an overseas jurisdiction, you've got to be careful that you don't expose too much risk to the core business. That was a strong lesson from Canada.' Unlike many companies that have foundered in North America, Stagecoach had got only a bloody nose and, interestingly, almost went back for another dose. In March 1997, on a visit to Canada, Souter negotiated with his old pal Huisman to buy Greyhound Canada. Cochrane and Scott, who knew all the people, were dispatched to Calgary and Toronto to thrash out a deal. Scott says, 'I found myself in Canada again, trying to buy this coaches-to-airlines company, which I was not sure would be wise. But we lost out.' The successful bidder was Laidlaw, which runs school buses throughout North America.

Despite this failure, Souter is proud that he was able to go back to a country where he had a bad experience as well as a lot of disputes with the Toronto Transit Commission and yet the people welcomed him: 'That's the secret of Stagecoach. It's built on relationships with people. I laugh at those who say we have this aggressive reputation. How on earth can you do all these deals if you don't get on with people? It was through the personal relationship with Huisman that we nearly bought the company. We stand by our word and we don't have a reputation for chicanery, or changing our minds. When we shake hands on a deal, our word's our bond.'

Derek Scott reckons that the Canadian experience was also a demonstration of Stagecoach's ability to cut and run: 'It's an example of Stagecoach being pragmatic. A lot of companies would have been tempted to pump more equity in rather than taking the hard decision. We only used CCAA because of the dispute over tickets and maintenance, but it was a very useful device.'

During the Canadian kerfuffle, Stagecoach had expanded in Africa through the acquisition of two Kenyan businesses. In November 1991, Stagecoach purchased majority holdings in the country's two largest bus operators, Kenya Bus Services of Nairobi and KBS Mombasa, from BET, which continued to demonstrate its lack of enterprise by not alerting Stagecoach to the proposed sale. BET had promised to tell Souter and Scott, who had done a recce of KBS in 1990, when other companies were being put up for sale. In fact, they only heard on the grapevine from KPMG that BET was preparing to sell the Kenyan businesses to a group of Asians in Mombasa who, Scott was informed, were just going to asset-strip them. They had offered £111,000 and Stagecoach topped that by £100,000 to gain control of a business with 325 buses, including the largest depot in the group, at Nairobi, which by 1997 was housing 300 buses.

Soon after takeover, there was a threat of strike action by the Nairobi bus drivers amid concern that Stagecoach would not honour long-service and pension benefits. Ann Gloag quickly went to Kenya to assure the workers and told them that the company was considering creating an Employee Share Ownership scheme (which, in fact, never materialised because of legal and tax difficulties). She succeeded in calming the Nairobi workers but was unable to satisfy the more militant Mombasa staff and, soon after her departure, 700 workers there downed tools and were promptly sacked by Stagecoach for going on an 'illegal strike'. After negotiations, most were offered their jobs back under new terms and conditions, which involved extra duties, a commitment to abide by management decisions and a six-month probationary period. Almost all the workers accepted this deal, but the company refused to reinstate a group of shop stewards and a few other union activists who were considered to be 'troublemakers'. Their cause was taken up by opposition MPs, who raised the matter in the Kenyan parliament, but eventually the row fizzled out.

Labour unrest broke out again in February 1995 when bus drivers in Nairobi went on strike during a visit by Gloag over a local management decision to charge drivers for damages in accidents for which they were responsible, but this time Stagecoach was forced to back down unequivocally. Gloag was furious at the local management for embarrassing her by trying to impose the contentious rule.

Despite the difficult conditions, Stagecoach completely reorganised the company, reducing the 3,300 staff complement by 400, primarily through cutting administrative support jobs where, as Barry Pybis, the chief executive of KBS, put it, 'duplication of duties had reached a fine art'. Stagecoach managed to increase ridership by 25 per cent in the first three years and imported a steady stream of new buses CKD – Completely Knocked Down, and therefore needing to be assembled locally – in line with the requirements of Kenya customs regulations, to replace older stock. A computerised management and booking system was introduced and productivity increased, such as getting 280 buses washed every night with the same staff as previously only cleaned ninety, thanks to the construction of a borehole and better organisation.

Mombasa, where the local council retained 49 per cent of the business, was always under too much pressure from unregulated competition and it had never been profitable, so Stagecoach sold it in 1996 for a small loss. However, Gloag, who again took a personal interest in the business, was keen to hold on to Nairobi, despite the difficult operating conditions and the unpredictability of having to keep up a relationship with another grisly African despot, Daniel arap Moi, prone, like Banda, to throw his opponents in jail. A photograph in *On Stage*, the company's house magazine, shows the President scowling so hard at the smiling Gloag while shaking hands with her that a lesser woman would have fled the country permanently. Perhaps the scowl was because he remembered that, the first time she met him, she said firmly, 'As a company, we don't pay bribes.' In fact, Moi views Stagecoach favourably, possibly because he used to run a bus company himself and he personally hosted the launch when Stagecoach reintroduced double-deckers in October 1995. They were not a great success because Dennis, the manufacturer, had not reckoned on the problems of operating at 6,000 feet in a hot climate on the equator. The buses suffered frequent breakdowns from overheating, and plans for a second consignment were scrapped.

Despite the constant problems with the 4,000 unregulated *matatus*, the Kenyan subsidiary had managed to stay in the black until 1998, though returns had long been on the slide. However, when Mike Kinski, who became Stagecoach's chief executive in April 1998, went on a fact finding visit to Kenya the following autumn, he concluded very quickly that it was not a market Stagecoach should remain in. He says: 'I was there a couple of hours and realised it could never be made to pay. Engineering costs were soaring because of the deteriorating roads and you have unlicensed *matatus* in front and behind undercutting you. So I went to Brian and said, "you have to sell it." He said "it's between my heart and my head." And Souter's heart lost, as Kinski quickly disposed of the business to its management, ending Stagecoach's adventure in Africa.

Kinski intends to stay out of such markets in the future: 'I perceive there being three types of market; the developed countries, the emerging economies such as China, and those in crisis such as parts of Eastern Europe, Africa and Latin America. While we see opportunities in the first two, we are keeping out of the third kind.'

Given the failure in Canada, and the vagaries of operating in Africa, Stagecoach's first straightforward overseas acquisition was its purchase in October 1992 of Wellington City Transport in New Zealand, which has become the company's most profitable bus operation, achieving a 20 per cent margin. The business, like many Stagecoach acquisitions, came through a personal contact. Ross Martin, the chief executive of Wellington City Transport had visited Stagecoach during a trip to the UK at the time of the 1991 Rugby World Cup. The business was very cheap, £2.56 million for a profitable concern with a turnover of £4 million and 270 vehicles, including some trolleybuses, trams and a funicular railway. Stagecoach got the company on recommendations, as the City had been reluctant to conduct an auction: 'They rang up the TGWU and even the National Federation of Bus Users, both of whom gave us glowing references,' says Scott. Stagecoach quickly expanded, taking over tendered operations in Auckland and a minibus operation in the Hutt Valley. By 1996–7, Stagecoach had increased turnover to £15.4 million, without any fares increase since 1990, and made £2.7 million profit with continued organic growth. Souter reckons New Zealand is a great place for public transport businesses: 'There is not the same stigma which public transport has in Britain. The New Zealanders are very environmentally aware, so they increasingly are choosing public transport. We could learn a lot from them.'

Souter is an admirer of the semi-deregulated system in New Zealand. Where routes are tendered, other operators cannot compete – preventing attacks like Stagecoach's on Moffatt & Williamson in Fife (see Chapter 5) – and where routes are operated commercially, they have to be registered in advance if the operator wishes to claim income from concessionary fares discounts. Souter reckons, 'New Zealand has the best of British deregulation, without some of the excesses.' Local authorities even have the right to override deregulation for environmental reasons. So Stagecoach has been able to win long-term franchises for its Wellington trolleybus operation, and buses powered by gas are looked upon favourably.

Stagecoach attempted to expand in New Zealand in 1998 with a bid to buy Auckland's £30 million Yellow Bus Company, but the New Zealand Commerce Commission blocked the bid because 'it was not satisfied that Stagecoach would not acquire or strengthen a dominant position in the market for scheduled passenger services in Greater Auckland'. The response was a result of Stagecoach's already having a small operation in the city. This was Stagecoach's first major brush with overseas regulatory authorities and Derek Scott feels it was prompted by FirstGroup's attempts to buy the company: 'Suddenly, we were getting the British interpretation of the market – that it only includes bus services and not cars or any other form of transport – into foreign jurisdictions.' Stagecoach is appealing and, if necessary, will may consider selling its small operation in Auckland in order to be allowed to bid for Yellow Bus.

The short-lived second Hong Kong operation was run from New Zealand and Souter envisages keeping his Pacific Rim headquarters, headed by Ross Martin, there while seeking expansion in Australia. Stagecoach already has a small operation in Queensland, involving school contracts, bought in 1997 from its old friend and former rival, Harry Blundred, who emigrated there after selling his Oxford business to Stagecoach.

Stagecoach's first entry on to mainland Europe was in June 1995 to Portugal. It was not an obvious market: the country is small and is a complex and relatively difficult environment for bus operations. The company on offer was itself a modest concern compared with the large municipals that Stagecoach was targeting in the UK. But it was to be a testing ground for bigger plans and gave Stagecoach a foothold in a country where the rail industry was also possibly scheduled for sale. Wary, after the Canadian débâcle, of risking too much on its own in an overseas market, Stagecoach sought a partner for its initial European ventures. Souter and Cochrane had followed the Portuguese privatisation process for a couple of years. The twelve companies that had made up the national bus industry were being privatised one by one but Cochrane felt that the earlier sales involved 'property values that were a bit toppy' and Stagecoach had kept out of them. With property prices falling, when the suburban areas around Lisbon came up, Cochrane and Souter were keen to bid and teamed up with two local companies, Baraqueiro and Vimeca, to put in a tender for what was the last of the companies to be sold off. Stagecoach also went in with a financing partner, Montagu Private Equity, part of HSBC, which meant Stagecoach had a 25 per cent share.

The sale was through a live auction on the floor of the Lisbon Stock Exchange, which Cochrane says was incredibly exciting and rather different from the staid, closed-envelope tendering processes in the UK: 'There were three groups of bidders and when one of them announced an offer, you had ten or fifteen minutes to confer and come up with another offer. There was a really serious bidding war as there seemed to be a bit of historic animosity between Barraqueiro, who we were in with, and one of the other groups. We were unhappy that they were bidding too high and we went to talk to the other guys who were bidding and tried to do a deal with them, to reconfigure our team possibly.' The battle went on all night, having started at 5.30 p.m. after trading stopped on the floor, and Cochrane felt rather foolish that he was booked on to an 8 p.m. flight that evening. Eventually, Barraqueiro, the Algarve-based market leader in Portugal, won with a bid of £26 million and hived off a section to Stagecoach.

Success meant Stagecoach became the first UK bus company to operate in Continental Europe. The purchase price of £6.3 million was shared between Montagu and Stagecoach, with the latter having an option to buy out its partner after two years from the start of operations in January 1996. The cautious approach, following the Canadian experience, was also demonstrated by Souter's insistence on keeping the Portuguese acquisition off the balance sheet until the costs of reorganisation and job losses could be assessed.

Following the acquisition, Stagecoach retained the Western part of the franchise area, leaving the rest to the two Portuguese partners. Cochrane explains that Stagecoach prefers having complete control of a particular area rather than being involved in joint ventures. As Cochrane put it, 'Joint ventures take up as much management time, but you're only getting a half or a third, or whatever – depending on the number of partners – of the returns.'

The Portuguese deal involved only 320 staff and 150 buses on routes based in Cascais, Estoril and Sintra, an area twenty-five kilometres (fifteen miles) from Lisbon and a bizarre old tramway, including a dozen Edwardian toastrack-style trams, which Stagecoach is refurbishing and reopening. The services principally feed into railway stations taking people in and out of Lisbon. There is also a sizeable tourist market serving the coast. Under the Portuguese system, Stagecoach received a monopoly licence to operate in its area, but the fares are capped. Apart from routes and route changes requiring approval from the local authority, services are run on a purely commercial basis.

Stagecoach quickly embarked on the usual restructuring of management systems as well as routes, and fifty new buses were introduced within the first year. The buses have been reliveried in the familiar Stagecoach colours.

However, turning the company round has been an uphill task. The area is not natural bus territory, with its many windy roads along the Atlantic seaboard, and much illegal car parking which occasionally blocks the roads. The increasing car ownership, due to the growing prosperity in Portugal, has made operating conditions difficult. Nevertheless, Souter says margins have 'increased from 8–18 per cent and passenger volumes are growing'. Two years after starting to run services there, Stagecoach bought out HSBC, in keeping with Souter's preference to function alone, taking full ownership of the Portuguese operation in January 1998.

Stagecoach's toehold in Portugal did not help it win a bid in the spring of 1998 for a stake in the local rail network. It lost out to a French/ Portuguese consortium.

The acquisition of Swebus which operated in the three other Scandinavian countries as well as Sweden, dwarfed all these foreign acquisitions, as it brought in a company with a massive 3,400 buses – Stagecoach had 8,300 prior to that – and an annual turnover of £316 million. Confident, after the success in Portugal, that Stagecoach could operate on its own, Souter eschewed finding a partner for what was a major acquisition costing £230 million, about half of which was debt which the Swedish railway sought to offload. The purchase was all the more amazing because within a week it had been upstaged as Stagecoach's biggest buy by the acquisition of the Porterbrook rolling stock company (see Chapter 8). The importance of the purchase of Swebus was rather missed because of the coincidence of timing of the two deals and consequently Stagecoach has got off rather lightly with its poor performance in Scandinavia.

Sweden was much more natural territory than the Mediterranean environment of Portugal. Souter and Cochrane had kept an eye on the Swedish market for several years. As Cochrane put it, 'We felt we could do business in Scandinavia. We had contacts with Linjebuss, the second largest operator, and we thought, this is a market we want to get into. The culture, ethics and language are all very similar to our own.'

Souter and Cochrane thought the price was good, about 66p for £1 of turnover, demonstrating why they were increasingly looking abroad for bargains. In the UK the price for bus companies was now around £1.20 to £1.40, which Souter reckoned implied that too much was being paid for the goodwill. Yet, again, the approach was incredibly cautious. Swebus's core business, representing 80 per cent of its turnover, is obtained through contracts with thirty-six city and county passenger transport authorities around the country. These are retendered on average every five years and the contractor receives a fixed amount, usually per vehicle/kilometre, for operating the routes. The tendering authority retains all the revenue and sets the fares level. Stagecoach, therefore, bid on the basis that it would win none of the retendered contracts, although Cochrane stressed that he did not expect this to happen: 'We wear our banker hat to analyse these deals and see if they still stack up. And the deal did.'

The business was, therefore, low-risk, but also low-yield. When Stagecoach took it over, the margins were around 3.5 per cent and Souter promised to reduce costs by 2–3 per cent, increasing margins within a year to 6 per cent and eventually to a more respectable 10 per cent. It was not to be. Stagecoach barely managed to move the margins, which rose to 4.6 per cent in the first year, and also found that it lost some significant contracts because of fierce competition. The target is 15 per cent, but few analysts believe that any more than 10 per cent can be reached in the medium term.

Stagecoach was hit by the remarkable deflation in Sweden during 1996–7 when prices actually went down. The contracts are linked to the Consumer Price Index and therefore the amounts Stagecoach received were reduced. Yet costs were rising. Cochrane explained, 'We had wage deals in place that had been negotiated by Swedish Railways, the previous owners, for two years and resulted in 3 per cent increases for the drivers. We were stuffed.' Fuel prices also went up in the first year. Nor could Stagecoach change the terms of the contracts coming up for renewal, such as by trying to specify cheaper rolling stock, because their competitors are happy to work within the existing constraints with onerous contracts that specify every detail of the operations, right down to type of bus.

According to the managing director of Swebus, Lars Mattsson, in the first year Stagecoach retained contracts for about the same number of buses, but in 1997 it lost franchises for 150 more than it gained, reducing its fleet by nearly 5 per cent. Mattsson said the problem was that Swebus, which has around a third of the market, faced increased competition from other operators including consortia of local authorities. The industry was not opened up to competition until 1989 and was still maturing. He said margins for the twenty largest operators, 'had fallen from 8.5 per cent to 3.5 per cent between 1993 and 1996' because of the fierce competition and that pressure shows no sign of abating. Indeed, the market for new tenders is becoming even more competitive because of a change in the law that allows local authority companies to operate outside their municipality, prompting them to be more aggressive. Groupings of smaller local-authority-owned companies have begun to bid for contracts, putting even more pressure on prices – winning, for example, a major contract in the West of Sweden against Stagecoach in late 1997.

Stagecoach's struggle in Sweden continued in 1999 when there was a national strike which involved both its local bus and intercity services. Negotiations are carried out on a national basis between an employers' federation and the unions. The drivers had pushed for an extra rest break to allow them to go to the toilet, which the employers federation claimed would increase costs by 6.5 per cent. The drivers were locked out for thirteen days but eventually returned, having partly won their case, helped by widespread public support for their cause. A compromise was reached whereby the decision over the breaks would be negotiated locally. Stagecoach reckons it lost £2 million on the strike, representing about half a per cent on its margins.

Kinski has taken a keen personal interest in the underperforming Swebus, having become chairman in June 1998, and aims to improve its margins. He feels that Stagecoach did not impose itself early enough after taking the company over: 'Perhaps they were distracted as the Swebus deal came at the same time as the Porterbrook takeover', he says. Stagecoach had instituted some changes when it took over. The senior management team was almost entirely changed, with Roger Bowker arriving in 1997 from the UK as deputy managing director to help the transformation. The small Norwegian subsidiary was sold quickly as a buyer was eager to take it on, the Danish section, also small, was sold later, and responsibility for the Finnish subsidiary was transferred to direct operation from Perth, because Souter was desperate for the Swedish management to concentrate on their core business. But with drivers' wages representing 50 per cent of costs, and subject to national agreements, the scope for savings is much more limited than in the UK. And Kinski feels that the Swedish managers 'persuaded Brian not to reorganise quickly'.

Kinski decided to do just that. He split the organisation into four regions, put in group procurement and engineering standards and brought the maintenance, which had been contracted out, back in house. With 85 per cent of Swebus's revenue coming from tendered contracts, Kinski's aim is to make sure that they are more lucrative. He supervises each tender and is negotiating with the regional authorities to reduce costs through using slightly older buses. Some contracts have been let on double digit margins, but Sweden is still proving an uphill struggle. The 1998/9 figures show that Kinski's efforts were beginning to pay off, with the operating margin going up from 5.3 per cent to 6.3 per cent, despite the strike.

One bright point in Sweden, stressed frequently by Souter, is Stagecoach's intercity service, Swebus Express, which has been greatly expanded through low fares promotions, but still represents only 15 per cent of the Swebus business. The market for coaches was deregulated in January 1999, but the strike soon afterwards resulted in the service losing market share back to the buses. Despite this, the annual growth rate during 1998/9 was 12 per cent.

According to Ann-Christin Sjolander, a Swedish journalist specialising in labour relations, Souter has made a good impression in Scandinavia with the trade unions. They were pleased that Souter immediately agreed to the national bus agreement with the unions, something he has ruled out in the UK. They liked, too, how he always spoke to drivers when he visited a depot before going to see the managers. Ironically, they even prefer dealing with Stagecoach than the previous owner, Swedish Railways. Souter, for his part, likes the Swedish situation, despite the difficulties and the strike, as he finds the standard of driver very high, commenting how helpful and well-educated they are. Souter's visits to the depots was more than just a way of improving relations with the workforce: in one Swedish depot, he found several new coaches parked up and asked what they were for. On being told they were for summer touring, he got them repainted and put on the express service.

The Swedish market is an interesting contrast to the British one because its model of partial deregulation and strong competition for tenders (but not on the roads) limits the scope for high margins and British Labour politicians look enviously to such a system. However, if they tried to introduce it in the UK, they would be fiercely resisted by operators such as Stagecoach, who fear for their margins. It is, of course, relatively similar to London, where routes are franchised out and Stagecoach's targets for margins are lower.

There is barely a country in which buses operate where Stagecoach has not, at one time or another, considered possible expansion. Souter has travelled to the Far East and Latin America where deals have been close to fruition. Despite his insurers' concerns, Souter even travelled to Colombia to try to set up a deal in Bogota and reckoned that his habit of dressing down and carrying a plastic bag rather than a briefcase guaranteed that the kidnappers took no interest in him.

Despite the patchy progress abroad – only New Zealand can be considered as an unequivocal success – expansion overseas is the only way for Stagecoach to match its growth pattern of the past decade. The value of these early foreign forays has been as a way of developing contacts and of gaining knowledge of alternative systems. The overseas subsidiaries, particularly Africa, were also used as a training ground. Promising managers picked up in UK acquisitions have deliberately been sent abroad to teach them to cope with totally different environments and to bring new ideas back to the UK.

Whether Souter and Stagecoach can really crack 'overseas' is the key to Stagecoach's long-term future and whether it will be a major transnational as well as a national player (see Chapter 11 for consideration of this issue).

7
On the rails

Stagecoach saved rail privatisation for the Tories, thanks to its early enthusiasm for the project, and then wrecked the party's flagship policy by making a mess of running its trains at a crucial time just before the General Election. And, between these two events, Stagecoach put the whole complicated edifice of the privatised rail industry in jeopardy by its move towards vertical integration through the purchase of a rolling stock company. But for Stagecoach, rail was to be the vehicle to double its size within a couple of years and to create for itself a milch cow, which the company is using to try to further its global ambitions.

Stagecoach's beginnings in rail were small-scale, innovative but short-lived and ultimately a complete failure. It was the first company to break the British Rail monopoly for forty-five years by running a private service. Souter had kept a close eye on rail even before the Tories retained power in —1992 on a manifesto to break up and sell British Rail. He had designs on ScotRail or InterCity, expecting that BR services would be broken up into its four main component parts rather than, as happened, into twenty-five sections. In December 1991, Souter met with the Transport Secretary Malcolm Rifkind to discuss the idea of running a couple of trains a day between London and Scotland. BR would have provided the trains and the drivers, but the on-board staff and the marketing would have come from Stagecoach. Richard Branson, too, had been talking about a similar scheme, inevitably getting more publicity because, ridiculously, he talked about on-board Jacuzzis, but British Rail, seeing such ideas as the thin end of the privatisation wedge, killed off the projects.

However, Tory ministers were keen to have a demonstration rail-privatisation project in time for the 1992 election and managed to persuade British Rail's InterCity arm to keep the communication channels with Stagecoach open. Souter spotted an opportunity when, early in 1992, InterCity announced that it would scrap seating accommodation on overnight trains between Aberdeen and London, forcing all passengers to pay for a sleeper berth. Souter spotted what he felt was a market gap and signed a deal to provide overnight seated accommodation from Aberdeen, Dundee and Edinburgh to London with Stagecoach buses feeding into the service from Fife, Perth and Inverness. The six coaches, leased from British Rail were to be decked out in Stagecoach livery, and attached to the normal British Rail sleeper train, making it the longest on the railway, which caused problems because the locomotives were taxed to the maximum. Chris Green, who was InterCity's managing director at the time and now head of Virgin Rail, said in a press release, that it 'was a classic case of a joint venture between InterCity and the private sector' but added, ominously for Stagecoach, that 'importantly for InterCity, we will have a guaranteed income which will enable us to fulfil our commercial remit'. After all, if BR could not make money out of selling these seats, leasing the coaches expensively – £1.5 million per year for the six, with maintenance and staffing on top – was hardly likely to be Souter's cleverest deal. Operating only four out of six coaches every night, with two spare, seemed amazingly profligate by Stagecoach standards.

The launch on 12 May 1992, just a few days after the Tories' surprise election victory, revealed the fundamental flaw of the service, highlighted unwittingly by the very minister who had been dispatched to inaugurate it: nobody wants to sit up all night in a train. The assembled journalists and the handfuls of genuine punters on the first train were treated to a speech by Roger Freeman, the Public Transport Minister, who said, 'Once I heard about it, I said I must be on the inaugural train.' Freeman, however, rather blew all his PR work when he promptly eschewed the pleasures of sitting upright all night and went off to crash out in comfortable sleeper accommodation, 'prop British Rail monopoly', as the delighted *Guardian* pointed out. 'I've got a full day's work in front of me,' he told the journalists rather testily as they spotted him tiptoeing off to his bed just south of Carlisle. 'I am fifty years old and I didn't feel like sitting up all night.' Mr Freeman's duplicity demonstrated what a difficult market Stagecoach had got itself into. Souter, though, made of sterner stuff, stayed up all night chatting and pointed out that he had been trying to get British Rail involved in a scheme like this for the past six years.

At least the launch attracted Stagecoach's best run of publicity since the company's creation over a decade previously, which was a boost, given that flotation was being planned for the following year. Stagecoach had even wheeled out seventy-four-year-old Isabella McRorie, who had been the first customer aboard Stagecoach's coach from Dundee in 1980 and was given a free ride on the inaugural train. There were acres of newsprint, pointing out that this was the first privatised – albeit semi-privatised – train to run on BR lines since nationalisation in 1948. Inevitably the train arrived twelve minutes late at Euston. There was a bit of ribaldry, too, at Stagecoach's expense as some bright spark had put in the publicity leaflet that the tea would be free 'until it runs out'. Brian Cox, who was in charge of the project, admitted to the *Sunday Times*, 'It is not the best way to start a railway; we just hope all the passengers go to sleep; it has all been done in a hurry.' Soft drinks were free but there was to be no alcohol sold by Stagecoach's trolley staff, in line with Souter's religious philosophy.

Tickets from Aberdeen to London were £38 single, including a free evening meal and a bap for breakfast, compared with a foodless £65 for BR in its sleeping accommodation, but despite all the publicity, sales were slow. Chris Green reckons that there was little scope for Stagecoach to make money. The Stagecoach Rail service had 232 seats to sell every night in each direction, and Green reckons that demand would always have fallen well short of that level of provision. He says, 'There was a summer market, but not a winter one, and Scotland has nine months of winter. We negotiated a price that was good for InterCity but proved too high to sustain the business for Stagecoach. At the end of the day, overnight seating is a natural coach market. You aren't going to get four hundred people each night. There's probably three or four coachloads of people on the Scotland–London market on a winter's night. The coaches are dark and there isn't such a problem with security as on trains.'

Interestingly, while praising Stagecoach's professionalism, Green feels there was a weakness in the company's approach: 'Stagecoach have a blind spot on marketing. They don't believe in it. Part of their manage-ment philosophy is that they provide a visible product, like a bus, and they do not advertise it or spend money on marketing. It doesn't work on the railways, where we doubled off-peak travel through advertising.'

Cox accepts that the concept was flawed from the start: 'We had no control over any of the product. Sleeper trains notoriously run late. It's not uncommon for them to arrive six hours late. There were big problems because the trains were very, very heavy and the line between Edinburgh and Aberdeen has steep gradients.' He also complains that Stagecoach ran up against the BR bureaucracy: 'Because they were selling our tickets, two hundred and seventy-five staff had to be briefed on how to do it and it was a nightmare.'

Cox is more sanguine, however, about BR's role than Souter, who thinks that its managers stitched up Stagecoach. He says BR started marketing the option of getting a seat on a Glasgow train from London, and then changing on to another seated train to Aberdeen, effectively a rival service: 'I suspect that there was as much cock-up as conspiracy in it, but Brian [Souter] thinks it's mostly conspiracy.'

The scheme, therefore, was a total disaster, cleverly disguised by Souter through the flotation, and abandoned soon after because of ongoing losses. Even the summer season, when loadings should have been high, was a flop with fewer than half the seats being sold when Stagecoach, which blamed the recession, had reckoned it needed 70 per cent to make a profit. The only upside was that Stagecoach got, as Cox puts it, 'a lot of bloody good PR as we were hardly known in the south'.

Therefore, on Stagecoach's prompting, the scheme was restructured in November 1992. The service between Aberdeen and London reverted to InterCity control with Stagecoach being responsible for selling only a quarter of the tickets, and a similar arrangement was extended to a new Glasgow service. Now, however, Stagecoach and BR were competing and, although some commentators were fooled into suggesting the change was an expansion, effectively it marked the beginning of the end for the ill-fated idea. Most important, the restructuring allowed the flotation prospectus to say, 'The relaunched services have been successful in moving the operation closer to profitability', even though break-even was out of reach. It was no surprise then, when, with Stagecoach safely on the Stock Exchange, the scheme that had been launched with such a fan-fare fewer than eighteen months previously ended with a whimper in October 1993.

Kindly, British Rail allowed Stagecoach to walk away from its three-year contract, having really fulfilled only the first six months. Green says, 'They signed a deal virtually on our terms, so we let them off in the end.' Souter had already admitted losses of £500,000 at the AGM in July and announced a further £175,000 at the interims in December 1993. The embarrassing failure of Stagecoach Rail did not deter Souter from seeing rail as a major opportunity, as long as he did not have to deal with British Rail ever again.

Souter already had his eye on the main BR operations, which had been the subject of a White Paper published in July 1992. He kept on telling the world that he was interested in ScotRail, long before the company was due to come on to the market. The Tories had come late to rail privatisation after a long line of utility sell-offs. Perhaps Mrs Thatcher's dislike of trains had influenced the decision not to sell the railways, but it was only when John Major took over the leadership in 1990 that the issue reached the political agenda.

Major, ever the soppy romantic, sought to restore the big consolidated companies, remembered from his youth, which had dominated the interwar period with their evocative names like Great Western and LMS. He was talked out of the idea in favour of a much more radical approach by Malcolm Rifkind, his Transport Secretary until the 1992 General Election. The model that appeared in the White Paper published soon after the election was straight out of Thinktankland. The plan was to break up the services into forty groupings and franchise them out to the bidder who asked for least subsidy. The infrastructure was to be hived off to a separate company, Railtrack, which would, for the time being, be retained in the public sector. There would be open access on the lines to ensure that other companies could compete against the operators and there would be no obligation for any company to take another's tickets. There would be no controls on fares, which would be left entirely to free-market forces.

The potential bidders, like Stagecoach and Virgin, who made the most noise in the lengthy period during which the legislation was drawn up and taken through Parliament by Rifkind's successor, John MacGregor, expressed strong opposition to this model. They wanted to have control of the infrastructure as well as train services because otherwise they felt their profitability would be dependent on the performance of another company. Brian Cox, who was to head Stagecoach's bidding team and is now in charge of South West Trains, told the *Evening Standard* in September 1993 that the proposals were 'over complex'. In particular, Cox wanted vertical franchises where operators had control of the infrastructure because having a separate company 'was the stuff of which nightmares are made'. He also wanted open access to be scrapped and 'a stable environment to attract the private sector'. Souter was still pushing the point about Railtrack after the legislation had gone through. In July 1994 he told the *Evening Standard*, 'We are still interested but we have learned that we will need control of the infrastructure and firm warranties on all BR figures.'

Inevitably, the initial scheme was watered down in the face of such views and the considerable political opposition both within and outside the Tory party – indeed, it had been a Tory MP, Robert Adley, who had dubbed rail privatisation as 'the poll tax on wheels'. Cox and Souter, and the other potential bidders, won some of their points. Open access, for example, was abandoned because the Government realised that no one would bid for franchises if rivals were able to cherry-pick the best train paths. Network benefits, such as through ticketing, were retained and some fares, notably season tickets and standard returns, were controlled. But Cox and the other bidders lost the most important argument: they would not be allowed to control the infrastructure. Railtrack was to be hived off and moreover, instead of the company being kept in the public sector, it was to be sold off before most of the lines were privatised to bring in much-needed cash for pre-election tax cutting. The twenty-five franchises were to be mostly for seven years, a lot shorter than the private bidders had wanted.

The legislation was eventually passed in the autumn of 1993, but there was a lengthy delay as the franchising director, Roger Salmon, worked out how to get the process going. Although around forty companies, including management buyout teams, applied to pre-qualify as eligible to take on a franchise, there were only a handful of serious bidders for each of the initial operating companies because of the complexity of the process and fear of the unknown.

The franchises for train operators are bizarre constructs. The franchisee does not own the trains (which belong to a leasing company), or the track (which is Railtrack's) but has a requirement to run a set level of services in exchange for subsidy (only a few lines, like Gatwick Express, involve the payment of a premium rather than the receipt of a subsidy). They can, also, run extra trains above that basic requirement. Therefore, taking on a franchise requires very little capital investment, apart from a bond of 15 per cent of passenger revenue placed with the franchising director, and is an obvious target for management buyout teams, but few outside bidders could get their heads round the concept.

In particular, there was little serious interest from the private sector during the run-up to the letting of the first three franchises: South West Trains; London, Tilbury and Southend; and Great Western Trains. They were scheduled to be let in early 1996, which was already a cause for embarrassment since it was two years behind Freeman's initial promise of the spring of 1994. The Government wanted to avoid handing over all the franchises to management buyout teams, as the public would argue that after the hassle and expense of the sale, the same people were running the show.

The lack of potential bidders meant Tory ministers, who had faced a barrage of flak over both the privatisation process and the delays, were deeply grateful to Stagecoach, which had managed to be shortlisted for all three of the first franchises. GWT was initially allocated to a start-up company called Resurgence Railways; LTS was to go to the management team; and a shortlist of two, Stagecoach and the management, was announced for South West Trains. Then Resurgence collapsed because it emerged that one of its backers had been involved in a failed double-glazing business and it was unable to prove that it could raise the capital, and GWT went to the management team, backed by FirstBus and venture capital.

The two bids for SWT were incredibly close, a matter of just £200,000 for a franchise that was to receive £350 million subsidy during its seven-year contract. The Stagecoach bid, according to Steve Norris, the junior Transport Minister at the time, was slightly better than the management team's on cash, but was based on 'a far more credible management plan'.

Brian Cox admits, however, that the franchise could have gone either way: 'Our bid was marginally better than the management's but I don't think it would have been difficult for OPRAF [the franchising director] to have found reasons to give it to them rather than us. Politically, though, it suited them as well to have an outsider in because at that point there was very, very little interest from outside. Other than Sherwood [of Sea Containers] there was no sign of anybody apart from us.' Stagecoach had been very lucky. Cochrane recalls that at the crucial board meeting, at St Ermin's Hotel in Westminster, 'we were all sitting in a room and working out the NPV [Net Present Value] and saying, "We'll take a bit off here and a bit there".' They could, so easily, have taken off too much.

The PR disaster that accompanied rail privatisation continued when it was revealed that the first privatised train would, in fact, be a bus, running as a train replacement on a GWT service from Fishguard to Cardiff. Then a ticketing fraud emerged at LTS, which scuppered the management team's bid and delayed the letting of the franchise, just before the weekend launch of privatised services. GWT's misfortune meant that the first proper private train was to be the 5.10 a.m. from Twickenham to Waterloo on 4 February 1996, operated by Stagecoach. Souter and Gloag were conspicuously absent from the early-morning journey but Sir George Young, the Transport Secretary, had been quickly whistled up as the ticketing fraud threatened to overshadow the celebrations. SWT rather misread the market, too, by doubling the length of the service, only to find that the expectations of hordes of trainspotters never materialised because they were antagonistic to privatisation. The first train, therefore, had barely a dozen real passengers and one of these was a fare-dodger who, clearly unaware that the train was undertaking a historic journey, was rather surprised to find a clutch of revenue inspectors at Waterloo station because normally, at 6 a.m. on a Sunday, the station would have been as deserted as the train.

The Labour opposition was apoplectic about Stagecoach's entry into the rail industry. Brian Wilson, who took every opportunity to criticise the company, which he saw as the personification of what was wrong with the Tories' privatisation policies, was livid: 'It is particularly ironic that privatisation, which began with rhetoric on competition, has ended up with the first franchise going to a ruthlessly anticompetitive company.' As I wrote in the *Independent* at the time of the announcement of Stagecoach's victory, 'If the government had wanted to choose the most controversial candidate as the flagship for the privatised rail programme, it could not have done better than going for Stagecoach.' Steve Norris confirms this: 'Awarding the franchise to Stagecoach was really taking the fight to the enemy, giving Brian Wilson a field day. It was the most aggressive decision we could take, and if we had tried to dress privatisation in its most acceptable form, it would have been better to award it to almost anyone else.'

Nevertheless, Stagecoach's success in winning SWT did the trick for the Tories and led to other companies becoming more seriously involved. And, according to Steve Norris, the Government was deeply grateful: 'Brian Souter was in there early and you should not underestimate the extent to which he took a leap in the dark. Would the process even be completed by the General Election and the inevitable Tory defeat? What would happen to his balance sheet if he had to spend five years in court fighting the government through the European courts for compensation? But as the process went on, more and more people saw the potential. At first they wondered how Souter could justify his figures, but then, as the process unfolded, they saw he was right.'

Of course, being there first, Stagecoach got the best deal for a franchise. In league tables of the profitability of the franchises, compiled by industry insiders, SWT is always at or near the top. The contract was a straightforward plain vanilla deal with little investment required of Stagecoach which, in turn, made few commitments above the basic franchise specifications. SWT was also a healthy addition to the profit-and-loss account, with a turnover of £262 million and the largest passenger revenue of any of the franchises. As franchises involve no capital – the trains, track and stations are owned by other companies – the company cost only £156,000 and Stagecoach's acquisition costs were less than those of other bidders, thanks to its normal unwillingness to pay for costly advisers and consultants, with its own managers doing much of the preparatory work on finance, traffic patterns and engineering. SWT has a good mix of commuter and longer-distance traffic, which makes revenue more stable, as it is not so dependent on levels of office employment in central London as other franchises in the south-east. And there was plenty of lovely subsidy, with Stagecoach receiving £63.3 million in the first year, falling only to £34.1 million at the end, not enormously different from what BR would have got.

Later franchisees faced much more onerous terms, with the subsidy not only starting off at a lower level, but also reducing more sharply during the course of the contract, as Roger Salmon was able to squeeze better deals from bidders who faced more competition. Cochrane is delighted at SWT's performance and prospects: 'If you look at what the analysts are predicting for it, compared with what they say about other groups who got four or five franchises, SWT is still worth more to us than four to five franchises are worth to other people.' Indeed, an analysis by David Myrddin-Evans of Dresdner Kleinwort Benson in June 1996 put SWT at the top of the profitability league of the twenty-five rail franchises and showed that Stagecoach would only need to prevent an annual loss of 1.4 per cent of its revenue to pay its way. The *Independent* calculated that South West Trains would see an operating profit of £100 million per year by the end of the franchise in 2003 if passenger revenue grows at 4 per cent.

The City, which had been sceptical of rail privatisation, quickly understood what a good deal Stagecoach had got – its share price jumped around 70p to 350p in the few days after the announcement in the run-up to Christmas 1995. However, Stagecoach's pioneering role in attracting more interest in rail privatisation was to prove its undoing in terms of winning any other franchise. Stagecoach set up a small team, headed by Cox and Cochrane, to bid for the other twenty-two lines, which were being franchised out over the following year by a Government anxious to ensure that the process was complete by the 1997 General Election. Stagecoach's successful bid for SWT had been cautious in terms of estimating the required subsidy and the potential growth, and that approach was maintained throughout the process. With the exception of Gatwick Express, all the franchises were to get subsidy from the government, at least initially, and without exception franchises went to the bidder seeking least financial support.

According to Cochrane, his team developed a model to project forward what Stagecoach could do with the franchise, and from that worked out the level of subsidy required. He felt that all the other bidders would make similar assessments on how much cost could be taken out of each franchise and success would be down to who made the most optimistic assumptions on revenue. And Stagecoach refused to play ball, missing out consistently because its bid was for more subsidy than its rivals. Stagecoach bid for all twenty-five train operating companies but gained only one other franchise, the tiny Island line on the Isle of Wight, which, uniquely, came with its own infrastructure as an integrated railway. No one else had been very interested and for Stagecoach there was the advantage that the trains connected, by ferry, with Stagecoach's SWT services. Stagecoach came closest to winning GNER, the recently refurbished east-coast main line between King's Cross and Scotland, which Cox admits the company would love to have: 'We were close on that, and on some of the regional railways, which are very dependent on subsidy, which meant our conservative assumptions about revenue were less of a factor. But we were miles out on the other InterCity lines, the most classic being Branson's at the end.' Branson put in a stunningly optimistic bid for the much-neglected west coast and, although Stagecoach, according to Cox, 'stuck our neck further than we had before, we didn't get in sight of it.' Indeed, Stagecoach's bid was over a billion pounds more in terms of subsidy over the length of what was a fifteen-year franchise. Yet, amazingly, in the summer of 1998, Stagecoach bought a 49 per cent stake in Virgin Rail.

Even though the railway has boomed since privatisation, with passenger growth rates of 6 to 8 per cent per year across the network, and larger increases on some lines, Cochrane has no regrets about the conservative approach which cost Stagecoach the chance of being the biggest operator on the network. He points out that revenue has always dropped dramatically on the railways at times of recession: 'We believed that in a way we were insuring the UK government's revenue risk. Previously, in a recession, if revenue went down, the government would just put more subsidy into the railway. So what we were doing was insuring that risk, because the government had a quantified subsidy level for the next seven years, whether there was a recession or not.' Publicly, Stagecoach said it was seeking a 9 per cent margin on South West Trains, and it was prepared to go lower, but not, as Cochrane insists, 'down to the 1 or 2 per cent levels because a very small swing in revenue can take you from profits to losses'. However, with hindsight Stagecoach may have underestimated the extent to which people are now being driven off the roads by the permanent gridlock affecting the large conurbations and much of the motorway network, which could bring about a permanent increase in rail usage.

Perhaps it was fortunate for Steve Norris and his ministerial colleagues that Stagecoach failed to build on its success with South West Trains because in February 1997, horribly close to the General Election, the Stagecoach management made a basic mistake in organising the service that was to lead to 2000 trains being cancelled in the space of two months and a PR débâcle of Premiership League proportions. Like all the new train operators, Stagecoach renegotiated deals with its staff, doing away with old restrictive practices and complex bonus systems in favour of a higher basic – and, importantly, higher pensionable – wage. The drivers liked it, as they got £25,000 per year, becoming one of the highest-paid groups of blue-collar workers, tacit recognition of their industrial muscle – it takes forty-four weeks to train a new driver, and therefore any threat of industrial action has to be taken seriously. The managers liked it because of the greater flexibility they gained, such as ensuring that there were enough drivers for Saturday and Sunday working. Because of increased productivity, the companies decided to make a few drivers redundant and Stagecoach allowed seventy to go, around 10 per cent of the driving workforce. It was too many, and suddenly SWT found itself short of people to operate the trains.

The new drivers' rosters were introduced on 9 February 1997, just a few days after the first anniversary of SWT taking over the franchise, and within a couple of days Brian Cox realised that there was a fundamental problem: 'It was not that we did not have enough bodies. We needed around seven hundred fully trained and utilisable drivers and we had seven hundred drivers, but the problem was they were not fully trained and utilisable. We were never short of bodies – we were short of *warm* bodies.'

As a BR apologist might have put it, Stagecoach had 'the wrong sort of driver'. Drivers need not only general training, but also 'route knowledge' for sections of track they go on, which involves going in the cab with another experienced driver to ensure they know the location of every signal, crossover and junction. They also need to have 'traction knowledge', ensuring they know how the particular rolling stock works, and they have to learn how to operate each type of vehicle. Stagecoach learnt the hard way that it was not like a bus driver who can be told to 'take route number 34 and follow the road round the town'.

By offering voluntary redundancy, Stagecoach had unwittingly encouraged those with the longest service to leave because they would get the largest cheque, and, of course, they were the ones with the required route and traction knowledge. There was, too, a history of militancy among

SWT drivers and a reluctance to help the management out in this time of difficulty by being flexible over rostering and working on days off. Cox warned darkly of a 'hotbed of Troskyism' in a letter to the Commons Transport Committee. He says there was a fundamental clash between Stagecoach and SWT: 'SWT's culture was particularly backward. People regard Stagecoach as having its own culture, and my conclusion was that we are at one end of the cultural spectrum, far out at one end, and they are at the other. The gap between us was therefore really twice as big as we actually thought it was.' There was a particular problem with the Waterloo drivers, who not only regularly had disputes with management but were also in constant battle with their own union, Aslef.

The press got hold of the story within a day or two of the change in rosters and Cox decided to come clean with OPRAF, which oversees the contracts with the train operators. After a few days of cutting services in a random way, which meant some much-used Portsmouth–Salisbury trains had been cancelled, prompting a host of complaints, Cox went to the franchising director, John O'Brien, to get his blessing for a programme of planned cancellations. They agreed a plan by which SWT cut thirty-nine trains per day, 2.6 per cent of its 1500 daily total, in addition to the 1 per cent or so unplanned cancellations that result from routine mishaps such as sick drivers or breakdowns.

John Watts, the Transport Minister, could hardly contain his anger, calling Stagecoach's management 'inept'. But under the rules, there was nothing much that O'Brien could do until the cancellations had actually happened, and this inaction compounded the anger of both ministers and the public at SWT's mistake. The rules, drawn up by a Tory government anxious to find anyone to run the railway, were too lax to ensure quick action. Finally, in mid-March, the embattled O'Brien, under pressure from ministers, started talking a bit tougher: 'SWT have until the end of April to convince me they are operating a proper service and will continue to do so. Otherwise they face a fine of a million pounds with the possibility of further sanctions, including franchise termination.' But O'Brien, who says he prefers dealing by negotiation rather than through punishments, knew from his conversations with Cox that SWT would have enough drivers by then and the fine was never levied. Even then, a £1 million fine would have represented barely a week's subsidy and there was never a realistic chance that O'Brien would take the franchise away from SWT for cancelling a few short-hop trains, however much the press was on the attack. SWT paid £750,000 as a routine poor-performance payment in February, but O'Brien could not use his powers to impose an unlimited fine (£1 million was his suggestion) because this required a continuous eight-week period of poor performance and, with extra drivers coming on stream, Stagecoach managed to get its act together just in time.

These subtleties, however, escaped the press, which lambasted Stagecoach, SWT and rail privatisation in general. The *Daily Telegraph* was typical: 'It has not taken long for rail privatisation to come off the track. Barely a year after being handed a £54 million subsidy to run South West Trains, Stagecoach is cancelling 39 trains per day and receiving no more than a light tap on the wrist from the regulator.' Labour joined in gleefully. Glenda Jackson, the party's transport spokeswoman, chirruped: 'Railway privatisation is in meltdown. It's the final humiliation for Major and his flagship privatisation policy.'

Souter poured petrol on the fire by suggesting that some of his customers had nothing better to do than to write letters of complaint in office time and wondered whether their bosses knew they were doing this. It was an attempt at a joke, because he added that bus companies were used to getting bricks through the garage windows when their customers were dissatisfied. But it was a bad one. He was surprised that SWT received 40,000 letters of complaint a year, not realising rail commuters, unlike the impoverished pensioners, downtrodden women and benefit claimants who use buses, include the great and good who know full well how to go about complaining and have access to the media and even Parliament. Lynda Lee Potter, the *Daily Mail* columnist and SWT commuter, went berserk, even though Souter had made the remark about letters of complaint a year previously: 'Brian Souter is the multi-millionaire boss of SWT but instead of hanging his head in shame and apology, he's jolly cross with us.' She confessed to having written a couple of letters of complaint herself: 'I was incensed and driven to the brink of gibbering fury by the blundering service that we are being offered by varying private companies.' She longed for the return of BR 'when we had the greatest railway network in the world'. All this in the paper that prides itself as the Tories' house magazine.

Cox did not help by saying that 'critics were fully paid-up members of the hindsight club'. There was even an uprising among the commuters. A businessman, John Taylor, refused to accept that a train was being prematurely halted at Salisbury, rather than running through to Exeter, and refused to get off, forcing SWT to run the train through to its planned destination.

Even Souter's attempt to appease SWT's passengers with a day's free travel, at a cost of £1.5 million on 20 February, backfired as the press found out that some canny punters had booked themselves free trips on Eurostar or up to Scotland. Stagecoach's lack of an in-house public relations or press officer, who might have counselled Cox and Souter to be more temperate, contributed to the damage caused by the affair.

The City began to take note, too, not least because many of the analysts and brokers use SWT trains. The shares dropped 25p on the day that O'Brien rattled his sabre and the share price, which had reached a peak of 801p just before the débâcle, was in the doldrums for all this period, staying for a long period in the 600–700p range and the *FT* Lex column even suggested that it was overvalued and really worth only 540p. 'Stagecoach has come to the end of the line as a stock market darling,' said Anthony Hilton, City editor of the *Standard*, a sentiment that was widely echoed through the City. It was not to be until the autumn that Stagecoach's share price nosed above 800p again and the episode heightened the City's general concern about Stagecoach's future being too bound up with Souter's ability to keep all the balls in the air. The 'what would happen if Souter fell under a bus?' (possibly even one of his own) query put a damper on the share price.

The initial error in calculating the rosters was traced to a couple of middle managers who quickly left the company, but there was a more fundamental problem, a management deficit at the company. Souter and Cox had both taken their eye off the ball for understandable reasons. Souter was not on the board of SWT because of the potential conflict of interest between the train operator and Porterbrook, the rolling stock company (see Chapter 8) that Stagecoach had bought in the summer of 1996. Cox was still heavily involved in bidding for train operators and, although he was managing director of SWT, he admits that 'between November '96 and January '97, we were really stretched because we were at the height of bidding for the most complex and last franchises. West Coast was incredibly complicated. And just at the same time we were at the point where the rather tardy work which SWT had been doing on restructuring was beginning to come through.' He says that there was more reliance on the existing SWT management than he would have liked. Crucially, the MD, Peter Field, who had been retained by Stagecoach after the takeover in February 1996, was removed after a few months, leaving the company short of railway expertise. Graham Eccles, another seasoned railwayman taken on by SWT after he had lost a management buyout bid for a neighbouring franchise, was also concentrating on the franchise bids rather than running SWT.

Cox reckons that if another twenty drivers had been kept on, the crisis would never have happened. He claims that, despite the hullabaloo, there was not much passenger inconvenience, as most of the cancellations were on little-used lines or on those like Guildford to West Croydon, where services were duplicated by another train company. However, the press certainly found sufficient numbers of commuters who had suffered to fill their pages for day after day with anti-SWT stories.

It was just what the Tory Government, preparing for the election, did not need. The SWT crisis emerged on the very day that the Government announced the letting of the last franchise, which meant that, yet again, the 'good news' on privatisation was swamped by bad publicity. Steve Norris reckons those few weeks of chaos on SWT wrecked any advantage from the whole five-year rail privatisation programme and his bitterness still shows through, despite his admiration for Souter and Stagecoach: 'We in the Conservative Party were very happy at the way rail privatisation was going – new investment, new ideas, new services. When Tony Blair had said the election would be fought on renationalising the railways, I knew that was the one prediction which was absolute balderdash. When Labour started looking at the way they were going to handle rail privatisation in the 1997 General Election, they realised they would not be able to criticise privatisation because of BR's poor customer service.

'SWT instantly unwound all that. It was so obviously a grave error of judgement, so obviously to the disadvantage of passengers, and so clearly an act committed by a private company. It left a bad taste instantly in people's mouths about SWT. Even now, the intelligent non-transport buff will remember SWT and it will take years to get SWT out of the political lexicon.

'That was a cardinal sin. To have committed it at that particular time in the electoral cycle was not just bad luck, but appalling, and it gave Labour the entire rail issue. They didn't deserve to have it. History will say that rail privatisation was one of the great privatisation successes.'

Indeed, Daniel Hodges, who worked as a researcher in Glenda Jackson's office until the 1997, confirmed Stagecoach's unwitting role in presenting the rail issue on a plate to Labour: 'Stagecoach saved us. We were in deep trouble over privatisation because we thought that the Government would be able to present it as popular. Then the South West Trains thing started happening and it was disastrous for them. We were deeply grateful to Stagecoach.'

Stagecoach did escape one punishment. The Commons Transport Committee had announced that it would summon Souter and Cox to Parliament to explain what had gone wrong, but once the election was announced, Paul Channon, the patrician Tory chairman of the committee, realised that short-term political considerations had to prevail and announced that the hearing would be cancelled: 'A lot of members thought it was wrong to debate a highly contentious matter when a General Election has been called,' he said. After the election, Gwyneth Dunwoody, the Labour MP for Crewe and Nantwich, who took over the chairmanship, thought that there was no point raking over old coals and Souter and Cox escaped their session in the stocks.

Although the fiasco in February and March was well covered in the press, the fact that Stagecoach nearly found itself in the same mess again a few months later that year was not revealed at the time. Too many drivers were down for taking their holidays in July and August and a few heavily used peak trains had to be cancelled. For ten days, in fact, the situation was worse than in February, but the press missed the story. Cox realised he had to avert another major crisis, which this time, with Labour in power, might result not only in a massive fine but also in the potential loss of the franchise. With its share price at last beginning to recover, Cox dreaded the prospect of another bout of anti-Stagecoach publicity. He decided to throw money at the problem and buy the drivers off: 'For about ten days we had got ourselves into a position where we were about to have a mega PR disaster, apart from the fact that we'd have been in real shit with the actual franchise agreement. It was obvious that the following week was going to be very tight. The trouble is, it gets exponential. If you are 5 per cent tighter, you might start losing 20 per cent more trains. We realised we had to do something really decisive. Within four days, we could have clocked up sufficient additional cancellations that we couldn't have recovered the position in the period.' (The performance tables are based on thirteen annual four-week periods.)

On a Friday afternoon, with a weekend crisis looming, Cox called in Aslef and offered to pay the drivers a bonus of £1,000 for working on their rest days for a fortnight. And that was on offer for three successive fortnights, with an extra £1,000 for working all three – in other words, £4,000 on top of the normal overtime wages for working eight extra days: 'We knew we had to get them by the goolies immediately. And we got a huge number of people signing up to that. They would lose the bonus if they didn't turn up for any of the days. Sickness went down to nothing, which proves something about sickness.' Cox also agreed to allow people to postpone their holidays.

By September, the crisis had eased, but there were still some problems with too many drivers taking holidays and the offer was made again, but with fewer drivers being able to take up the scheme. By October, with fewer holidays and more newly trained drivers coming through, Cox was able to scrap the scheme. Cox, who had been only a part-time MD, took a much more active role and cleared out a number of managers, which meant that by the end of 1997, only one of the original twelve senior managers Stagecoach had inherited from BR remained.

The restructuring deal – and the costs of the fiasco – hit SWT hard. In addition to the £1.5 million incurred as a result of the free travel, almost half SWT's £8 million profit for 1996–7 went on restructuring costs, as did £6.8 million out of the £7.8 million that SWT made in the following six months. There was, though, underlying growth throughout this period. Turnover went up from £262.5 million in 1995–6 to £283 million the following year, and passenger numbers were rising by 6.5 per cent (and passenger mileage by 8.1 per cent, showing that many were longer-journey passengers fed up with congestion on the roads). The increase was partly a result of doubling the number of 'revenue protection officers' to 250, in an effort to reduce ticketless travel. Costs had been cut by 6 per cent in the first year, too. And, of course, there is no capital investment required by Stagecoach in the franchise.

By 1998/9, SWT was living up to its promise. In the year ending April 30 1999, there was an operating profit of £34.4 million on turnover of £338.8 million. Passenger numbers had continued growing at the same pace, increasing, since the franchise started, by an annual rate of around 7 per cent, with particularly strong growth on inner suburban routes. With no more restructuring costs, SWT was at last becoming a significant contributor to Stagecoach's profit figures.

Interestingly, costs were up by 11 per cent in two years, showing that the new private rail operators like Stagecoach were finding it difficult to find the kind of cost savings which had occurred in other privatised industries. Indeed, SWT had begun to take on more revenue protection staff, cleaners and drivers during its second and third years, reversing the trend of its first year.

Therefore, while the long-term prospects for SWT remain good as long as the economy keeps booming, Stagecoach found it slower to turn the company round compared with bus acquisitions. Cox admits that Stagecoach has found it difficult to 'crack the rail industry'. He says, 'Rail is much more complicated than the bus industry. It's so process-driven, so much reporting to OPRAF, the regulator, Health and Safety, Railtrack and so on. There is also the safety culture, which infiltrates everything we do in South West Trains. You need a lot more white-collar, functional non-line people than the bus industry and it's much more difficult because of the technical complexity and one-offness of each of these jobs. It is much more difficult to scythe them out than it is in the bus industry. We could go into a bus company now and sort out the staffing by tonight. It's as easy as that. After two years at South West Trains, we haven't finalised it here.'

Although SWT has been such a chastening experience, Stagecoach's commitment to running passenger rail services was demonstrated in June 1998, when Souter surprised the City by announcing a tie-up with Richard Branson to invest in Virgin Rail.

The deal was conducted in a typical Stagecoach fashion, very quickly and by personal contact between the main players. Souter had noticed that Virgin Rail was about to be floated and realised that Branson might well favour an alternative source of funding since his previous experience with the Stock Exchange had been fraught. Branson had originally floated his Virgin Group in 1986, but withdrew a couple of years later and Souter felt that with the market 'high and wobbly', Branson might prefer to avoid another float. Many analysts were also sceptical of Branson's willingness to go to the market. Just days before the planned launch of the flotation in May 1998, Souter rang up Branson, whom he did not know personally apart from the odd brief encounter, and set up a meeting. Souter realised that Branson might be unhappy about floating and, as Branson says, 'Brian pointed out that public life had its hassles and he thought he could deliver what we would get by going public and up our stake so that we had ultimate control'.

The two have eccentric but contrasting images and backgrounds: the bearded public school educated pseudo-hippy who thrives on publicity, and the quietly spoken and devoutly religious working class Scot whose rare media forays, like his appearance at the Scottish TUC, are carefully stage-managed. But both are engaging characters and clearly charmed each other to bits. It is easy to understand why the two got on: neither much likes having to go cap in hand to bankers and they are sceptical of the value of all those consultants and analysts who offer their services at a premium. They are both 'can do' people, eager to do deals.

Branson had Souter checked out before their first meeting and the reports all said that 'he was a delightful man, the sort of man who would be good to meet'. Souter recalls 'picking up my plastic bag and going to see Richard. They opened up their books and we did the deal in record time.'

The initial meeting at Branson's Notting Hill house lasted an hour and was followed up by another two weeks later at which the deal was virtually agreed. Branson reckons, 'I have never seen anyone move as quickly as Brian did. The whole deal was set up within a couple of weeks which for a deal that size with bankers involved is amazing'. Since Virgin was so close to announcing its float, all the necessary figures and due diligence were available, making a quick deal feasible. Souter says that the Virgin flotation document was on 'draft number 12' and that they were just a few days from issuing the document.

Both say that they get on well with each other. Branson has even been on holiday in the Virgin Islands with Ann Gloag and her family. Branson accepts that Souter is tough but says: 'He is very fair. You do not survive unless you have some toughness as he will have 99 per cent of the world trying to take some of what he has got off him and put it in their pockets. But we are in the driving seat. He can't take over the company.'

Under the terms of the link-up, Stagecoach invested £158 million into Virgin Rail, largely from funds it had raised for two other purchases, Road King and Prestwick Airport (see Chapter 11), giving it a 49 per cent stake. The deal seemed to benefit both sides. For Branson, it kept Virgin out of the City and away from prying analysts' eyes and, moreover, gave him the chance to expand his holding company's stake from 41 per cent to 51 per cent, getting rid of the venture capitalists who wanted out anyway. For Souter, it was an opportunity to expand Stagecoach's rail interests and to use some surplus cash.

The deal also gave Virgin a bit more capital than it would have got from a float – valuing it at £276 million rather than £250 million – which means that Branson managed to extract quite a high price, as well as obtaining a majority share. Derek Scott says: 'We put a bit of extra value on the company compared with the predicted flotation, but generally companies are floated at 10–20 per cent below their worth to give the shares a chance to rise afterwards. We merely ensured they got that extra value straight away.'

Virgin Rail operates two former chunks of BR, the West Coast Main Line and CrossCountry. As mentioned earlier in this chapter, Virgin's bid for the West Coast was predicated on very optimistic assumptions of growth. Not only does Virgin have to lease around £1 billion of new trains for the two lines, but it has said it will double passenger numbers to around 50 million per year by the end of the franchises in 2012. Moreover, from receiving a subsidy of around £200 million per year for the West Coast Main Line, it will pay out a similar amount annually to the Treasury by the end of this period, a tall order which placed a question mark over the company's ability to float. Hence Branson's welcome for Souter.

When Souter lost out on the franchise bid in 1997, he said that Virgin's offer was based on over-optimistic figures. So what had changed? Souter points out that the two had been relatively close to each other on the franchise: 'We were only £140 million different in terms of NPV [Net Present Value].' Moreover, two developments helped Souter take an interest: the deals which Virgin had made with Railtrack and the rolling stock suppliers and the increase in passengers during the first years of the franchise: 'When we bid, we were afraid of the risk of Railtrack not building the new line in time, and the risk of the manufacturers delivering the trains late. We took those risks and factored them in, but Virgin was much more bullish and judged that they could defer the cost of this risk onto Railtrack and the manufacturers. We discovered that Virgin had, for both the upgrades, managed to transfer most of that risk onto Railtrack. And they also transferred most of the risk for the rolling stock.'

Souter was impressed too with the annual rate of growth of 12 per cent in passenger numbers on the West Coast line (though Virgin's other franchise, CrossCountry, is weaker with only 6 per cent growth). He had visited railways in Europe and has seen similar growth on intercity lines: 'There is structural growth, natural organic growth on these services', he says. Virgin Rail was, therefore, profitable, and represented a good investment.

While both those factors are true, there is an element of rewriting history here, showing Souter's eagerness to get hold of more of the railway network before the industry matures. Even though some of the risk of delays to the improvements have been offset, the massive reductions in subsidy make the investment quite risky, something felt widely in the City which did not warm to the deal. The investment was announced on 22 June 1998, the day that Stagecoach officially reached the FTSE-100 but its share price went down by 57p to £13.63 because the analysts were unclear about the advantages for Stagecoach. One told the *Financial Times:* 'Souter has a reputation of knowing the downside of any deal. But this is an aggressive deal. I don't feel comfortable. The subsidy profile is extremely demanding. Before, Stagecoach was a defensive stock. It changes the nature of the company quite a lot.' Souter admitted to the *FT* that the franchise was a 'wee bit different' but retorted, 'for the first three years [when the subsidy is still high] only an idiot couldn't make a few bob. Then the new trains come in.' The *FT* editorial said the deal marked a turning point in the industry marking the shift 'from coping with problems it inherited from its state-owned past to coping with the problems of the future'.

Now that the two transport entrepreneurs have got together, other joint deals may well be possible, especially as Souter is interested in airports and Branson runs airlines. Asked if the partnership would survive until the end of the franchise term in 2012, Branson said in May 1999: 'My guess is that we will be working on a number of projects together. There's lots of opportunity out there and we are good friends.'

But the situation is not stable in the long-run. Souter sees the link-up as a 'strategic investment', with Stagecoach not having an operational role, at least initially. However, Stagecoach generally prefers to operate alone using its own methods – although, admittedly, more recently it has entered into several partnerships – and it is well placed to increase the size of its stake in Virgin Rail in the future. The most likely outcome is that Souter will eventually achieve his aim of getting control of the two rail operations.

As Roger Ford, editor of *Rail Privatisation News* put it, 'Souter is a strategist and Branson is an opportunist. Stagecoach may well take over the whole of Virgin Rail if Branson gets bored of the stick he is getting from it, or it goes pear-shaped. It may be in five years time, but Souter is playing a long game, something he is good at.'

Neither Souter nor Branson are on the board of Virgin Rail but they meet every month or so according to Branson 'to plot and plan about what needs to be done. It is not necessarily the big issues. It is things like product improvement and how many people pay their bills on time, and making sure that everyone pays.'

Indeed, Virgin's train service continued to attract criticism at the start and well into 1999 both for the poor performance in terms of punctuality and reliability, but also for the awful catering on board which contrasts badly with the much more popular GNER service on the East Coast Main Line. Chris Green, the former BR manager who, in turn ran InterCity, Network SouthEast and Scotrail, was drafted in early in 1999 to beef up the management structure. Mike Kinski claimed that the rail management had concentrated on signing the train procurement contracts until then and had not been able to focus their attention on improving the service. There were doubts in the industry, however, whether Green, a visionary rather than a details man, was the right choice and even Branson said: 'I interviewed Chris first and put him up to Stagecoach to see if they agreed. You always have some reservations about people, but taking everything into account, we felt it would be a good appointment.' A big chunk of the reputation of both Virgin and Stagecoach rests in Green's hands.

Despite all the hassles with SWT and the potential risks of the Virgin tie-up, rail privatisation has proved a fantastic bonus for Stagecoach, even if its train operating company was so troublesome. One of the reasons that Souter's eye had been off the SWT ball is that he focused on what he saw as the big opportunity in rail: the rolling stock companies. Buying one would be Stagecoach's biggest deal and the one that really set the City analysts' eyes popping.

8
The £826 million coup

There are few bargains in the £826 million price range, especially those which cost only £527 million six months previously, but Porterbrook was certainly one of them. If there is one deal that illustrates that Souter is head and shoulders above most businessmen of his generation, it is the purchase of Porterbrook for what many City analysts thought was an extremely high price but which, in fact, turned out to be a bargain and a fantastic generator of profits. It was Souter's ability to see through the complicated structure of the privatised rail industry that enabled him and Stagecoach to take advantage of an opportunity missed by much of the City and all of the transport industry, and which was to be Stagecoach's biggest and most important deal.

Porterbrook was one of three rolling stock companies set up in 1994 in preparation for privatisation by the Government. The idea was that by allocating British Rail's 11,250 coaches and locomotives to three roughly similar-sized companies, with Porterbrook getting 3,700, a market would be created that would ensure there would be competition for leasing the trains. The Government was keen to avoid the situation of creating another monopoly, given that it was impossible to divide up Railtrack in such a way that there could be competition. In the Byzantine structure of the rail industry created for privatisation, the idea was that the rolling stock companies (Roscos) – Porterbrook, Angel and Eversholt – would take on all the existing BR stock on leases of, on average, eight to ten years. The stock was divided up to ensure that each of the twenty-five train operating companies leased trains from at least two of the Roscos.

The Roscos were an essential component of the rail privatisation because rolling stock has a thirty- to forty-year life, while the Government wanted to let franchises for only seven to fifteen years. Therefore, there needed to be a mechanism by which companies could lease their rolling stock and be confident they could get out at the end without being lumbered with the trains. The Roscos were a key part of the jigsaw of over a hundred companies which emerged from the poor old dismembered British Rail.

As well as trying to ensure competition between the Roscos, the Government also saw them as one of the principal ways of raising cash from the BR privatisation. To make them saleable, the government did two things. First, it created a pricing regime which made the older rolling stock as expensive as the newer, with the idea of encouraging the train operators to invest in new trains rather than keeping their older – but cheaper – stock going for ever. The idea, too, was that these lease payments would generate large surpluses to the Roscos, which would be reinvested in the railways. Yet, oddly, the Government imposed no regulation on the Roscos. There was nothing to stop them taking these large surpluses out of the industry or simply rewarding their shareholders with dizzyingly large dividends. The high level of lease payments, particularly on the older stock, had the added advantage of increasing the potential sale price of the Roscos.

Secondly, the Government took much of the risk out of the deal by guaranteeing 80 per cent of the income from the initial leases, which mostly run out in 2002 to 2004. In other words, if a train operator went bankrupt, or simply decided it did not want the particular trains any more, the Government would pick up the tab. Despite these inducements, and the seeming ease with which a Net Present Value could be calculated from the income stream, the Roscos proved hard to sell at the right price. Hambros, the government's advisers for the sale, toured the world and sent out 400 prospectuses in an effort to generate interest, but train leasing was a new business, as no other country had progressed so far in privatising its railways, and none was even considering the same complicated model that had been adopted by the Tory government.

Hambros had initially managed to attract the interest of the large transnational leasing companies but they all withdrew at the last moment, frightened off by the uncertainty surrounding rail privatisation. The Americans, in particular, with no understanding of the sabre-rattling nature of much of British politics, especially the speeches of the opposition, were terrified by the political risk. The Labour politicians, with Clare Short as Shadow Transport Secretary, were at the peak of their noise-making about renationalisation and many in the City were gullible enough to believe them, despite the fact that such a policy would run counter to everything Tony Blair appeared to stand for. As Steve Norris, who was a Tory transport minister at the time of the sale, put it, 'There was no area in rail privatisation where prices were more depressed by the then opposition than the sale of Roscos. The market wanted in general to walk away, and Labour made it clear that they regarded this as the one element in the system which was quite unnecessary and warned it would be the first to march in the tumbril.'

The Tory Government pressed on regardless. According to a subsequent highly critical report by the National Audit Office into the sale of the Roscos, published in March 1998, ministers had already concluded that the success of the overall rail privatisation programme depended on an early sale of a major component of the industry and they selected the rolling stock leasing companies for this role. What's more, the Government was desperate for the cash. Kenneth Clarke, according to a memorandum leaked to the *Independent*, had indicated that the Roscos were a crucial part of his budget strategy for 1995–6 and therefore it was essential that they be sold, as scheduled, by the end of 1995, however low the price.

Thanks to Souter's ability to spot a good deal, Stagecoach was to be a grateful beneficiary of the government's error. The Roscos were, as Professor Bill Bradshaw, adviser to the Commons Transport Committee put it, 'a steal', but very few people, apart from Souter, had spotted that. Souter had examined rail privatisation carefully. He was, of course, interested in the train operating companies, but very early on he realised that the rolling stock companies represented the best potential deal. He looked at the structure of the industry before and after rail privatisation and, in particular at where the subsidy was going. Before privatisation, the Government put in around £800 million per year to keep unprofitable services running. To ensure the industry was saleable, it was fattened up for market with an extra £1 billion subsidy, and Souter wanted to be in there. Souter says, 'I looked at the structure and the big question was, where did the extra billion pounds go? I reckoned three to four hundred million went to Railtrack, two to three hundred to the train operating companies and all the subcontractors, and three to four hundred to the Roscos. And so from very early on, I knew that there was a great deal of value in the Roscos, and a great deal of value in Railtrack.'

One of Souter's colleagues phoned Hambros and got a snooty response. Souter, a good mimic, puts on an upper-class voice: 'Oh, yes, well you need an awful lot of money. Really over a billion pounds for each one.' A total of £3 billion was what Hambros thought the Roscos were going to go for at the time, because of the interest from the major leasing outfits, but the eventual price achieved was considerably lower. Stagecoach had a market capitalisation of only £280 million at this point and therefore the Roscos seemed out of its league, as did the other potential best deal, Railtrack. But Souter kept on badgering Hambros and, as the year went on, he realised the price seemed to be getting lower. A few weeks before the bids were due in, Souter received a call from a small firm who had been in the bidding but had dropped out, and he got a flavour of the numbers.

Realising that the early interest had largely petered out, Souter decided to work on a late bid. Stagecoach first went in with the management of Angel Trains to bid for that company, but soon found out that it had been beaten. Souter had wanted to bid £100 million more but could not find the backing and decided, belatedly, to go for the other two. Keith Cochrane was hauled away from his holidays in September 1995 to help prepare the bid, which was done in a fortnight. So then Stagecoach, with HSBC Montagu and Baring, put in late bids for the other two, Porterbrook and Eversholt. The Eversholt bid was too low, at £520 million, against £580 million by the winning team, but the Porterbrook one of £600 million was £17 million higher than the outside bid and £73 million higher than the winning management buyout team offer. Derek Scott admits that 'what Brian and Keith were doing was a bit cheeky' and was not surprised that the Department of Transport rejected both Stagecoach's late bids on the grounds that it did not want to be seen to reopen the process and that due diligence had not been carried out.

Apart from Stagecoach's late offer, there had been only two bids for each of the Roscos, one from each management buyout team and one from a consortium which bid, individually, for all three, the Great Rolling Stock Company, led by Nomura. Since GRS was allowed to win only one, it was given Angel, as the differential between its bid and that of the MBO team was greater than on the Porterbrook deal. So the Porterbrook team, led by the chairman, Sandy Anderson, started out knowing that GRS was prepared to pay £56 million more for the company, and that Stagecoach's consortium had offered £73 million more. At the press launch of the sale in December 1995, an adviser cornered me and pointed to Anderson: 'Watch out for him, he's a canny bastard.' And so it proved. Anderson was to become the fattest cat of them all for a very small personal investment.

If Stagecoach's Perth HQ is modest, Porterbrook's offices are positively Spartan. They are housed in a small, modern, redbrick building in Derby, cramped and mean with a scruffy entrance and no receptionist, merely a notice saying 'For Porterbrook, use white intercom'. There is still a sign outside saying BRITISH RAIL BURDETT HOUSE and even a year after BR's demise, there were still plenty of British Rail staff instructions on the wall. Indeed, the desk of Sandy Anderson is still littered with files saying 'property of British Rail'. It is not theft, but parsimony. He bought the company from BR, as part of the management buyout team, and sold it on to Stagecoach. There are still only forty-seven people working there, amazing for a company with a turnover of £270 million. That's the way leasing works. Lots of money, not a lot of people.

Anderson was not exactly impoverished when Stagecoach came along and made him a multimillionaire. His first nest egg also came from a management buyout, when he was with TIP. Anderson sports a moustache, the beginnings of a tubby tummy and the relaxed air of a man who knows that he need never work again but enjoys the intellectual challenge it offers.

Right from the beginning of rail privatisation, Anderson felt the Roscos were an essential part of the new railway, the mechanism by which private capital could go towards funding the much-needed investment. Indeed, Anderson, like Souter, had perceived the Roscos as being full of value and a big opportunity to make money. So much so that he deliberately sought a job with a Rosco, even though at the time, in 1994, the Government did not intend to sell the Roscos for about five years. He had worked for British Rail before, after university, and then worked in leasing, ending up with GE Capital, the world's biggest leasing company. The circumstances of his return to BR were hardly auspicious: 'A lot of my friends thought I was absolutely nuts. I had a really top job with GE and I'm leaving that to go to work for British Rail. If it hadn't been privatised or something had happened, I would have been left there working as a British Rail manager, which wasn't too attractive or creative.' Anderson even took a £25,000 pay cut to rejoin BR.

Nevertheless, the pickings seemed so rich that he felt it worth the risk. And when ministers decided to bring forward the sale of the Roscos, Anderson was delighted: 'I thought I was going to have to be there working for BR for four and a half years, and I remember saying to my wife after three months that it was driving me barmy.' BR had stuck Anderson and his small team – at the time Porterbrook employed only thirty-nine staff – in an old office in Sheffield. He had originally been allocated a job with one of the two London-based Roscos, but then BR said that somebody else who couldn't move wanted it, and was he prepared to go to Sheffield? 'I said, "If you pay me," ' says Anderson, 'true to my Scottish traditions.' He also realised that there would be a better chance of winning an MBO if he was out of London because 'you get all these Americans who will fly into London and do due diligence on the London Roscos but will they be bothered to go to Sheffield or Derby or whatever?'

Anderson quietly sat in his decrepit Sheffield office and helped prepare the Roscos for privatisation, creating thousands of leases which initially were between the Roscos and British Rail, but were to form the backbone of the company when it was privatised. Indeed, Roscos are little more than a bundle of leases, which is why they need so few employees. The heavy maintenance is all contracted out, and the train operators are responsible for the day-to-day upkeep of the trains.

Anderson was not exactly sad to see the price of the Roscos visibly plummet as Labour kept up the pressure by threatening renationalisation: 'If anybody says to me, why was I able to get Porterbrook so cheap, I say I'd like to thank the Labour Party.'

There had to be a lot of Chinese walls. On the one hand, Anderson was going round the country giving dozens of presentations to encourage bidders, while on the other he was preparing his management team's bid. As he puts it, 'It was very, very hard to do. On the one hand you want to buy the business; on the other hand I certainly didn't want to do porridge.' Anderson says that he was aware that there was not a great deal of interest for the Roscos: 'Hambros did a pretty good job of keeping it pretty tight that there was only four. But we had a pretty good feeling there was only five.' And, as he knew the five included the three management buyout teams, that meant at least one Rosco would have to go to an MBO and Anderson worked hard to ensure that it would be his that emerged successful.

The three Roscos were sold in January 1996 for a total of £1.8 billion, much less than Hambros's original calculation of £3 billion. The National Audit Office reckoned that £2.5 billion, even on very conservative assumptions, should have been achieved. (On resale, all within two years, the three Roscos realised £2.65 billion.)

The speed of the sale, the lack of valuations, the failure to impose any clawback arrangements on subsequent resales, and the fact that £56 million was wasted because the Tory government refused to allow any bidder to acquire two of the companies all combine to make the sale of the Roscos the worst scandal of the rail privatisation process. It was carried through at great speed by a government anxious to ensure that the whole industry was in the private sector by spring 1997, the expected time of the General Election.

According to the National Audit Office report, taxpayers were cheated out of, even at a very conservative estimate, some £700 million and probably much more if the sale had been carried through with less haste and with the aim of maximising receipts rather than getting rid of the companies as quickly as possible. In particular, had the sale been undertaken after the rest of the industry had been privatised and the identity of the Roscos' clients, the train operators, had been known, there would have been much more interest in the City.

Porterbrook was an obvious bargain, as the higher bid from GRS had to be rejected to stop it getting two Roscos, and Anderson's team got it for £527 million. Eversholt also went to a management buyout team, while Angel went to GRS.

Souter had never believed Labour's blustering about renationalisation. He realised straight away that there was no prospect of it, despite Clare Short's hardline speeches, and felt that he could exploit the effect of the political climate in depressing prices. There was, too, another source of extra value in the Roscos, which Souter was equally quick to spot. Apart from the assessments of the political risk, the main difference between the real worth of the Roscos and the (much lower) price paid for them by the initial buyers was the value ascribed to the rolling stock at the end of the leases. Some of the bidders, not understanding the rail industry, considered this to be as little as £1 million, a ridiculous assessment for some 3,500 locomotives and coaches in each company. Souter, understood that, of course, there was considerable residual value because the train operators would still want to run their services on the day after the leases ran out. The relationship between the operators and the Roscos is indeed a complex one. The operators need trains to run their services and, mostly, they have no choice but to continue using the existing ones. From the Roscos' point of view, however, they need to let out their trains and probably have very little scope to find an alternative user. Therefore future negotiations between the two will be like big games of poker with bluff and counterbluff ('I'll take my puff-puffs away if you don't pay me five million pounds more ...'), but certainly the trains have a definite residual value at the end of their leases, which Souter was confident of being able to estimate.

Therefore, despite his failure to buy any of the Roscos first time round, Souter never lost interest in them and knew that management buyouts are always on the lookout for purchasers. Through his involvement with South West Trains, one of Porterbrook's clients, he came across Sandy Anderson and in the course of a routine conversation suggested that perhaps he would like to buy into the company, say 20 per cent.

Anderson was a fellow working class Scot brought up in a council house whose father, like Souter's, had petty capitalist tendencies. Anderson Senior, too, like Souter's father, had started out as a farmworker but then ran the local shop in the village in Caithness where Anderson was brought up. Coincidentally, Anderson had been a contemporary of Souter's at Strathclyde University, although they never met, as he was in a different year and studying geography and economics, rather than accounting. But clearly they spoke the same language. They hit it off straight away, as they like to do business in the same direct way, without all the paraphernalia of lawyers and advisers. One suspects there is a bit of rivalry, too, as they watch each other's success: 'I've got a lot of catching up to do,' says Anderson, whose holdings are worth about a fifth of Souter's wealth.

They met for breakfast in March 1996 at the Hilton in London's Park Lane where Souter was, unusually, staying, his usual haunt being the more modest Tower Hotel by Tower Bridge. Unbeknown to Souter, Anderson already had his eye on the Perth busman: 'Immediately I heard Brian Souter had missed out on the Angel company, he was my first port of call. But I didn't make it as blatant as that. I just went in on the pretence of seeing him about what might be useful for doing a deal with him on South West Trains for rolling stock.'

Over the cornflakes, Souter asked Anderson about how Porterbrook, which he had bought only six weeks previously, was doing. As Anderson describes it, they were both 'fishing'.

Souter followed up the meeting with a phone call: 'Well,' said Souter, 'I wouldn't mind having a wee bit of this.'

Anderson was dismissive: 'You don't get a wee bit of it, Brian. You either have all of it or nothing.' Anderson did not want Stagecoach to have leverage over his company, putting Souter in a position where he could block somebody else from bidding.

But Anderson was keen not to put Souter off: 'We're paying down debt like no tomorrow. We're in a really good position.' Porterbrook had signed up the first train order under privatisation to Chiltern Railway, worth only £12 million but a good pointer to the future. He also told Souter how Porterbrook had moved into freight with an innovative sale and leaseback deal with Freightliner, involving 400 wagons.

By then, too, Nomura had changed the rules of the game by securitising the debt. In a clever wheeze which, in retrospect seemed an obvious thing to do, the purchase of Angel was financed through the issuing of bonds backed on the future stream of earnings from the leases. Since 80 per cent of this income was backed by government guarantees, it was not too difficult for Nomura to get itself the precious triple-A rating that was essential to obtain the best interest rates for the money. With this government backing, Nomura had no problem securitising the debt. Essentially, this meant it sold the rights to the income stream for several years into the future – ranging from one to seven years – and in return received a lump sum immediately from institutional bondholders, who have first claim over the income. Moreover, Nomura had also cleverly managed to securitise not only the government-backed money, but obtained the much cheaper triple-A rating for part of the remaining 20 per cent.

Souter had been watching from the sidelines and realised that Nomura's move changed the whole picture since it meant that a Rosco could be purchased without bringing on board a mountain of debt. He was keen to replicate the arrangement if he were to succeed in purchasing a Rosco.

Before Souter's arrival on the scene, Porterbrook had been about to securitise its finance, like Angel, as this would have removed the enormous debt from the balance sheet, and sharply reduced the level of interest payments. What was already a highly profitable company, which had made £86 million operating profit on a turnover of £263 million before the buyout, became potentially even more lucrative. So when Souter came along, aware of the advantages of securitisation, Anderson had a scheme ready prepared by Goldman Sachs: 'We thought, Let him buy our company and look smart rather than us do it. We weren't going to get any more money for doing it and it's going to look much neater for him to do it.'

Given the size of the Porterbrook deal, the discussions between Souter and Anderson over the spring of 1996 were incredibly informal. There were no lawyers or advisers involved until heads of agreement had been thrashed out and many of the details had been settled. Anderson quickly agreed to allow Souter to be the sole bidder, getting, in return, a commitment that he would be allowed to continue working for Porterbrook. The informality did not stop Anderson trying to get as much as possible, starting the negotiation at over £900 million, well above the final price of £826 million. Anderson could not lose, since he had always intended to cash in his chips by floating Porterbrook in 1998 or 1999. It took Souter and Anderson just three meetings and a few faxes to cook up what was one of the biggest business deals of the year. There was Geoff Arbuthnott from Charterhouse, the venture capitalists who had financed 80 per cent of the management buyout, and Sandy Anderson on one side of the table, and Souter and Keith Cochrane on the other.

As Anderson explains, the final figure was somewhat arbitrary: 'We had lots of people who came in and said that we should do this or that and we just said no. We just said, "Look, that's the number." '

Stagecoach initially paid for Porterbrook with a bridging loan, but knowing that the securitisation would come through in October, two months after the original deal was announced. Stagecoach also raised £111 million in a rights issue to pay for the rest. The combined family shareholdings of Souter and Gloag, therefore, were diluted from 39 per cent to 28 per cent of the company.

There was, surprisingly, no trouble from the regulators. Souter had to give six undertakings to the Department of Trade and Industry, promising, for example, to offer other train companies the same terms on leases that would be given to Stagecoach's company, SWT. Stagecoach also had to promise to create a Chinese wall by not using information obtained by Porterbrook in its bids for remaining rail franchises, and to co-operate fully with rival bidders' requests for information. Souter was happy to give these undertakings to the minister, John Taylor, as he had expected far worse – a total ban from obtaining any more train operating companies. He says, 'I was quite sure that, rather than blow our brains out on the rest of the franchising process, we should go and buy a Rosco, even it meant that we had to give an undertaking that we wouldn't buy another franchise.' This rare show of sympathy from the Government for Stagecoach turned out to be valueless since all the company's subsequent bids for train operators failed.

The £826 million figure for the purchase price was in fact £476 million plus a huge raft of debt which quickly disappeared through the securitisation, undertaken by Stagecoach's underwriters, UBS, rather than Goldman Sachs. Again, as with Nomura, there were two classes of bond, one for the income stream from the Government-backed leases, and the other, at a higher rate of interest, for the rest of Porterbrook's income. But following Nomura's example, Keith Cochrane managed to get triple-A rating for some of the non-government-backed debt. Out of £545 million which Porterbrook securitised, £515 million was triple-A and only £30 million triple-B.

The City was impressed. As the *Evening Standard* commented,

> This is the first time that acquisition finance and securitisation finance have been yoked together in this way, and it is what made the deal doable. It is a deal for our time. A small bus company borrows £500m from a rich bank, buys a company, sells the victim's prime asset, and thereby raises the

£500m it needs to repay the bank. It is left owning the company for nothing. Not only that, but thanks to the Government guarantee, the bonds will have a triple A rating. Stagecoach might have found difficulty achieving that rating on its own. Neat.

Moreover, Souter reckons that the failure to get Porterbrook first time round had not cost him that dear. Between December 1995, when Porterbrook was first sold, and when in July 1996 the deal was done, the shares went up from 293p to 434p and continued soaring to 570p by October 1996, when the securitisation and the rights issue went through. Therefore, as Stagecoach was paying for much of Porterbrook with its own paper – which, in any case, it could not have done when buying the company off the government – the real cost increase was not that great. Souter says he calculates the extra 'at around fifty million pounds' and he admits that 'we'd have really struggled to find the money at that time [i.e. late 1995]'.

There were, though, some critics still unhappy about this little bus company that had got rather big for its boots. The *Financial Times* pressed for an OFT inquiry on what it called 'this audacious takeover' and said that 'Stagecoach is a company that needs firm handling'. A different writer in the *Evening Standard* likened Stagecoach's behaviour to the bad old days of the eighties, comparing Souter to fallen heroes such as George Davies of Next and John Ashcroft of Coloroll. The paper said, 'Souter is using his highly valued paper to buy other companies cheaply. This generates a quick boost to earnings, plus a further rise in the share price, paving the way for the next deal.'

The *Independent* was full of disbelief, saying the expansion was being funded 'with an avalanche of Stagecoach paper and extended borrowing facilities' and that, while the market had not blinked, 'shareholders may be enjoying the ride now. But experience tells us that such helter-skelter expansion will surely end in tears.'

The deal attracted widespread coverage not only because of the huge numbers involved, but because Stagecoach had created the fattest cats of all the privatisations. It was unprecedented for such a large sum to be shared by so few people so soon after privatisation. Sandy Anderson received £33.6 million, half in shares and half in loan notes. As the shares kept on going up, and doubled by the end of 1997, Anderson became the man who benefited most from any privatisation. He clearly cannot quite believe his luck since, in talking about the deal and the company, he still occasionally confuses 'millions' for 'billions'. Ray Cork, the finance director, received £15.5 million and the other two directors, got £13 million between them. The remaining forty-five staff shared around £20 million, and in a separate deal, the commercial director, Ian Cairns, who had left Porterbrook before the takeover, received £6.3 million. In addition, Anderson, who joined Stagecoach as chairman of Porterbrook, received the hardly needed golden hello of £250,000. At first it was widely reported that Anderson and his fellow directors had each invested several hundred thousand, making a total of £15 million, and put their houses at risk. The *Daily Telegraph* reported that Anderson 'stressed the risk he had taken in [the] management buyout, including his home and hundreds of thousands of pounds in savings'. However, Anderson declined to tell the paper how much (or little) he invested and clearly the reporter was taken in by the confusing statement from Anderson that 'I got a remortgage on the house and I had done a management buyout before and had several hundred thousand pounds saved from that'.

It later emerged, in the NAO report, that the staff and directors had put in a total of £300,000, which means that Anderson himself was in for just £120,000, a figure he later confirmed to me. The return on his investment of just seven months was 28,000 per cent and, as he had a nice nest egg from his previous business dealings, he had certainly not risked his whole lifestyle.

The initial confusion over how much the directors and staff had invested arose because most of the equity taken by the City institutions had been in the form of preference shares, which was little more than an alternative form of debt and was repaid as such, without the massive premiums attracted by the ordinary shares. Of the total £75 million in equity, only £2.5 million was in ordinary shares, of which the directors and staff held £300,000. Stagecoach paid £398.4 million for that equity, of which £83.7 million went to the directors and staff. Charterhouse told the NAO that it 'attributed the size of [the management-employee buyout team's] gain almost entirely to the willingness of Stagecoach Holdings to pay a premium to obtain control of the company'. In other words, Stagecoach was happy to buy off the Porterbrook directors and staff because it knew that the deal gave the company access to remarkable profits over the next few years.

The investors also flourished. Charterhouse got £276.5 million for a £52.7 million stake. Several Charterhouse directors realised they were funding a goldmine and personally put in £88,864, for which they received £32 million.

After the acquisition, Stagecoach set about trying to reduce costs.

Porterbrook's business is divided into two main activities, leasing and maintenance. The company has contracts for the 'heavy' maintenance from the train operators, such as major refurbishment of engines, stripping down carriages and so on, while the light maintenance is carried out by the operators themselves. The heavy maintenance is then, in turn, contracted out.

The bald figures of the business are staggering and huge. Since Porterbrook has securitised its debt – at a fixed rate of interest averaging 7.4 per cent – the only opportunity to cut costs is in maintenance. In the first eight months after the takeover, Porterbrook made £80 million operating profit on a turnover of £180 million, compared with £64.6 million on a turnover of £176 million. The main cost is maintenance, on which Porterbrook spends around £100 million per year. Stagecoach, therefore, had managed to reduce costs significantly in Porterbrook.

Porterbrook has also won far more orders for new trains than the other two Roscos. Of the three Roscos, it is the only one that is fulfilling the Tories' original aim of reinvesting its profits in the industry and it has an order book of £420 million. According to Anderson, 'Porterbrook will be investing the profits for the next five or six years.' Indeed, Roger Ford, editor of *Rail Privatisation News*, says 'Porterbrook won the first seven or eight orders from the train operators and is reinvesting the majority of its profits, whereas the other two Roscos have struggled to get any orders at all.' He reckons Anderson is, like Souter, 'a deal maker who gets things done. He agrees on a deal, shakes hands, and that's it. No messing about.' As Porterbrook has won so many orders, its ability to produce high profit levels once the contracts run out in 2002–4 is assured. Stagecoach again used securitisation to pay for a large chunk of the investment. In April 1998, Porterbrook raised £363 million to fund the purchase of 113 new trains, of which £273 million came from the issue of bonds secured on the basis of future leasing payments for the trains. Although the deal was similar to the way the original purchase of Porterbrook was funded, it was the first time that such a deal had been done in Britain simply to buy trains.

But all the train orders for the British rail industry are almost completely in now for the next five years, as most of the franchises run out in 2003–4 and no company is going to order any new trains in the last few years of its franchise. Anderson is therefore also trying to look for new types of business and is prepared to change the terms of the business, possibly altering, by agreement, some of the leases to a kind of contract hire arrangement whereby the train operators have a 'no train, no pay' deal. And he has plans to expand: 'Next step for us is abroad. We've already planted the seeds in a couple of countries in Europe. There's no point in building up a rail leasing business just in the UK. You need to be in on an international basis.' Initially, Anderson had planned to leave the business but, as long as there are deals to make, he will stay, though a leasing expert, Keith Howard was appointed as managing director of Porterbrook in Febuary 1999 to run the day-to-day business.

But even without innovation, Porterbrook is guaranteed terrific levels of operating profits at least until 2002–4, when the existing leases run out. And after that, Porterbrook will be in a very strong position. It will have the upper hand when renegotiating the leases because, at the end of the day, the train operators will not be able to run services without rolling stock. If rail travel keeps on booming and the amount of new stock coming into the railway remains at below the replacement levels that have prevailed since privatisation began in 1994, there will be a shortage of trains, boosting Porterbrook's hand in the big game of poker.

It is hardly surprising, therefore, that these fantastic levels of profits, a 46 per cent margin and a 9 per cent return on assets compared with regulated utilities, which are allowed only 7 per cent, have led the Labour Government to look at ways of regulating the Roscos. After Stagecoach announced in December 1997 that Porterbrook had made a £63 million operating profit on turnover of £136 million in six months, John Prescott, the Deputy Prime Minister and Secretary of State for Transport, told the Commons Select Committee on Transport that his review of rail regulation would include the Roscos because they had been sold at a 'knockdown price' by the previous government, and had no controls and no requirement to invest in new rolling stock. He said that while the Roscos said it was not in their commercial interest to abuse their market position, 'I am determined that they will not do so. They must not get rich again at the taxpayers' expense.'

The statement sent Stagecoach shares plummeting, and Souter immediately attempted to pre-empt any government action. He threatened to call in lawyers to challenge any decision to try to alter the existing contracts. He accepts that the contracts are very profitable 'but they are contracts under English law, used for securitisation for an international bond. Most of the beef about Rosco regulation is attributable to corporate jealousy.'

And he said that after the contracts ended, there would be 'a competitive open market for rolling stock – you can buy direct from the manufacturer, lease from a Rosco, lease from a manufacturer or go to a leasing company and get them to bid on the train.'

John Swift, the rail regulator, who had the task of reporting to Prescott on possible ways of regulating the rolling stock industry, largely agreed with Souter's analysis when he published his report in May 1998. Swift decided to leave things as they are. He said that 'regulation of the rolling stock market should be introduced only as a last resort, if problems of dominance and potential abuse cannot be successfully addressed through encouragement of further competition.' The Roscos will be asked to draw up a code of practice but Swift recognised that this would effectively have to be voluntary. And he lavished praise on Porterbrook: 'The fact that Porterbrook has been more successful initially than its rivals does not suggest that Porterbrook has market power, but its verve and initiative has shown the way to its rivals, now subsidiaries of financial institutions of great power and resource, who are now starting to win contracts.'

Swift's report removed any lingering doubts over the future of Porterbrook. There never had been any possibility that the Government would attempt to unravel the contracts between Porterbrook and the train operators, but the inquiry had created uncertainty, which even prompted some pessimistic analysts in the City to issue 'sell' notices on Stagecoach shares, a move that cost their clients dear, as the price rose from £8.50 in the autumn of 1997 to £12.80 in May 1998. This, incidentally, gave Stagecoach a market capitalisation of £3 billion, well into the Footsie 100, but with Souter and Gloag retaining 26 per cent of the company, later reduced to 21 per cent following further acqusitions. They are, in a way, the fattest cats of them all, more so even than Sandy Anderson. Their company has been built up out of purchases from the public sector but because the acquisition process has been incremental and they have retained their holding in the company rather than cashing it in, they have escaped the wrath of the tabloids.

The debate over regulation arose because there were fundamental flaws in the creation of the Roscos. The government created a highly profitable edifice, backed by guarantees for the leases, in order to encourage investment in rolling stock, but made no effort to ringfence the money to ensure that it would stay in the industry. So a lot of it ended up in the pockets of Sandy Anderson, and the other directors of all three Roscos, and there is nothing to stop the profits from lining the pockets of the new owners even further. Stagecoach is profiting from the Tories' error, generating extremely high margins thanks to the creation of highly priced leases on old rolling stock, much of the money coming from the taxpayer. Derek Scott argues that this is justifiable because Stagecoach is investing £420 million over the space of three years in new stock and that without reinvesting Porterbrook would disappear. Nevertheless, there are no controls on what Stagecoach does with the money and, as Steve Norris puts it, 'Souter now has a source of financing. He has bought his own financing company with its own access to banking sources.'

Souter was so ecstatic about his purchase of Porterbrook that soon after the deal, he regaled a bunch of railway bigwigs with the following ditty sung to the tune of Teddy Bears' picnic, poking fun at Sir George Young, the Transport Secretary, who was based in Marsham Street in Westminster:

If you go down to Marsham Street, you'll never believe your eyes;
If you go down to Marsham Street, you're sure of a big surprise.
The Porterbrook sale was never expected,
Poor Sir George is feeling rejected,
And Mr Watts will never be re-elected.

Souter was right. John Watts, the Junior Transport Minister, defected from his perilous Slough marginal to nearby Reading East, which was supposedly safer, but he was swept away in the Labour landslide.

9
Piracy in Darlington

Darlington used to be famous for its railway until Stagecoach made it infamous for its buses. And as a result of the saga, Stagecoach found itself pilloried in the media, becoming a byword for the excesses resulting from the Conservatives' privatisation policies.

The bald story is that Stagecoach bid to buy the local municipal bus firm, Darlington Transport Company (DTC), but lost out in the protracted tendering process to Yorkshire Traction, which had offered around £1.44 million for a business that comprised fifty buses, the depot and the goodwill built up over its ninety-year history. Stagecoach, which had bid £1 million, had already registered routes in the town through its Busways subsidiary and, instead of taking the defeat with good grace, sent in a fleet of buses and ran them for free, claiming it could not wait for the forty-two-day statutory delay imposed by the Traffic Commissioners between registration and starting the service. Moreover, Busways offered inducements to the drivers of the blighted DTC of a £1,000 bonus to come and join them, and promised wages nearly 3 per cent higher than they were getting. The municipal bus company could not survive the onslaught and within three days, on 11 November 1994, went bust. DTC's last bus was called in, symbolically, at 11 a.m. on Armistice Day. To compound the matter, the free bus service ended on 28 November as the Traffic Commissioners gave permission for Busways to start charging because they feared the other companies might go bust. That left everyone angry at Stagecoach: the local councillors because they had lost at least £1 million; the passengers, who felt that they had been cheated out of a free service; the rival bus companies, who had no chance of surviving against Stagecoach; and the media, which saw Stagecoach's behaviour as the worst kind of bully-boy tactics.

The episode is interesting not only because it attracted national condemnation of Stagecoach, but because it illustrates both the ruthless way the company was prepared to operate and its justification for that behaviour. Stagecoach has never apologised for Darlington, even though privately its executives accept that it was not exactly the company's smartest bit of PR. Indeed, according to Stagecoach executives like Souter and Scott, Darlington, and the damning report of the MMC into the events there (which was called *The supply of bus services in the north-east of England* because it also covered four other smaller local bus wars involving Go-Ahead and Busways), only serves to reinforce their view that the very basis of what the OFT and MMC have been trying to do in the bus industry was misguided and wrong-headed.

The longer version of the story of Darlington is rather more multifaceted than the one outlined above and the issue of who was to blame for the downfall of the municipal company is more complicated than the way it was presented in the media coverage at the time. Darlington Transport had happily bumbled along for most of the eighty years prior to deregulation, providing a reasonable, if unadventurous, bus service for local people. Following deregulation, in August 1986, United, a former subsidiary of the National Bus Company, with its roots in the surrounding area, decided to compete in Darlington with a fleet of some sixty minibuses, enough to duplicate most of the incumbent's services. The bus war went on for three years, with intense competition between the two. Both companies played cat and mouse, changing routes, timings and frequencies, but neither reduced its fares. After three years, competition died down, apparently through some tacit agreement between United and DTC, with DTC retaining 60 per cent of the market. After the period of severe losses, both companies were then able to make a small profit.

Then, all-out war sparked up again with the entry, in May 1993, of Your Bus, a company launched by two former United managers with a twelve-vehicle fleet. The motive for the launch of Your Bus seems to have been personal, as one of the managers had been made redundant in unpleasant circumstances by United. This time there was also a price war and Your Bus cleverly attracted many pensioners by offering them a free pass – a move that hit DTC hard – in exchange for the tokens issued to them by the local council, which Your Bus redeemed for £48.

While bus users were happy at the frequent transport service they were getting, there was increasing concern about overbussing, with High Row, the main street in the town centre, attracting up to five buses a minute for much of the day. On the first day of the Your Bus service, there was a row of buses stretching 400 yards through the town centre, a relatively compact area given the town has a population of just under 100,000. The diesel fumes threatened to choke the shoppers who were supposed to be the users of the services. Timetables were disregarded and buses sometimes waiting at one stop in the town centre, changed their destination board, and headed off to a fuller stop with more people waiting. The residents of Springwell Terrace in Haughton staged an anti-bus protest, barricading the road and refusing to let any more through. The police and the Department of Transport became embroiled in the row, with the latter announcing that Darlington had the worst bus-caused congestion problem in the country. Darlington residents adapted the old joke about waiting for buses for forty-five minutes and three coming along all at once. In Darlington, they said, you wait three minutes, and forty-five buses all turn up together.

Inevitably, all three operators – United, DTC and Your Bus – were incurring losses, and this prompted the council to put DTC up for sale. The local Labour council had considered this move some years before, but had been reluctant to proceed. The mounting losses forced the council-lors' hand.

The announcement of the sale was made on 12 July 1994 and the council's advisers, worried about the unstable conditions, pressed for a quick sale. The bus-war madness continued. In August, United responded by pouring in yet more buses and DTC attacked back by buying yet more rolling stock, funded by an £80,000 loan from the council.

Busways, which had been bought by Stagecoach on 26 July, had already expressed interest in moving into Darlington and Stagecoach quickly identified Darlington as a prime area for expansion. To signal Stagecoach's intention to enter the market, in September Busways registered a four-route, twenty-vehicle operation due to commence on 12 December.

Darlington, according to Souter, was an obvious target for Stagecoach's acquisition process in the north-east, building up a large operation from a number of smaller companies, as it had done on the south coast: 'We had got Busways, the municipal company in Newcastle, Sunderland and South Shields, I knew Hartlepool was doing a deal with us, and we were about to exchange contracts with Cleveland, which also gave us Hull. So we were going to end up with all of the municipal companies in the north-east and Darlington, in a sense, was finishing a piece of the jigsaw.'

When, on 24 October, Stagecoach heard it had lost out on the bidding to Yorkshire Traction, Souter was full of disbelief. 'We were suspicious. We knew that the business could never be sustained at that level.' He claimed that Yorkshire Traction, with its base in Barnsley, and historic profit margins of around 3 per cent, would not be in a position to compete with United in a loss-making market and was a stalking horse for its friends at United, who would then have a virtual monopoly.

Souter saw the Darlington Transport Company as a lame-duck outfit which was ripe for plucking: 'Darlington Transport was like a Hastings or a Portsmouth [see Chapter 4]. It was tottering on the verge of receivership. It was running an appalling service and the councillors were being badly advised. We were not at all sure that we really wanted to be involved in the bidding for it, as it was such an appalling asset. So we registered bus services and everybody said, "That's a bully-boy tactic". In fact, what we were saying was we're not sure we want to bid, but we're going to be in Darlington anyway, whether we buy or not.'

Enter the Transport and General Workers Union. Souter claims the role of the union was never outlined at the time in the press and that the MMC report completely ignored its importance. According to the MMC report, Busways' finance director, John Conroy, received a phone call from Charles Tait, the T&G chairman at DTC, who said that the workforce was unhappy about the selection of Yorkshire Traction as the preferred bidder because his members wanted to work for Stagecoach. Yorkshire Traction had a poor employment record, with an anti-trade-union ethos, and the union did not trust its intentions because the bid seemed too high to be viable. Tait later told the MMC that he had been surprised at Stagecoach's good industrial relations record, as its reputation had been as 'a bad employer'. On phoning round his counterparts around the country, he discovered 'in almost every area, the conditions were better than our members enjoyed at DTC'.

Tait had expressed his preference for Stagecoach as early as 19 September in a letter to the council and that, 'our members had made it very clear to me that even if their preferred choice of Stagecoach did not succeed in the bidding process, they would still resign from DTC and join Stagecoach rather than put up with the uncertainty of the threat to their employment'. The workers had received only one 3.5 per cent rise between 1988 and 1994, and Stagecoach, in an advertisement placed on 27 October, was promising an increase of 3 per cent (to £4.26 per hour), as well as the £1,000 bonus – which Stagecoach argued was not a bribe but was offered because that would be the cost of training outside entrants – a guarantee of no compulsory redundancies for three years, a profit-sharing scheme and a recognition of existing seniorities.

Not all the drivers were convinced by Stagecoach's intentions. Tait had organised a meeting, which the three bidders had been asked to attend, but only Stagecoach turned up. However, Frank Carter, the head of Yorkshire Traction, claimed he had not been invited and one driver told *World in Action*, which made a TV programme on the affair, that the T&G officials had stitched up the deal. He pointed out that Tait was rewarded with a supervisor's job.

As a result of the T&G's readiness to deliver its workforce, Stagecoach registered more services, effectively matching all DTC's routes. It simply photocopied its rivals' registrations, merely changing the relevant details about the name of the applicant – a common industry expedient during the bus wars, according to Stagecoach, but one that seemed at odds with its claim that it does not merely duplicate its rivals' routes. The services were all due to start on 12 December, the date originally scheduled for the commencement of the limited four-route Busways service.

As soon as Stagecoach had announced it was coming into town, DTC was doomed, even before a single free bus service had been run. Stagecoach's registration of the routes prompted the bidders for the purchase of DTC to withdraw. The plan for free buses appeared in the local press on 1 November and Yorkshire Traction pulled out the following day. Badgerline (FirstBus), running third in the bidding, had withdrawn and even United, which originally had bid despite the council's opposition, pulled out. Busways, the Stagecoach subsidiary, put in a token offer for the assets of the company, much as Stagecoach had done in Lancaster, but this was rejected. Stagecoach arrived in Darlington all guns blazing on 7 November with forty-eight buses drafted in from other companies and the seventy drivers it had recruited, fifty-five of them from DTC. The free-fares policy was seen as a dirty trick by Durham County Council, which banned Stagecoach from using the bus lanes on its roads. The bored local youth, though, loved it, and there were reports of arguments between drivers and teenagers who enjoyed riding round town for free all day.

Facing a loss of £30,000 per week, the directors of DTC called in the administrators on 10 November and the following day the ninety-year-old life of the bus company was extinguished. The cost to the ratepayers was reckoned to be £40,000 in addition to the foregone £1.44 million for the sale to Yorkshire Traction, though there were a few sellable assets such as the depot and the newer buses. Stagecoach had entered Darlington for the cost of three weeks' free bus service – £90,000 – and £55,000 in bonuses to the drivers poached from DTC.

After the demise of DTC, and Stagecoach's decision to start charging fares, the war between the remaining operators continued for a few weeks. West Midlands Travel, which later became part of National Express, first purchased United, which had been weakened by the long Darlington bus war, on 24 November and then also bought Your Bus out a month later, leaving just the two operators, United and Stagecoach.

Early in 1995, Durham County Council, tired of the bus war, voted itself extra powers to regulate the bus companies and brokered a deal between United and Stagecoach to reduce the number of services, and the two companies also agreed to accept each other's tickets. In March 1995, the OFT reported – late as ever – on the bus war between United and Your Bus, finding United's action predatory, but taking no action because Stagecoach was now on the scene. The noise and pollution have been reduced and peace has broken out. Stagecoach bought the Haughton Road Bus Depot from the administrators in June 1995, and sold it, at a profit, a few months later to Glendale Developments for a superstore.

Without the widespread publicity, the Darlington bus war might have remained as obscure as many of the other battles that Stagecoach fought over bus territory. Stagecoach blames me for having been the first national newspaper journalist to have covered the issue (in the *Independent*, on the same day as the *Guardian*). As both papers ran large features, the issue was then widely picked up in the national media and, notably, in a highly critical report on BBC2's *Newsnight* and a subsequent *World in Action* programme. Indeed, Stagecoach had got away with similar events in Inverness and Lancaster with virtually no national newspaper coverage, but the company was to be permanently associated with Darlington. The MMC report, which was published in August 1995, a thin time for news, made the front pages because its language went beyond any previous criticism of the company, calling its behaviour 'deplorable, predatory and against the public interest'. The political outcry was louder than anything previously, with calls for Souter's head. Brian Wilson, Labour's transport spokesman, called for a nationwide inquiry: 'Stagecoach knows that the OFT are toothless. By the time each critical report comes out, they have done exactly the same thing in another ten towns. Their whole approach needs to be looked at nationally, rather than on a localised basis.'

There is no doubt that at times Souter has misread situations and ignored the political and public relations implications of his actions. Darlington is the most obvious example. Souter admits that on Darlington, the 'PR damage by far and away offset any benefit that the deal brought us'. Even the trade press, which has largely been an admirer of Stagecoach and Souter, felt he had gone too far in Darlington. An editorial in *Buses* magazine was typical. While reminding readers that it had frequently praised Stagecoach for its investment, its relationship with its workers and record of service to passengers,

> A single act has caused us to question our judgement. How can one describe what has gone on in Darlington? Here is this large operator committing a gross act of piracy in Darlington. We don't suggest Stagecoach has done anything illegal. But it is a sad day when an operator which has gained a good deal of respect in a comparatively short time should descend to such low tactics.

Derek Scott admits that Stagecoach mishandled the PR: 'It didn't look very good but who cared about PR? We were trying to run a better bus company for our passengers and shareholders. We were never a very good company in PR terms at that time.'

But Souter remains somewhat bemused to this day about why Stagecoach was attacked so fiercely: 'We did a deal with the trade union which we felt was entirely fair game. We did not think it was immoral to leave the town council with the rust-bucket buses that they had, because we thought they had been badly advised by their accountancy people in the first place. Yorkshire Traction could never have signed that deal in the state the company was in.'

While Darlington and the SWT fiasco have attracted equally bad publicity for Stagecoach, the two episodes are treated very differently by the company's executives. While on SWT the management put up their hands and admitted they were at fault, in Darlington, despite all the criticism, they still protest their innocence.

The defence at the MMC inquiry was robust. Peter Nash, Busways' commercial director, felt that Stagecoach should not be blamed for DTC's demise because it made a late entry to a market in which three companies were losing money: 'This is a bit like blaming the train driver who runs over the damsel tied to the tracks, rather than the villain who tied her there.'

He concluded, 'Far from destroying competition, in Darlington, we believe that we have prevented United becoming the only operator of Darlington town services ... we are beginning to wonder whether we would have been better branding our Darlington services "Scapegoat Darlington".'

That 'hard done-by' feeling, so well expressed by Nash, is much felt by Stagecoach executives who see the criticism of Stagecoach as misconceived and motivated by one or more of the seven deadly sins, from greed to jealousy.

Souter reckons the MMC was forced to take a hard line because there were twenty other bus companies still in the hands of local councils and the MMC felt that there would be repetitions of the Darlington scenario throughout the country. But Souter argues Darlington was a one-off: 'I can understand that it was politically unacceptable that the eighteen companies who had chosen not to be privatised, on the basis of that tactic, could have fallen one after the other. My argument to the MMC was that it wouldn't happen. Darlington was a one-off. The Darlington staff had been ignored by the council, buffeted from pillar to post, put in the hands of a very unacceptable new owner, and then they took precipitate action because we gave them a fire escape to run down and I don't actually believe that would happen across the country.' In any case, Stagecoach would never dare to try another Darlington, given the damaging publicity. The MMC did not agree. Its report said, 'There was widespread concern that all publicly-owned companies were now under threat. One said that Stagecoach had demonstrated that it was no longer necessary to pay large sums of money for goodwill. It was cheaper to force the municipal operation into receivership.'

The people of Darlington did not take to Stagecoach. Six months after the takeover, Busways commissioned NOP to carry out market research on bus services in the town. The previously unpublished report found that 42 per cent of bus users thought they had deteriorated in the past year, while only 28 per cent reckoned they had improved. People felt there were fewer buses and lower frequencies. In other words, they rather liked the bus war.

Despite this, there was praise from an unexpected quarter. Moir Lockhead, the chief executive of FirstBus, probably Stagecoach's most disliked rival, praised Stagecoach's services in Darlington saying, in August 1995, 'Now, when you see the quality of services that are being provided [in Darlington], I think that has got to be in everybody's interest. What happened has produced newer vehicles and the quality of service to the public is better than it was before.'

Darlington was Stagecoach's worst brush with the regulators. In the decade after deregulation, Stagecoach was referred to the Office of Fair Trading some thirty times. Of these complaints, eight resulted in MMC hearings and seven – Portsmouth, Hastings, Lancaster, Sheffield, Strath-clyde, North East (including Darlington) and Ayrshire – found Stage-coach's actions were 'against the public interest', forcing it either to divest or to be the subject of specific regulatory action. Only in Chesterfield was the merger found not to be against the public interest.

Stagecoach was so regularly hauled up in front of the regulators that Souter and Scott developed a routine. They used to have a chat over lunch in a Holborn McDonald's before going across to the MMC offices in Carey Street, where the hearings were held. They treated the process as 'an occupational hazard' and, while they took it seriously, their low expecta-tions of being given a proper hearing meant they dispensed with lawyers and put on a bit of a show. The chairman would kick off by saying to Souter, 'You are no stranger here; you know the way we operate by now.' At the Sheffield Mainline hearing, for example, asked why he was expanding into urban areas, Souter said that he was sick of being told by Bryan Carsberg, the director general of the OFT, things like 'you have got all the public transport in Cumberland'. He said, 'That is right, but there are a million sheep and a hundred thousand people around there.' And promising a paper on the group's purchasing policy, he said he would be happy for the Commission to have it 'as long as you don't sell our secrets'. Souter, the schoolboy clown, was still at it and that attitude can hardly have endeared him to the portentous members of the Commission.

According to Derek Scott, Souter gave up going to the hearings because, 'he said, "What's the point?" They didn't seem to want to listen to the economics tutorial he was giving them but I think I got the benefit of our work because I stuck with it for two or three years after Brian, and I began to see a bit of a change.'

Criticism by the MMC and the OFT and the subsequent coverage in the media has, effectively, created the public image of Stagecoach: the ruthless, aggressive, big company run by a couple of heartless Scots pushing smaller operators out of business and forcing venerable publicly owned companies into bankruptcy. It was an image that occasionally Stagecoach relished. As the *Glasgow Herald* put it in December 1994, when Stagecoach was at the peak of its regulatory hassles, 'letters from the Office of Fair Trading are usually a sign of business success, so it was no surprise that the Stagecoach bus group yesterday reported soaring profits.'

There is widespread consensus, both inside and outside the bus industry, that the competition legislation on which the criticism was based was flawed and unable to cope with the newly deregulated bus industry. To separate Stagecoach from its image and to ascertain whether its public pillorying has been justified, it is necessary to try to assess what the OFT and the MMC were trying to do and what type of bus industry they saw as ideal. The principal criticisms of Stagecoach and its activities also need careful examination.

The OFT and the MMC operate to the competition and fair trading legislation, as well as the Transport Acts. They are the authorities responsible for the promotion of effective competition in the supply and consumption of goods and services. The Fair Trading Act 1973 empowers the MMC to investigate references made to it in relation to monopoly or merger situations that may be expected to operate 'against the public interest'. The MMC can also investigate references made to it by the OFT in relation to anticompetitive practices, as defined by the Competition Act 1980.

The definition of 'public interest' was taken narrowly, essentially in terms of whether actions were 'anticompetitive' or not, and with little reference to what passengers or employees wanted. The regulators' bible was the Tebbit Guidelines for merger policy, drawn up around the same time as the *Buses* White Paper – when Thatcherism was at its ideological apex – by Norman Tebbit, the Trade Secretary. The guidelines make the presumption that more competition is better than less, and so if an operator is removed from the marketplace by a merger, there is less competition than there used to be and that is bad, *per se*. Ridley's aim was to have myriads of tiny operators, each owning its own bus, a model that was obviously impractical and inefficient.

It was the legislation on mergers and anticompetitive behaviour that brought Stagecoach to the attention of the regulatory authorities. To qualify as a situation worth investigating, the merger must result in one operator controlling at least one quarter of the supply of bus services in a substantial part of the UK. 'One quarter' and 'substantial' both gave the lawyers many happy and lucrative days' work. The MMC has usually taken the view that a quarter refers to the proportion of total vehicle miles operated in the reference area by buses – disregarding any other form of transport in the area.

The issue of whether the reference area constituted a 'substantial' part of the UK went right up to the House of Lords in a case involving South Yorkshire, which had a delaying effect on deciding the regulatory consequences of Stagecoach's takeover of the local Hastings bus company (see Chapter 4). The Lords, overturning the Court of Appeal, ended up defining the area with the rather tautologous statement that 'a substantial area should be a part of such size, character and importance as to make it worth consideration for the purposes of the Act'. That meant the MMC could investigate relatively small areas like Hastings, Ayrshire and Chesterfield.

For the competition investigations, the procedure is that the Director General of Fair Trading receives complaints about the actions of a company. He investigates them and, if he finds a company's conduct to be anticompetitive, he can ask for undertakings and, if not satisfied, can refer the matter to the MMC for a further report. Defining the 'public interest' is also problematic in the bus industry but the MMC is supposed to be concerned with maintaining and promoting effective competition. The regulatory authorities were also always on the lookout for 'predatory behaviour', defined as reducing fares or increasing service levels to the extent that the operator incurs losses with the intention of driving competitors out of the market. The OFT frequently came up with a problem of definition because the distinction between predatory behaviour and a vigorous competitive response is a fine one, such as with Stagecoach's use of discounted Megarider fares.

Even when the OFT and MMC found against a firm, the action that the regulatory authorities can take on anticompetitive behaviour is weak and often so long after the event that it would be counterproductive. In several of the Stagecoach investigations, the aggrieved party had either gone out of business or decided to give up competing with Stagecoach by the time the report was published.

On mergers, of course, the MMC can recommend divestment and it did so in Glasgow. But if the MMC found evidence that there had been action 'against the public interest', the extent of the punishment was up to DTI ministers. In three instances ministers went further than the MMC's recommendation by requiring divestment – Portsmouth, Hastings and Mainline. As we have seen, Souter sees this as evidence of hostility from Tory ministers towards Stagecoach. However, Jonathan Evans, the Corporate Affairs Minister who recommended divestment of Stagecoach's holding in Mainline, the Sheffield company (see Chapter 5), when the MMC had suggested only not allowing Stagecoach to increase its share, says he saw his role in very limited terms: 'If the OFT found that there was a potential operation against the public interest, then it would be up to the minister to decide whether to refer it to the MMC or not. Every judgement was made in accordance with the legislation in order that competition works effectively. If MMC came back and said there is operation against the public interest, it was up to me to decide whether it was acceptable or not. The judicial decision is made on the basis of the

MMC's finding.' He said that the decisions were carried out on a judicial, and not political, basis. Therefore he was not working to a concept of what he wanted to see happen in the bus industry, but merely on whether the actions of a particular company had breached the legislation or not. Asked a more general political point about what he was trying to achieve, Evans declined to answer. 'Decisions were not made on a political basis, but on a judicial one.' He could not remember the specifics of the Mainline case.

Partly as a result of such attitudes, the OFT and MMC got themselves hated by both sides. Many of Stagecoach's smaller rivals complained that they were completely toothless and unable to act. Indeed, in a TV interview for BBC South, Sir Gordon Borrie, the Director General of the OFT from 1979 to 1992, admitted that the competition policy had failed: 'Unfortunately, the reality today is a number of very large companies have been able to see off their competitor rivals by predatory tactics and by takeover bids, and it's been very difficult for anyone, including the OFT, to do very much about it. There is no doubt that the regulators failed, and because they were perceived as failing, new entrants to the market felt they would not get protection against the likes of Stagecoach and other large operators. Therefore the barriers to entry into markets whose importance the regulators had repeatedly stressed, existed largely as a result of their own impotence and incompetence.'

For its part, Stagecoach, while treating references to the authorities as an 'occupational hazard', was constantly critical of their findings and were always considering legal challenges to their decisions. Souter and Scott argue that the MMC reports and the accompanying criticism from politicians characterise the failure of the regulatory authorities to understand what was happening in the bus industry in the decade following the deregulation and privatisation brought in by the 1985 Act.

The bus industry in general, while occasionally frowning at Stagecoach's excesses, has been highly critical of the regulatory authorities' role in the fraught deregulation and privatisation process since 1986. Two aspects of the role of the regulatory authorities that most angered the bus industry were their definition of the market and their belief that there were no economies of scale in the bus industry.

The regulatory authorities defined the 'market' in a limited way. They did not consider that other forms of transport were relevant and therefore did not accept that the private car was the main rival to the bus. Instead, they insisted that competition between bus companies was the only yardstick against which to measure the competitiveness of the market.

Veronica Palmer, director general of the Confederation of Passenger

Transport, feels that the OFT was completely unprepared for what was happening in the bus industry after 1986 and developed case law as it was going along: 'They had to interpret the law in an almost academic sense and they haven't come to terms with defining the market either geographically or economically. The market could be a substantial area of the UK, as in the South Yorkshire case, or a tiny bus route in East Sussex. There is no other industry exposed to such widespread definitions of the market.'

Even more important was the failure to recognise that other forms of transport such as the car, motorcycles, rail or even cyclists were in constant competition against the bus. The only recognised form of competition against the bus were other buses, according to the regulators. Because of this view, the regulatory authorities stamped on any type of co-operation between bus operators on timetables, joint ticketing or fare arrangements, as it was considered anticompetitive. Under the Transport Act 1985, it is illegal for operators to get together to produce such joint initiatives and the regulatory authorities were fierce in policing that aspect, despite their impotence in regard to much else that was happening in the industry.

The argument about economies of scale in the bus industry is quite bizarre and has its roots in Nicholas Ridley's 1984 White Paper, which said, oddly, that 'it is generally agreed that this industry does not show economies of scale'. Indeed, the tone of the Paper was against large organisations, saying that they tended to have 'very large overheads' with 'policies and standards for the whole organisation which may fit ill with local circumstances or operational needs'. The problem for Ridley was that at the time he was writing this, the only large bus organisations were in the public sector, but he extrapolated from this to imply that there were no economies of scale in the private sector. This informed the regulatory authorities, whose policy was to protect the smaller operator, not believing that the larger one could have an edge in a competitive battle because they were making savings as a result of their size.

The argument about economies of scale angers Stagecoach. Indeed, Stagecoach has made large savings through its size, helped by the fact that it has kept central administration to a minimum with only thirty people working at its HQ in Perth. It buys buses by the hundred and has a central unit for many other purchases. Scott told the Darlington hearing that there were a host of ways in which Stagecoach saved money such as 'insurance premiums, uniforms, fuel, the ability to standardise the fleet so that parts procurement can be structured, and the cost of capital'. Even good pensions could be provided more cheaply and lessons could be learnt from different subsidiaries, a process that the management consultants call 'benchmarking'. Souter reckoned that Stagecoach had a 20 per cent advantage in costs over national and regional averages.

Stagecoach's argument on the issue of competition is sophisticated and controversial. Souter reckons that in most areas and routes there is no room for competition, unless the rival operator is offering a different service. Only when the number of buses reaches more than eighteen per hour on a particular route is there room for a second operator. Souter has identified around fifty such corridors across the UK – twelve in Glasgow, eight in Birmingham, six in Manchester and so on.

But is it not hypocritical for Stagecoach, whose very existence is owed to the fact that the market was opened up to competition, to then argue that it should be allowed to scare off smaller opponents? Souter argues it is not and maintains the right of Stagecoach to defend its territory: 'If you're the main company and somebody comes in and runs two minutes in front of you, is it reasonable that we should just allow them to split the market with us? Well, the answer to that is no. We must have the right to improve our frequencies to try to retain our market share. Nobody sits back and lets a new operator run two minutes in front on their busiest service. So we would respond, and there were very mixed reports on this from the OFT about what was a reasonable response and what wasn't. If someone can come in with an eighteen-year-old Leyland National and run two minutes in front of our new, super, low-floor, well-invested vehicle, then our industry is on a very, very terminal route indeed.' But Souter accepts that new operators can get customers if they have new ideas, which is how he justifies the launch of the latest Glasgow war (see Chapter 11).

Derek Scott feels there is an element of class bias in the way that the Tories attacked Stagecoach, particularly when it had the unions on their side: 'You had Conservative politicians wanting competition, but when they actually get competition, they didn't like it. It didn't accord with their sense of fair play. If you play the trade union card, as we did in Darlington, they feel it is dangerous. It's one thing for white-collar workers to jump ship in the City and go work for another bank, it is another for blue-collar workers to do that. I think there is a class agenda here and we are up against a very elitist bunch of lawyers in London who do not go out for more than one day to look at the situation locally.'

Much of the analysis in the MMC reports about Stagecoach is about fears that the company would take advantage of its monopoly position to increase fares and to withdraw unprofitable services. The report into the

Hastings & District Transport takeover is typical: 'We do not believe that competition from other operators, or potential competition from new entrants, or the sensitivity of passenger behaviour to price increases, or frequency reduction are sufficient to constrain the performance of Stagecoach. The creation of a dominant position in Hastings and Bexhill as a result of the merger removes a main constraint on the fares and tender prices that can be charged, and the main stimulus to efficiency and to the improvement of services, and the merger may therefore be expected to lead to higher fares and tender prices, and lower standards, quality and frequency of service, and less choice than would be expected to occur in a more competitive situation.' That is a good summary of the regulatory authorities' perspective on Stagecoach.

Interestingly, in this example it is possible to assess whether the MMC's dire predictions were correct or whether Stagecoach's defence was correct, because ultimately, as a result of the delays from the South Yorkshire case, Stagecoach was never made to divest Hastings Buses, although originally it was ordered to do so by Peter Lilley. A local Labour councillor and bus user, Patrick Shergold, reckons Stagecoach has not improved services and its fares 'have gone up faster than inflation' since the competition was bought out. Caroline Cahm, who is chairwoman of the National Federation of Bus Users and lives on the south coast, reckons 'Stagecoach's reputation is good: they have not cut services and their fares have gone up less than other companies. But I'm increasingly jumpy about their need to keep on increasing profit margins.'

Souter is unequivocal about competition from smaller operators. He differentiates between those providing extra services and those duplicating existing ones. 'I have little patience with new entrants to the market who copy everything that everybody else has done and just run old buses and copy services. I don't think it's a moral issue. It's a business issue because if that operator runs the right product, at the right price, in the right place, then he can get a living. If we run a good product and he is only copying us, then I don't think he's got much chance of survival.'

However, some of the bus companies which Stagecoach has forced out of business, notably Easy Rider in Bognor and Orion Omnibuses in Fife, were running services not provided by Stagecoach. Both Orion and Easy Rider were providing services that created new markets for passengers on new routes. Indeed, Easy Rider had built up substantial customer loyalty, and Souter admits that it was providing a good service. The ultimate logic of Stagecoach's argument is that in provincial areas there is a need for a network that can be provided only if there is a monopoly. Although

Souter does not believe in 'political' – i.e. dictated by local councils – cross-subsidy between loss-making and profit-making routes, he accepts that 'some commercial cross-subsidy has helped to retain comprehensive networks'. Therefore, in order to keep whole networks of interlocking services intact, Stagecoach has to see off smaller operators, even if they are efficient or innovative. And increasingly, the smaller operators will not even dare to attempt to tread on the toes of the big boys. This creates the problem for councils when putting out subsidised services for tender as there may be a shortage of smaller firms to compete with the larger companies.

The truth is that over the past ten years, in most areas, the public monopoly has been replaced by a private one. Stagecoach has a policy of trying to keep fares low by screwing down costs but its self-imposed requirement for high margins – the target is 18 per cent outside London – means that there will always be pressure to cut marginal services. Stuart Murray of the Transport Resource Unit in Manchester, a long-standing Stagecoach watcher, feels that the commercially led concerns of the private operators mean that ultimately 'the network of bus services needed to cater for all residents will not be provided by Stagecoach or large operators like them. There are many examples of failures to link communities to shops, employment, leisure and health-care opportunities and needs.' Services on Sundays have not improved, despite increased demand from shoppers, and 'evening access to many areas is worsening'. It is not so much an abuse of the monopoly position but an overemphasis on commercial considerations that Murray is concerned about.

And while Stagecoach is widely recognised as a relatively benign and efficient operator, what would happen if it were taken over by a more short-term company, concerned only with immediate profitability? The present regulatory framework does not give scope for the regulators to do anything about such an abuse of the system. No smaller competitor can, realistically, enter an area dominated by Stagecoach or another major operator.

The regulators' constant desire for what economists call 'perfect competition' is a Nirvana that is both unattainable and unwanted by anyone. Apart from the Glasgow war launched by Stagecoach in 1997, and the consequent retaliation by FirstGroup in Fife and Ayrshire, there have been very few instances of major groups taking on each other in bus wars because they know that both would lose out. As the MMC report on the north-east reveals, 'we found little evidence of active competition between large operators; indeed, the evidence of several parties suggested that large

177

operators consciously refrained from competing against each other. They appear to take the view that, in what is still a declining market in most areas, if hostilities were to break out between two large operators, both would be worse off as a result, at least in the short term. Active competition takes place between small operators, or between a large and a small operator.'

Therefore, the competition that was supposed to be an integral part of the bus industry after the 1986 deregulation is largely non-existent. The question is, then, to what extent does Stagecoach exploit its situation?

Derek Scott says that Stagecoach's performance around the country shows that it does not and that its good record has begun to make the MMC more kindly disposed towards the company: 'At the early hearings, such as Portsmouth, we had no track record for the MMC to evaluate us but by the time of our later mergers, the last inquiry in Chesterfield in 1995, they were actually able to look at our fares policy in places a number of years after the acquisition and they could see that we didn't put fares up. They are beginning to give us credit for our investment record.' In January 1996, the Chesterfield report, the most recent MMC inquiry into Stagecoach's bus acquisitions, found that the merger was not against the public interest and waved it through, despite some concern about whether Stagecoach would stick to its low-fares policy in the long term.

Scott and Souter feel that the MMC particularly targeted Stagecoach because of its reputation. Scott argues that the MMC took a softer line on rival companies, notably FirstBus when it took over in Glasgow: 'If they had looked around in Aberdeen, Sheffield, Leeds and Bristol where FirstBus operate, they would have found evidence of fare increases well above the national average. If that had been us, they would have thrown the book at us.'

Scott points out that Stagecoach's record is better than the industry average: 'Between 1991 and 1996, the industry average fares rise was thirty-two per cent. Inflation was fifteen per cent and Stagecoach increases were thirteen per cent.' Scott was particularly incensed in February 1997 that National Express, which was a major coach operator in Scotland, was allowed to bid for ScotRail while Stagecoach had been effectively ruled out of the race because the Director General of the OFT had told the company that if it won the franchise, there would be a referral to the MMC. National Express was only referred after winning the franchise, which Stagecoach complains was a breach of the rules because the bid should have been cleared in advance.

The later reports from the MMC are, indeed, studded with references to

Stagecoach as a well-run, efficient company providing good services. Take this example from, of all places, the report into the Darlington affair, which recommends against divestment because it says local people 'are now served by Stagecoach, an efficient operator which has already invested substantially in the provision of new buses for its Darlington services'.

Although the battles with the regulatory authorities have died down because Stagecoach has stopped acquiring British bus companies, Souter predicts there will be further conflict following the passing of the Competition Act 1998, which he fears will bring in harsher rules on competition – rules he feels are inappropriate to the British bus business (see the final chapter for a discussion on this issue).

10
What about the workers?

When Stagecoach began taking over bus companies, panic swept through the unions and the workforces of target companies. Stagecoach had a reputation of union bashing, fostered by the fact that it had helped to break a TGWU strike at the Scottish Bus Group in 1987. In the City, Stagecoach's tough reputation did no harm to its share price, even though it is not entirely accurate. Souter can, indeed, be tough with the unions and has several times brought in drivers from other areas to break the resolve of workers bent on industrial action, but in fact he recognises trade unions throughout the group, both in the UK and overseas. Stagecoach is sometimes positively supportive of unions – for example establishing its European Works Council long before most other UK companies – but it is resistant to national agreements and negotiations (except in Sweden, where such agreements are universal and Souter immediately accepted the status quo).

Souter himself (as we saw in Chapter 1) was a committed union member, who had even been on the committee when he worked as a bus conductor in Perth and East Kilbride, and he still feels a bit of that class loyalty that saw him go on strike despite personally voting against industrial action. Indeed, Souter proudly showed his union credentials to the Scottish TUC in April 1998 where he became the first private-sector employer to address the conference. Souter received rapturous applause when he sang a bowdlerised version of 'The Red Flag' on which he had worked for several days on the piano at his mansion in Crieff and which revealed his strong support for nationalism:

At eighteen years I made a start, wis in a cauld December,
A big conductress said to me, best be a union member,
The meetings wir at dead o' night,
The shop steward, he wis dynamite,
But boy could he negotiate,
He could cut the hours and raised the rate.

New Labour his a wide appeal tae a the posh 'n' arty,
I see yer still payin' every week tae fund the Labour Party
Am glad tae see that Donald's [Dewar] here,
So raise yer hats an gie a cheer,
Am sure the man wis heaven sent
Tae gie us oor ain Parliament.

It's guid o' ye tae ask me here despite being awfy wealthy;
Am sure that ye wid still agree it's better tae be healthy.
Jock Tamson's bairns are a' the same,
If ye think am daft ye've Bill [Morris] to blame,
It's kind of yees tae lend an ear,
But keep the red flag flying here.

Famously, Souter always goes to talk to workers first whenever he visits a subsidiary or a company targeted for acquisition. This is not a pretence. Souter has an affinity for the shopfloor workers which only someone with his humble roots can genuinely feel.

Yet, despite his friendliness with the workers, Souter also expects a lot from them. Several of his colleagues, including his brother David, from the early days describe how hard he expected everyone to work and, although he has softened slightly as success has materialised, hard work is an ingrained part of Souter's ethic and he expects his staff to show the same commitment. Talking to him about this, one senses a touch of unease between the man who feels a genuine affiliation with the working class and the driven capitalist out to maximise profits who is also deeply influenced by his austere and dutiful religious ethic. That ambivalence is reflected in the attitude towards staff. He will meet them, talk to them, but, if crossed and he feels they have betrayed their loyalty, he is quite prepared to try to smash any industrial action. The contradiction was best expressed in one of the few times he has spoken about his ethic, in *Scotland on Sunday*, in December 1991. He said, 'If we were to apply the values of the Sermon on the Mount to our business, we would be rooked within six months. Don't misunderstand me, ethics are not irrelevant, but some are incompatible with what we have to do because capitalism is based on greed. We call it a dichotomy, not hypocrisy.'

Souter played a key role in weakening the Scottish Bus Group strike of 1987. Brian Cox, who was working for SBG at the time, says he hired Stagecoach buses on a contract basis to operate some of the long-distance services hit by the strike. Cox says Souter made use of the fact that coach drivers were not organised: 'By then he had bought Hampshire Bus, which was unionised, and he used its staff to drive the non-union Stagecoach Express services and, in turn, the non-unionised Stagecoach Express staff drove the replacement services I needed.' Souter was too knowledgeable about the sensitivities of organised workers to try to break the strike directly with union drivers and it helped that Hampshire Bus was RMT rather than TGWU.

Souter's readiness to talk to unions has, at times, been very useful from a business point of view. It was the union organiser who advised him of the situation in Inverness, and the role of the union in Darlington was also crucial. In Chesterfield, where the bus employees had bought the business, the union supported Stagecoach's bid to buy the company and staff voted 99 per cent in favour of accepting the Stagecoach takeover, after Souter had promised a three-year deal of no compulsory redundancies or wage reductions. Similar support for Stagecoach bids was received at Busways, Western Scottish, Cleveland, Hartlepool, Hull and Manchester. And, at times, overseas companies looking for UK buyers have approached the union and been recommended to Stagecoach.

When John Mair, the TV producer, wrote to the TGWU hoping to get help in finding cases where Stagecoach had misbehaved for a TV programme he was making, he was surprised to receive a letter back from Stagecoach's lawyers. The T&G HQ had sent it out to regional officials but several were on such good terms with Stagecoach that they sent copies to Perth. Souter is extremely proud of this: 'John Mair thought we had a bad relationship with the unions and contacted them to see if Stagecoach had done anything dirty. But the union gave us copies of the letters because we are on such good terms with them.'

The national union is surprisingly positive about the company, so much so that some of its members, who are more sceptical about Stagecoach's intentions, are highly critical of the relationship. Graham Stevenson, the national secretary, says, 'We would prefer to deal with Stagecoach than with individual managers who had done an MBO. Our members moved from total hostility to Stagecoach, to ESOP companies [employee buy-outs] coming to me and saying, "We haven't got capital, we're facing competition, what do we do?" I'd say, "Stagecoach is not the best thing since sliced bread, but go to them." '

As well as recognising unions, Souter and Gloag have tried to involve staff more widely in the company through share ownership. The philosophy is almost straight out of the New Labour handbook of stakeholders, reminiscent of the old Fabian philosophy. Scott, who was involved in several small co-op enterprises in the 1980s, says it is a way of trying to increase staff loyalty: 'This is a labour-intensive industry and we'd like employees to have a long career with us. The way you secure loyalty is by having good pension schemes and by giving them shares in the company. Maybe having shareholders in the canteen can help change attitudes. If there is a group employment situation and one or two people are not pulling their weight, and they are all sat in the canteen moaning about life in general, the shareholders will say, "Come on, we're in this together. If you do that, the company share price is not going to go up, it's going to go down." '

Stagecoach was setting up an employee share scheme in Malawi and decided to create one in the UK. In November 1991 Stagecoach set up a BOGOF scheme – buy one and get one free. Souter, Gloag and Scott toured round the subsidiaries having meetings in depots to encourage take-up, and around a thousand employees bought an average of 2,000 shares each, matched by the same number free, at 35p. By August 1998, they were worth £12 but Scott can trace only a few workers who have held on to them throughout. The shares were available tax free as long as they were held for five years (later reduced to three years).

In 1994, Stagecoach gave 150 free shares to every employee and after that started paying 3 per cent of profits each year as shares to its workers. In 1997–8, therefore, each worker got fourteen shares, worth around £110, which means that 94 per cent of employees are shareholders. Scott is amazed that 6 per cent, including a very few who refuse on principle, do not take up the shares, as all they have to do is fill in the form once to receive them. The Inland Revenue will not allow Stagecoach just to distribute the shares.

In October 1998, Stagecoach became the first major UK company to hold a European Works Council, in advance of the European legislation which requires companies with more than 150 workers in two or more member states to undertake such meetings by 1999. The meeting was held in Buxton and, although such councils are little more than a talking shop, Graham Stevenson, the national secretary of the Transport and General Workers' Union reported that dialogue had been 'constructive and open'.

And at the dinner, they were treated to one of Souter's party pieces, a rendition of 'Daisy, Daisy, give me your answer do.'

Unions are seen as a useful way to deal with large workforces of people doing the same job and therefore requiring the same wages. Derek Scott says the company's philosophy is that it needs the unions: 'You cannot run a depot with three hundred employees without trade unions, as you can't deal with their individual concerns. Trade unions are a channel of communication. There's good and bad, but Brian [Souter] would far rather have them than do away with them.'

Stagecoach has made extensive use of profit-related pay, which allows up to £4,000 of wages to be paid tax-free, a saving of up to £920 per year. However, it is a moot point whether this is a bonus to the workers, or whether as the unions argue, it is a way for Stagecoach to reduce its wage bill. Scott admits that the scheme is 'tailor-made' for the bus industry since profits are predictable. Indeed, it is more a way of paying part of the wages tax free than a genuine sharing of the company's performance. When the scheme is phased out completely in 1999, Stagecoach may be forced to increase wages to meet the reduction in take-home pay, or face industrial unrest.

Overall, in the bus industry wages have been squeezed hard since deregulation and privatisation in the mid-1980s. There has been a sharp downward pressure on wages from the new owners of the industry like Stagecoach. Stagecoach, however, unlike some of its rivals, does provide a very good pension plan, which is one reason it has a good reputation with the TGWU.

Although Stagecoach usually makes a lot of white-collar workers and some engineers redundant when it takes over companies, very few bus drivers have ever been 'let go'. Souter recognises bus drivers as the backbone of the business, without whom no profits are possible.

The vast majority of Stagecoach's employees are bus drivers, traditionally unionised, and were, in the past, not averse to the odd bit of industrial action. By the end of the 1996–7 financial year, Stagecoach had 17,500 employees, including around 15,000 drivers, and abroad it employed 12,000 people. With another 3,700 in the domestic rail industry, the total number of staff was over 33,000.

While each subsidiary deals with unions locally, the main national negotiator is Barry Hinkley, the executive director, who has a reputation throughout the industry as a hard man who takes no prisoners. He says Stagecoach believes in unions, but makes no pretence that it sometimes makes decisions irrespective of the feelings of the workforce: 'Sometimes we consult, and sometimes we have decided what to do. There are certain things that we have to do in the commercial interest of our business that aren't up for negotiation or consultation, like getting rid of layers of bureaucracy. It's a very clear management decision.'

He believes in straight talking: 'If you have bad news to tell to somebody, don't embellish it. Give it to them straight, the full extent of it, and how you propose to resolve it. You also give them the opportunity to consider that if they have a better way of achieving the same objective, we will be happy to listen to them.'

Stagecoach might accept unions, but its workers have still had a hard time over the past decade. One of their complaints is that Stagecoach expects its drivers to be smart and courteous as part of its customer-care philosophy, and, with wages falling and longer hours, they do not always feel cheery and customer-friendly. Ann-Christin Sjolander, a Swedish trade union journalist who visited Darlington two years after Stagecoach's takeover, was amazed at the way the staff were treated: 'They were forced to wear ties, and even in summer they were made to keep the collar of their top button up, even though they didn't have to wear ties. They felt they were being treated like children. I was amazed by the disciplinary rules. We would never have that in Sweden. The workers felt that when the council owned the company, their views were listened to, but now they were being treated like small children.'

More importantly, many of the terms and conditions obtained over decades in the public sector have been abolished at Stagecoach, which was building up its business mostly at a time of high unemployment, when labour was cheap and plentiful.

Reducing costs is the first part of the Stagecoach strategy when it takes over a company and begins to try to improve its margins. And staff, typically, represent 60 per cent of costs. One example of how life for the workers changes after a Stagecoach takeover was at Ribble, one of the group's least successful companies. The Preston-based subsidiary struggles some months to earn an 8 or 10 per cent rate of return on its turnover, let alone the 18 per cent now demanded by Stagecoach's main board. In the 1980s, Ribble was always a bit of a dog because it covers a swathe of suburban and interurban routes, while the more potentially profitable main town networks in its area like Blackburn, Preston and Blackpool are still in the hands of small companies which are either controlled by the local council or have been recently bought out by management and employees. The company, which was already losing £200,000 per month on takeover in April 1989, had its position worsened when, the following year, some of its northern routes, covering the Lakes area, were reallocated by Stagecoach HQ to Cumberland to balance out the sizes of the two respective companies.

The situation is frustrating for Michael Chambers, the managing director, an accountant who had been with Ribble as finance director for only seven weeks when it was bought out by Stagecoach in 1989. He would love to get his hands on the local municipal operators to form a unified network across East Lancashire, much in the same way that Brian Cox carved out Stagecoach South along the south coast. But he can't. There is no doubt that if Souter and Stagecoach's main board gave him permission, Chambers could launch fierce attacks on those outfits and drive them out of business, in the same way as happened in Lancaster and Darlington. If Stagecoach competed on every route on a network, it would drive the incumbent out of business within weeks, if not days. But after the Darlington fiasco, and the report in which the MMC specifically outlined this scenario, such aggressive action is impossible because Stagecoach would be pilloried across the nation. Stagecoach's swashbuckling days are over.

Instead, Stagecoach is in the middle of a long war of attrition, gradually trying to boost business by keeping fares down and quality up and picking up any of the municipal companies that become available. Chambers, in the meantime, has the main board on his back. He isn't meeting the targets for margins, but has one hand tied behind his back in the battles with the local rivals, which are eating into his profits. Therefore the pressure to cut costs was intense and the agreements with the workers were completely restructured in 1992. Chambers is unapologetic about the fact that wages and conditions have deteriorated sharply: 'In 1992 the Ribble cost base was too high, the wage bill was too high and some of the terms and conditions cost too much. The wages were negotiated down, and we introduced flexibility. Yes, people have to work harder, there's no denying that, and no apology. If they wanted to make the same level of income, they had to work five or six hours more to get it and hopefully try to maintain their earnings level. On average drivers lost thirty pounds per week.' Chambers says that the reduction in wages was inevitable because the high rates paid by the previous owners, together with good terms and conditions such as paying for break time and avoiding split shifts, made the company unviable: 'Ribble would not be the size of company that it is today if the wages and agreements hadn't been renegotiated.'

Chambers stresses that the wage reductions were negotiated without the drivers going on strike, though he accepts the negotiation was tough: 'If they were prepared to sign new contracts of employment, we made them a one-off payment which effectively covered their loss of earnings for twelve to eighteen months. The minimum was five hundred pounds, the maximum three thousand five hundred. If people didn't want it, we offered a severance payment and some took that, but most stayed.' Ribble took about 75p per hour off the wages and, in 1998, paid around £4.58, one of the lowest wages in the group.

What happened at Ribble is viewed with concern by staff working for neighbouring companies that are still independent. Ribble is in acquisitive mood. One way of solving its profitability problem would be to buy out those companies that occupy the holes in Ribble's Polo mints and rationalise the whole region's bus services. However, while these companies are supposed to be run at 'arm's length' by the local council to comply with Tory legislation, the local burghers very much still see them as their fiefdoms. Every bus running round the town centre is a symbol of pride for the local councillors, tangible evidence of their importance. They are proud of their businesses, which stretch back to the early decades of the twentieth century, and are loath to sell out. And, most importantly, there is a strong relationship between these Labour-run authorities and their strong unionised workforces who fight tooth and nail against privatisation.

With good reason. They know that if their companies are taken over, they will face a stark choice: lower wages, or longer hours for the same money, or redundancy.

Stagecoach has managed to pick up three since acquiring Ribble: Lancaster, Hyndburn and Burnley & Pendle. The purchase of the last by Stagecoach was fiercely resisted by one of the owners, Labour-controlled Burnley Council, and resulted in a Parliamentary debate and a lengthy controversy which has left a legacy of bitterness among its workforce.

In October 1995, the ruling Liberal Democrat councillors in Pendle decided to sell their 50 per cent share in the jointly owned company because they wanted to spend the receipts on other council services. Burnley councillors, backed by the workforce and a 13,000-name petition of local people, did not want to sell their half. However, the Liberal Democrats pressed on and Stagecoach cleverly offered what looked like a generous deal. It said it would buy Pendle's share for £2 million but would pay an extra £850,000 if Burnley agreed to sell within three years. Burnley, too, would get £2.85 million. And, of course, money talked. Pendle agreed to sell in January 1996, and Burnley managed to hold out for only nine months, suddenly announcing a change in policy in October when the prospect of the money seemed too good and the councillors were presented with a prediction that the bus company needed £6 million of investment in the next year, which the council could not afford.

I met a group of Burnley & Pendle drivers, under conditions of strict anonymity, on a cold winter's evening in Burnley, a town whose soul and centre seems to have been ripped out by half-finished road schemes. Their anger and sense of betrayal poured out as they told how they had tried to prevent Stagecoach from coming into town. Stagecoach wants to reduce their hourly rate from £5.82 to the Ribble rate of £4.58: 'Why should they come and reduce our wages by twenty per cent? How are we expected to live off that. We've all got mortgages and children, and we just can't afford it. These people are bandits – they should wear masks. They are trying to take our money away.'

The workers tried desperately to stop Stagecoach coming and even subjected Souter to an icy meeting. He came to talk to a group of shop stewards, who decided beforehand to remain silent: 'It was embarrassing. No one said anything to him. All he said was that in the end money would prevail. We didn't want to hear that message.'

The working conditions of the Burnley & Pendle drivers were guaranteed by Stagecoach for a three-year period after the takeover, but, as the company kept losing money, Chambers tried to buy out the drivers' conditions, offering £2,500 as an immediate payment to compensate for drivers moving from their former old wage rates to the Ribble one. The money would largely have compensated for the loss of earnings until the guarantee ran out and Stagecoach offered the sweetener of £10 per week in profit-related pay, as it often does in such disputes.

At first, very few of the 156 workers took the money. The disgruntled workers who all had long service records, were determined that they could stand up to Stagecoach, even though they are doing battle with a multinational company with a track record of similar action throughout the UK. They still have a strong sense of that old northern working class solidarity which once motivated Brian Souter and will not listen to the fact that their wages are higher than any in the Stagecoach group. As one put it, 'All they are interested in is their rate of return. They want a 15 per cent return, which means they have to screw down our wages. It's not fair.'

But gradually, faced with such a powerful employer, the workers of the small bus company gradually succumbed. The matter was brought to a head when, in January 1999, the Ribble workers, angry at being one of the worst rates in the group, went on strike over a £6 per hour wage demand.

They held three one day strikes on successive Mondays, with Stagecoach responding by running a few buses driven by inspectors and clerks and offering passengers a flat fare of 50p. On the third day of the walk-out, however, tragedy struck when Frank Dean, a picket at the Blackburn bus depot, was killed by an inexperienced bus driver who took the corner into the yard too tightly and crushed the unfortunate man against a wall. 'The lad's death took the stuffing out of us', said one of the workers. 'We were shell-shocked. After that, we just crumbled.' The drivers accepted Stage-coach's offer of £5.03. And with the failure of the Ribble workers, the Burnley and Pendle drivers gave up the ghost. Twenty-nine of them had been holding out against the wage reduction on offer, but they were coming under increasing pressure, although legally Stagecoach could not force them to sign the new contracts. Eventually, they took the lump sum to buy their contracts out, which was worth £2,650, and their wages went down to the new Ribble rate following the strike, £5.03 both for normal hours and overtime. One of the Burnley & Pendle workers said: 'As we used to get £5.82 for normal hours and £6.78 for overtime, we are losing around £40 or £50 per week. You can imagine how that hits us.' Most irritatingly for the workers who had held out longest, the drivers who had signed earlier were given a further 'loyalty bonus' of £1,500 when the new contracts were introduced in April 1999.

Barry Hinkley defends Stagecoach's drive to push wages down, saying the situation in Burnley & Pendle was unsustainable: 'There is a market rate for any sort of staff in any area. The market rate in Lancashire is the rate that we are paying at Ribble. Burnley and Pendle drivers were paid 27 per cent more than Ribble ones because the council found it difficult to say no to people.' He says that drivers' wages were taking up 50 per cent of turnover at Burnley & Pendle, compared with 38 to 40 per cent of the revenue elsewhere in the company: 'We had this small depot in Burnley paying themselves more than anywhere else outside of London. That's not on.'

What happened in Ribble and Burnley & Pendle has been mirrored throughout the Stagecoach group, although Souter stresses that 'in most cases, the companies have been in a better shape and we've been able to drive a less hard bargain'. Stagecoach has inherited companies where the workers have been paid more than it is prepared to pay thanks to historic agreements with their old owners, either the National Bus Company or local councils. As a result, Stagecoach's cost-cutting has led to the workers facing wage cuts, longer hours, abolition of paid meal breaks and the scrapping of other non-financial benefits.

There has been the occasional defeat for Stagecoach. In Stroud, Gloucestershire, for example, in January 1997, the local union, having put in a pay claim for 3 per cent, found that instead the local Stagecoach operation, Stroud Valleys, responded – in a document as thick as the Old Testament, according to the union – with a demand that their earnings should be reduced by £18 per week, holidays be reduced from five to four weeks and sickness benefit cut by 50 per cent. Des Trehearne, the local district secretary, said, 'It was they who were demanding money from us. The firm argued that they needed to boost the profits of the depot from 10 per cent to 17 per cent in accordance with their national targets. They said they needed to save between sixty thousand and eighty-five thousand pounds per year.' The drivers, however, responded with an overtime ban and a ban on rest-day working. Stagecoach brought in drivers from around the country, including places as far afield as the North East and Kent, in order to break the action, but the workers maintained their ban for several months. Eventually, the managing director left and was replaced by a more conciliatory one who agreed not to implement the reductions. Such successes for the workers are, however, few and far between. Some Stagecoach analysts have been surprised at how few strikes there have been, given the reduction in wages and conditions that the company has imposed and the feelings of many workers. One driver, for example, wrote to me:

> I used to work for about eight hours a day and 39 a week. Now its 43 and away from home between 50 and 60. It's not uncommon to get home from work between 10.30pm and 11pm and to be leaving for work at 7.15am the next morning. It's almost unbelievable that a company that expects its drivers to run their fellow drivers in other companies off the road should treat them so badly.

Barry Hinkley said, before the Ribble and Swedish strikes, 'In ten years, we've had three strikes, including some at relatively small companies. East Kent, Selkent in London in 1996 for two days and in Swindon there has been a festering work to rule. If you look at the size of the business, these are relatively small areas and the record is a tribute both to the management and the unions.'

Hinkley stresses that Stagecoach pays the market rate for bus drivers wherever it operates: 'We have taken out the things that made the business too costly: for example, drivers being paid spreadover time, where they have a split shift and meal breaks paid all the way through. You can't afford to pay people for an hour's tea break or a meal break.

Changing the schedules so you increase the level of driving time, so that instead of driving five and a half hours, they are driving seven hours, you always expose yourself to the criticism of the driver of the 1970s, from the halcyon days, but at the end of the day, if you are paying somebody for eight hours and they are driving five and a half, then that's not right. Those are basic productivity improvements.'

The unions see the decline in wages and conditions as an industry-wide phenomenon. Graham Stevenson, the national secretary of the TGWU says, 'Bus drivers used to get seven per cent above average wages in the mid-eighties and now get thirteen per cent below. The quality of staff has been reduced. People come and go and no longer see it as a long-term job.' He says that initially conditions that had taken a generation to win, such as paid meal breaks, were given up by the unions with barely a fight because the companies threatened their jobs, saying there was no profit in the business. 'Stagecoach were very clever. They didn't directly attack the union, they just let the market do it for them.' But the workers were allowed to remain in their unions.

Hinkley explains that the bus industry is a declining one and therefore there is no spare cash available for improving pay: 'We are not in a business that's expanding. At best our business is standing still, or slipping by 2–3 per cent, so you cannot grow your revenue function to be able to give people a bit more pay, or spend a bit more on other things. On the other hand, we have to maintain the market rate, because if we don't, there will be no one to drive our buses.' Indeed, shortages were appearing in 1998 in several areas as the economy boomed. One driver wrote to me saying that the depot in Lewes, East Sussex, often had almost a quarter of its forty-five jobs vacant.

Wages and conditions are negotiated locally and, if the company has been faring badly, managers say there is no money available. One driver, who worked for Stagecoach South for a number of years, spoke of 'increases typically no more than 0.5 or 1 per cent per year' and the bulk of his increase in pay coming from 'surrendering bonuses such as shift payments, weekend bonuses, and overtime rates'. One common Stagecoach tactic, used widely in the industry, is to pay new drivers less than existing ones, with the idea of encouraging people to stay longer, but this can rebound, as the newer staff become resentful and leave quickly.

Stagecoach nearly faced a much more serious action, a national strike, in 1997 after a long wrangle with the TGWU. The staff of the union had been under pressure from the rank-and-file members to set up negotiations with Stagecoach on a national basis. The membership had been influenced by a prolonged strike by Badgerline drivers who were sacked after refusing to work extra hours for the same pay in Chelmsford in 1994. This had attracted national attention, even though eventually the drivers lost and most were sacked.

The TGWU tried to set up national talks with the three largest bus groups – Stagecoach, FirstBus (later FirstGroup) and Cowie-British Bus (later Arriva) – but the managements refused. Barry Hinkley wanted nothing to do with what he saw as the bad old days: 'In NBC days, there was the National Council for the Omnibus Industry, which met three times a year. All the fag-smoking people went to it, and it made decisions on pay, inflicting wage rates, shift payments, holiday entitlements on all the subsidiary companies from John O'Groats to Land's End. The deal imposed on weaker and smaller businesses conditions which were not sustainable. They were piling the cost on. That's where we come along, as a big bad ogre, and all we are doing is stripping out inefficiencies built in by national bureaucracy year in and year out. And we're not going back to national agreements.'

However, Graham Stevenson, the TGWU national secretary, said that he was never seeking a national agreement on wages, but only the opportunity to discuss matters such as the ergonomics of the cab, health and safety and uniforms – matters that can be influenced by group decisions. Stevenson says that Stagecoach had learnt to centralise some of its activities to its advantage and this had national implications for the workers: 'They made huge savings with bulk purchase of anything from buses to uniforms. But things like the uniform were lousy. They didn't issue enough of them and they fell apart. That sort of issue is very important for drivers and we should have the opportunity to talk on a national basis.'

Stevenson organised a ballot and, in November 1996, received a 94 per cent yes vote on a turnout of just under 50 per cent – 6,000 out of 12,850 Stagecoach members voting for industrial action: 'We don't want national pay bargaining. What pays in Newcastle doesn't pay in Newham. We just wanted a clear framework.' However, one of the demands was for 'a national minimum standards agreement on training, equal opportunities, safety and a £4.15-per-hour minimum.'

Bolstered by Labour's election victory, the TGWU threatened strike action and started organising another ballot. Stevenson is confident that his members would have backed it but eventually both sides compromised. The demand for a national minimum was quietly forgotten and Stagecoach came to the table prepared to create a liaison council, with sub-committees on matters such as bus purchasing and uniforms. Stevenson says, 'As they are quoted, they are vulnerable to opinion in the City. So they backed down.'

Hinkley's version is different: 'We set up the liaison committee on our own terms. We thought the time was right. The national union had been pushing for national agreements, but the rank-and-file members, who like locally negotiated terms, changed their view. I had never been against meeting them, but you can't use the tools of yesterday to solve the problems of tomorrow.'

The widespread process of wage cutting through the company is driven by the need to meet the rates of return demanded by the main board. Initially, in Stagecoach's early days, the target was 10 per cent because the best NBC companies were achieving 5 per cent and Souter thought that Stagecoach could manage double. By 1988, however, managers said that they were achieving this target so the board upped it to 15 per cent, which was what the best parts of most companies were already making.

At flotation, most of the companies were achieving 15 per cent, so the target was reset at 18 per cent outside London and 15 per cent in the capital because of the highly regulated system.

The unions feel that this target is unnecessarily high, putting continuous downward pressure on their wages. As one of the disgruntled Burnley & Pendle drivers put it, 'We are being asked to reduce our wages so that they can make more profits and go off and buy more companies around the world. Why should we be paying for them to make more money?'

Graham Stevenson, the national secretary of the TGWU, says that Stagecoach's establishment of a 15 per cent rate of return galvanised his members into action: 'That single act created a desire among members for a more active approach by the union. Instead of pay claims from us, we were getting pay claims from Brian Souter.'

Derek Scott denies that the target for margins is too high: 'The rate of return has to cover interest, taxation, dividends, retained profit and replacement costs.'

Scott explains that the average cost of a new bus is £80,000 per year. The average annual revenue from a bus also happens to be £80,000 per year and Stagecoach needs to make £12,000 profit from that in order to have enough money to pay for new stock when it is needed. That implies a 15 per cent rate of return.

Stevenson says the figures are unrealistic because the company borrows to buy new buses anyway. He argues that Stagecoach is merely using the high margins to fund its acquisition programme. Indeed, bus margins historically have never been as high and in Sweden, where they are much lower – about 6 per cent – because the system is regulated more strongly, they are high enough to ensure renewal of the fleet, according to the local Stagecoach management.

Scott argues that these Swedish margins are not high enough: 'It is prudent business practice to make the money now so that you can pay the borrowing costs. We will be happy to pay borrowing costs of 6–8 per cent in ten years' time and we put away money on that basis. If we made 10 per cent, we would not have the certainty that we could replace the vehicles when we wanted to and we would have no scope for expanding business overseas. Investment requests are lumpy. We might have to replace several bus garages at the same time. If we had lower target rates of return, then we would be making excuses all the time. We wouldn't be able to do it because our rates of return would not be enough.'

By the 1995–6 financial year, Stagecoach's core British bus businesses were achieving margins of 15.4 per cent but the company was unable to improve that figure for the following year. Scott maintains there is a limit to Stagecoach's desire to squeeze out margins. Souter would not countenance excess profits in one company to improve overall averages. The Stagecoach bus policy is that anything above 20 per cent is, as Scott put it, 'obscene', because 'you are covering your investment costs more than twice over'. Souter has said publicly that he would rather keep fares down in areas where the 18 per cent target is being met, rather than try to boost profits further. And, of course, in some difficult businesses, like Ribble, the 15 per cent target will probably never be met, unless Stagecoach manages to make further acquisitions locally to create a more efficient network.

With the loss of profit-related pay, the economic boom pushing up wage rates, and the possibility of new regulation with the White Paper, Stagecoach faces considerable pressure on the industrial-relations front. The next couple of years will demonstrate whether the company's relations with the T&G are really as solid as both sides like to make out.

11
The end of family Stagecoach

Although Souter had, by 1995, begun to shift his main focus of interest onto railways and overseas expansion, he did not neglect the British bus industry which was fast maturing. The consolidation was continuing and the larger groups' domination increased, but there were fewer acquisition opportunities for Stagecoach as prices increased. Stagecoach made a couple of significant purchases in 1996, with the acquisition of Devon General and Bayline, and Greater Manchester Buses South and it also picked up the small municipal companies, Hyndburn and Burnley & Pendle. But Souter, at the annual general meeting that year, stressed that there were few opportunities for expansion in the UK bus market. The challenge was to try to find ways of increasing or, at least maintaining, income in bus operations, given that increasing car ownership continued to mean a decrease in the number of potential users.

In Manchester, Stagecoach embarked on several experiments to test the potential for growth. Manchester was one of the most competitive markets in the country during the early 90s with eighty local operators attracted by Greater Manchester Buses' slow and inadequate response to deregulation. Nevertheless, GM Buses retained over half the market share and Manchester had long been a Stagecoach target. In 1993, the Government had forced Greater Manchester buses to split into two for sale and the following year, as we have seen, Stagecoach had been beaten in controversial circumstances by a management employee buyout team. Stagecoach had tried to resubmit a late bid, reputed to have been around £20 million but the employees got the company for £15 million. Stagecoach paid nearly three times that – £42.4 million – in February 1996, making millionaires of the six directors who had led the takeover, and gaining around £10,000 for each of the 1,800 employees who had participated in the buyout. The price shows just how much the bus industry had matured since Stagecoach's early acquisition, in 1987, of ex-NBC companies when Stagecoach was paying around 25–30 pence per £1 of turnover. Manchester cost Stagecoach around 110 pence per £1 of turnover and Devon General and Bayline, bought off Souter's old pal Harry Blundred, a similar ratio of price to turnover.

After Stagecoach bought GMBS, which had 750 buses, it began to look at ways of increasing its market share of 55 per cent in what was still an extremely competitive market. Stagecoach was planning to take a route where competition was fierce and apply a segmentation exercise. However, as the launch was being prepared for September 1996, the IRA blew up the Arndale centre in Manchester, creating an economic disaster in parts of the city.

The bomb only delayed Stagecoach's introduction of the ultimate in market segmentation – competition between different operations in the same company. Stagecoach selected the busiest route in Manchester, from the centre along the Wilmslow Road, to Withington where its splits off. Ben Colson, Manchester's commercial director, reckons it is Europe's busiest route, with a bus every 40–45 seconds at peak times and every 90 seconds off peak. Even at night, the frequency never falls below six an hour. Not surprisingly, there were six or seven operators, with Stagecoach the market leader with 55 per cent. In late 1996, Stagecoach launched a service called Magicbus (Souter's much used brand name) to compete against both itself and the other operators. The company repainted double deckers inherited from GMBS in blue and reduced the ticket prices, effectively offering a two-tier service. There was no external indication that the buses were run by Stagecoach although the company's weekly tickets, which allowed unlimited travel on all Stagecoach's Manchester buses, could be used on both and, interestingly, they were sold for £5 on Magicbus and £6 on the others.

Passengers have a choice between a single decker Stagecoach standard liveried bus costing 60 pence or the Magicbus which charges a third less, 40 pence. Stagecoach also entered into an agreement with a night operator to accept interchangeable tickets.

Colson says that the results show that there is more than one bus market. 'Some people will let a bus through to save themselves 20 pence, and others will let the cheaper bus through because they know if they get on the other single decker, it will fill up and then won't stop. Some people will pay more to stand if they can go quicker. But overall, there is a gradual shift towards the lower price, lower quality product. We have grown our market share from 55 per cent to 65–68 per cent and the market has grown overall in the process.' The scheme was extended to the Stockport Road corridor in April 1997 and to Newcastle, where Stagecoach's Busways (SB) is one of three major operators, the following month and by mid 1999, Magicbus was running on four of Manchester's main bus corridors. British Airways later copied the idea, launching its low cost airline, GO, in 1998.

Stagecoach is also trying other forms of innovation in its efforts to squeeze a bit of growth out of its UK bus operations, principally through launching new or different types of services. Most controversially, this has resulted in a bus war in Glasgow which has shocked many inside the industry who thought that the bad old days of bus wars were behind them. However, Souter defends the attack as a form of innovation.

Stagecoach went back into Glasgow, its third venture into Scotland's biggest city, in April 1997 when it launched an attack against the incumbent, FirstBus (later renamed FirstGroup), an amalgam of the Aberdeen based GRT and the West Country based Badgerline. Stagecoach's attack was prompted, ironically, by a Monopolies and Mergers Commission report into FirstBus's purchase of SB. Stagecoach, which had been forced to divest its 20 per cent holding in the company by the DTI, had done well out of the deal. As we saw earlier, FirstBus had to pay £23.9 million for Stagecoach's stake, bought only 18 months previously for £8.3 million. Then the MMC, reporting on FirstBus's acquisition, recommended that the company dispose of one of SB's four depots and the whole of Midland Bluebird in the east of Scotland. Stagecoach, according to Souter, felt that the prices for these assets, even if FirstGroup accepted Stagecoach as a bidder, would be too high and would run into regulatory problems, and therefore launched an attack instead.

So Souter sent in 70 buses in April 1997, with the promise that another 75–125 would arrive within a year. Stagecoach launched high frequency, good quality services using the motorway network around Glasgow, in particular the M77 and M80, to provide express services from such places as Ayr and Cumbernauld. The fares were cheap, 60 pence compared with £1.10, for example.

The move was met with consternation within the industry, already damaged by the poor publicity created by the bus wars of the late 80s and early 90s. Several insiders in the bus industry feel that his attack was motivated by a longstanding personal desire to control the main bus company in Glasgow, both because of his own relationship with the city where he went to university and worked on the buses, and because of his anger that Stagecoach was forced by the MMC to sell its 20 per cent holding in Strathclyde Buses to FirstBus. One neutral insider told the author: 'Stagecoach is growing up but what's happening in Glasgow worries me. Darlington was a gross error and they should have learnt that they don't have to be buccaneers any more. This will give fuel to the "let's regulate everything and get the profit making buggers off the road camp" that John Prescott [the deputy prime minister] is flirting with. It brings discredit on everybody and it's barmy.'

Souter argues that he is not copying services but innovating as this was the first time that a bus company had made use of the Glasgow motorway network and the services Stagecoach introduced were different from FirstBus's existing routes. They were limited stop services connecting some of the outer suburbs much more quickly with the City centre. FirstBus was vulnerable because 'the services have become very product-driven, rather than market-driven'. According to Souter, the FirstBus services were scheduled to run from one end of the conurbation to the other, 'stopping at every three lamposts' which means they were unpopular with through passengers going a long distance. 'This is a delight for the scheduler but a nightmare for passengers. You need to split the market, with express buses and stopping buses. Of course it's more complicated for the producer, you have to do more work and more marketing.'

Souter denies that his motive is personal. He says that Glasgow presents a clear market opportunity and Stagecoach's product is very different from the existing services: 'We are not going back to the old days of bus wars with old buses clogging up the streets. I don't call it a bus war. We see it as a market we've analysed and which needs two operators in it. It is a market you can't deny entry to another person because of the high volumes'. Souter stresses his 'corridor analysis'. He argues that on corridors where there are more than 18 buses per hour, competition between two operators is not only feasible but desirable and that is the motive behind the Glasgow attack: 'We are not trying to wrest control away from Strathclyde Buses which would be impossible. We are trying to establish ourselves with about 20–25 per cent of the market.'

A FirstGroup insider refutes this: 'We had a service registered to use the M77 before Stagecoach. It's not about innovation, it's about getting into Glasgow where Souter has an emotional attachment. And he is using inside knowledge of the network from his time on the board of Strathclyde Buses'. Consequently, FirstGroup responded by copying every one of Stagecoach's new services, often with a bus running two minutes in front of Stagecoach. And the company also retaliated in a limited way in Fife and Ayrshire, two Stagecoach fiefdoms, although a rumoured attack on Busways in Newcastle never materialised. The response in Glasgow outraged Souter: 'They put up fares three times in 15 months except on routes where we are competing. We would have a case under the new Competition Act against them.'

Stagecoach never launched its second wave of attack in Glasgow, partly because of the high losses from its initial attack and partly because of the industry's extremely hostile reaction. Instead, when Mike Kinski arrived as chief executive in April 1998, he took a sober view and reined back the operation, reducing the buses to 55 and scrapping the extension plans. Stagecoach, which had already invested close to £10 million in the city, was still losing money on the operation well into 1999 although Kinski, who clearly would not have sanctioned the operation had he been chief executive when it was launched, reckons it has turned the corner: 'It is in no one's interest to have Glasgows everywhere. We have taken Glasgow from being a big loss maker to breaking even by sensibly reviewing our network. We are not into big loss leaders, nor bus wars where everyone loses, including the passenger.' Kinski will look either for a dignified exit or a stable situation in which Stagecoach is making at least a small return on its investment.

Souter's intervention in Glasgow rebounded on him spectacularly. In July 1998, Margaret Beckett, in one of her last acts as President of the Board of Trade before she was replaced by Peter Mandelson, went against the recommendation of the MMC and decided to allow First Group to retain all its Scottish businesses. Ironically, she made the decision partly because Stagecoach was providing sufficient competition in Glasgow. Had Souter not launched the war, then he might have been able to pick up a piece of the Glasgow action.

But while the Glasgow bus war was waning, Stagecoach showed that even in 1999, it was still prepared to defend its territory with aggression when it felt threatened. While large operators, with concerned shareholders, will not take on Stagecoach, smaller ones occasionally continue to do so and the company's reaction is no less aggressive than in the bad old days following deregulation. In the Spring of 1999, for example, Stagecoach's Busways in Tyneside was referred to the OFT over its aggressive response towards a ten bus operation, Welco Transport Services, set up on a couple of routes in its area by a local operator, Harry Stewart. Stewart has a bit of a history with Stagecoach, as he worked for a company called Welcome which merged with Busways. After Busways was taken over by Stagecoach, Stewart was asked by Stagecoach to set up the operation in Glasgow that was aborted when Souter decided instead to take a 20 per cent share in Strathclyde rather than do battle. Stewart later worked for Stagecoach in Mombasa but fell out of favour and left acrimoniously.

After being involved in HMB, a company based in Gateshead that failed, Stewart set up Welco in Sunderland in early 1999, principally on a route from South Hylton, a nearby village, to Sunderland town centre.

Busways responded quickly by registering timings just before and after Stewart's services and a bus war developed. As the local *Shields Gazette* put it, 'It seems absurd to us that the village of South Hylton, adult population 7,797, which not too long ago had a reasonable four buses an hour now has, at peak, 34 an hour'.

In response, Stewart attacked one of Stagecoach's main profitable routes into the town centre and a mini bus war developed. Stewart claims that his routes initially tried to avoid duplicating those of Stagecoach: 'I am trying to make my living at what I know best. I tried to keep off their routes. Ten buses is hardly going to hurt them.' He claims that, 'Many local people are so angry about what Stagecoach has done that they refuse to get on their buses'.

At the same time, there was a similar spat between a small operator, George Bell Coach Hire, which had been asked by the passenger transport executive, Nexus, to run a service covering four local communities which had repeatedly asked for a bus service and Busways. Stagecoach, which according to Nexus had turned down the opportunity of providing the service, promptly ran buses in front and behind the Bell services. Marie Bell, a partner in the firm, was furious: 'We were asked to run this service, and then we lost money because Stagecoach treated us as rivals. We are not silly enough to try to compete with big companies like Stagecoach. Nobody with any reason would do that. Do they really think we are a threat?' Bell's eventually withdrew leaving Busways to operate the service.

Stagecoach's local managing director John Conroy is unapologetic: 'We have to defend our business. You can't have companies trying to run peak services with clapped out buses. Stewart's buses are not around at 10pm in the evening when we are.' Conroy claims that Stewart duplicated Busways' routes 'with little twirls at the end' while Stewart says that his routes were innovatory. By Easter 1999, Stewart had taken his battle to the OFT who launched an investigation. As for the Bell's episode, Stagecoach argues it was never asked to run the service but Nexus insists the company's representatives were present at meetings at which the new service was discussed. 'Stagecoach's argument is a meaningless irrelevance' said one local bus company insider.

These little local spats demonstrate not only Stagecoach's continued aggressive intent towards tiny rivals but the enduring weaknesses of the deregulation and privatisation of the bus industry. It is only the maturing of the industry into half a dozen major players who do not take each other on (*pace* Glasgow) that prevents a continuing series of bus wars.

Stagecoach also found itself head to head against another major group, Go-Ahead, when in July 1997 Stagecoach bought the rest of Transit Holdings, Harry and Janet Blundred's company which had owned Devon General and Bayline, for £8.2 million. This brought Stagecoach into direct competition in Oxford with Go-Ahead's City of Oxford subsidiary which had a long-standing rivalry with Blundred's outfit. Oxford is rare in that two major operators are locked into what seems like a permanent battle in a relatively small city. Bus use is high in the city thanks to the longstanding pro-bus policy of the council. While there is fierce competition between Stagecoach and Go-Ahead on the London–Oxford coach route (on which Stagecoach has invested heavily by buying 27 new low floor double decker MAN coaches), the rest of the area has largely been carved out between the two. Stagecoach and Go-Ahead have even agreed a deal to create a joint operator ticket but remain in competition in some parts of the city.

In its effort to boost revenues, Stagecoach has returned to the coach market, by operating an inter-urban Stagecoach Express network on such routes as Grimsby/Hull–Sheffield and Oxford–Cambridge. Souter sees this as important because it is a rare opportunity for organic growth in the industry. Stagecoach reckons that the local companies, which operate these services, can boost their income by up to 10 per cent if they take advantage of the opportunities. New routes are launched with a bit of a fanfare and promotions like 'buy one ticket, get one free'. They are potentially very profitable because of the long distances covered relatively fast, and Stagecoach has been using less expensive rolling stock with non-reclining seats in order to keep costs down – cheap and cheerful rather than the 'luxury' coaches promoted by National Express. London destinations have, so far, been avoided.

Such initiatives are one of the main ways Stagecoach can hope to achieve any growth in the British bus industry. The idea is to provide a different service, to segment the market in an effort to raise revenue in a market in which there is still a fundamental decline because of increasing car ownership.

Price is the other opportunity for growth. Stagecoach began to use the experience gained from its experiments with cheaper weekly priced tickets. During 1996/7, the Megarider concept was established widely across the Stagecoach empire in places as diverse as Perth, Thanet, Hastings and the East Midlands. In the old days of nationalisation, these tickets were sold with virtually no discount, but Souter sees establishing customer loyalty as essential and gives big discounts. Typically, with Megarider, the discount is around 40 per cent on the basis of 10 journeys. In Perth for example, a Megarider is £4.00 while a journey from the city centre to the housing estates cost 75p. Moreover, unlike the old system, the idea is that any family member or friend can use it as there is no photocard or any restrictions: 'The father can put the ticket on the mantelpiece after work, and the son can use it to go into town in the evening,' says Souter.

Conventional wisdom in the industry is that the elasticity is -0.3 – that means a 10 per cent increase in fares will only result in a 3 per cent loss in passengers and vice versa. However, the 1997 Annual Report suggests that creating cheaper tickets may have a long term effect of increasing passenger numbers and therefore the elasticity may be higher or asymmetrical: 'A pattern emerged where we see an initial loss of revenue, but a sharp increase in passenger numbers. Bus revenues then return to their pre-fare reduction level over the following year and in many cases have continued to grow in the second year.' And, the added advantage for Stagecoach is that such deals ensure that the company becomes almost competition-proof since no competitor could come in and match the reduced fares.

In another effort to keep customers loyal, Stagecoach has even introduced Bus Points schemes, the bus equivalent of Air Miles. Passengers keeping their old tickets can redeem them for goods from supermarkets or obtain discounts on trips to London or Disneyland. Typically spending £30 on bus tickets earns a £1 voucher.

However, Stagecoach's Megarider strategy is under threat. Souter is worried about two possible effects of the Competition Act which became law in the summer of 1998: being unable to respond to attacks from rivals and not being able to sell Megarider-type tickets.

The new law, which originated as a European Union initiative, gives power to the courts to fine companies in breach of the legislation up to 10 per cent of their turnover, a massive sum. Souter fears that this will apply to larger companies taking defensive action against attacks from small outfits: 'If a small operator puts on a bus two minutes in front of your service, using 20 year old Leyland Nationals, and you respond by putting a service in front of theirs, you can then become liable to a fine of up to 10 per cent of your UK turnover.' He reckons that means that anyone can go out with '£30,000 worth of smoky buses blowing toxic fumes and run against your well-invested £1.5 million of new low-floor buses'.

He is also worried that his new Megarider type tickets, which offer large discounts for regular users, will be described as a 'predatory ticket' because it offers a discount only to regular users and might be seen as an attempt to force people to use Stagecoach's buses rather than rival services. If the Competition Act were interpreted in this way, Stagecoach would be liable to a fine and its strategy to boost usage would be destroyed at a stroke. Souter says that the MMC took the view that such tickets were predatory in the MMC report on the North East, opening the way to wider action against Stagecoach. Souter notes: 'The OFT has moved from a position in the early days when they said you had to cover your variable costs, to avoid being accused of predatory pricing, to saying they now expect you to make a very substantial contribution of your profits from any route.' Souter tried to get the legislation modified as it went through Parliament but found that Stagecoach's reputation counted against him: 'Because of our regulatory record, we were not the best people to lobby on it'.

There is, too, another looming problem for Stagecoach's British bus operations. For Stagecoach, apocalyptic thoughts about the millennium are not about the year 2000 computer bug, but with the difficulties caused by the loss of profit related pay which will result in having to pay larger increases to bus staff to maintain their take home pay. There is also, the continued high employment which may push bus drivers' wages up in an environment where raising fares results in fewer passengers. As the Ribble strike in 1999 showed, there is some residual militancy among the workforce and, for all Stagecoach's readiness to deal with the unions, there is still some resentment about its hardline approach to industrial action.

Another area of uncertainty for Stagecoach in the UK is the Labour Government's emphasis on quality partnerships. The idea of quality partnerships is that local authorities and bus operators strike deals: the councils promise to provide better facilities such as bus lanes or bus priority schemes, while the operators agree to improve standards, with, say more investment in buses or the introduction of low floor or low emission vehicles.

Stagecoach was initially very lukewarm about the quality partnership concept. Derek Scott says that a lot is expected of companies by local authorities who have little spare money to invest: 'You end up making investments which you wouldn't otherwise and get less of a return on them. There has also been precious little about fare capping, which we think is the key issue for passengers.' And Stagecoach executives point to the Manchester experience, which suggests that, in many cases, bus passengers are seeking low fares, rather than a better quality of bus.

However, Stagecoach can no longer afford to eschew the concept of these partnerships as they are being seen by the government as a key way of attracting people on to public transport. Souter's philosophy is very much to 'make the policies of the government of the day work' and he felt that the March 1998 budget, in which the fuel duty rebate was restored, 'was the best budget for public transport for 18 years'. The Labour Party, which was so hard on Stagecoach in opposition, is doing the company favours in government. Quality partnerships, therefore, are being viewed by Stagecoach as a possible way of boosting passenger numbers. Labour's White Paper on integrated transport which seeks to boost public transport use by getting people out of their cars is seen by Stagecoach as an opportunity for growth, even though there are fears that ultimately Labour would like to reregulate the industry and, also, that the policy might result in forcing bus companies to invest in relatively unprofitable schemes.

Labour transport ministers took an interest in the situation in Manchester where Stagecoach, FirstGroup and the other operators actively worked together in the post-bomb redevelopment because it appeared to be a model project for the almost impossible task of reconciling integration with competition. Instead of having cut-throat competition with too many buses crowding into the central area, the companies have agreed to a form of self-policing for the Piccadilly bus station, with operators being granted slots, in which they can discharge and pick up passengers, not unlike the allocation system for takeoffs and landings at Heathrow airport. Moreover, the operators, together with the local council and the Passenger Transport Executive, have formed a company, Manchester Bus Quality Partnership Ltd with the aim of improving facilities for buses in order to encourage more people to use them. The target is to change the current 60–40 split between car users and public transport passengers to 50–50. Manchester is being seen as a possible model for the Government in its efforts to encourage a modal shift from cars to public transport. A travel information line, funded by the operators has been set up and all-operator travelcards are being sold, while the local authorities are providing a massive network of bus lanes.

The still unresolved problem, however, is over the conflict between competition and integration. On tickets, the Office of Fair Trading seems to have set out a clear policy: it has allowed the Manchester bus companies to create travelcards which can be used by all operators participating in the scheme, provided operators also offer their own ticket deals. However, Les Warneford, Stagecoach's local chairman, says that there are fundamental issues which are still not being tackled, reiterating Souter's point about underinvested rivals: 'What happens if the local authority provides bus lanes in return for investment in new floor buses by operators and good driver standards, and then some two-bit firm with old buses and untrained drivers wants to use them? At the moment, they could not be stopped. Stagecoach wants to compete to get the biggest market share, while the common interest of all operators is to boost the size of the market. But how is that to be achieved?'

While the type of initiative in Manchester and elsewhere may result in some extra bus patronage, and the Stagecoach annual figures for 1998/9 demonstrate organic growth in the UK bus market for the sixth successive year (albeit only 0.7 per cent), Stagecoach's only real opportunity of becoming Britain's biggest operator – a position currently held by FirstGroup with around 22 per cent of the market – is to take over one of its rivals. In 1998, Stagecoach, like all the big groups, had a good long look at MTL, a medium-sized firm which operates buses in Liverpool and London and has two rail franchises, but the price was not right, given that one of the franchises, North East, is a real dog that is losing money heavily.

Intriguingly, an all out bid for a company like FirstGroup, Arriva (which, like Stagecoach, has around 16 per cent of the market) or Go-Ahead (about 8 per cent) cannot be ruled out, even though the regulators would force Stagecoach to divest parts of such an acquisition. Souter would like to see Stagecoach achieve a 25 per cent share in the UK bus market, which is now impossible without a major acquisition. There is a feeling in Stagecoach that Labour might welcome further consolidation in the bus industry which will make it easier to bring about integrated transport, such as the bus rail links promoted by both the South West Trains and Virgin franchises. Kinski was at Scottish Power when, perhaps surprisingly, it was able to acquire Manweb and then Southern Water and he may see this as an example for Stagecoach to follow.

But in a way, British bus is Stagecoach's past. It will always be a sizeable chunk of the business, but the limits on squeezing out further profits and Stagecoach's global ambitions mean it will play an increasingly small part in the company's future. Stagecoach's diversification out of buses is therefore not seen as an optional extra, but as an essential way of maintaining its growth.

With no bus companies becoming available at the right price, Stage-coach diversified into trams with its purchase of the operations of the Sheffield Supertram, which cost just £1 million for a 27-year concession (to operate assets built at taxpayers' expense of £270 million). Although annual revenue was around £7 million, the operation had a troubled history and was a loss making operation. As one rival bus executive put it, 'Stagecoach's purchase of such a loss making operation shows how few opportunities remain in the UK for the company.' The Supertram's chequered history, is a result of the poor route network whose gestation period was so long that it extends to parts of the city where the housing has largely been demolished. Competition from buses, and hostility from the local press also affected profitability. However, it has very well-designed rolling stock and Stagecoach has improved ridership through cheaper fares. It has even joined forces with the rival bus operator, FirstGroup (which, as we have seen, bought Stagecoach's share of Mainline when Souter was forced to divest it, and later bought the rest), to offer integrated tickets. Although the service is still losing money, the target is to break even by the end of 1999 and there is now talk of extending the line.

Although the pace of acquisitions slowed in 1997, it picked up again in 1998 with a burst of activity, following a pattern which Stagecoach has exhibited previously – a feeding frenzy followed by a quiet patch. In April 1998 Stagecoach announced a couple of major purchases, a 28 per cent stake in a company called Road King for £107 million and Prestwick airport for £41 million. Therefore, at a stroke, Stagecoach entered two new areas, creating two divisions to run them and raising £160·5 million on the Stock Exchange to pay for them. Road King, listed on the Hong Kong exchange, is seen as having enormous potential because of the rapid economic growth in China. The company operates highways in conjunction with provincial governments and already has nearly 1,000 kilometres of toll roads in eight provincial areas. The roads are built by the local governments who then enter into an arrangement with Road King to collect the tolls. Souter says that when the private company takes over, 'the amount received goes up by 30 per cent immediately because the governments are no good at collecting the money'.

Souter sees Road King as a way into the People's Republic of China which has not suffered from the Asian crisis: 'The growth rate in China is still 6–8 per cent but because of the Asian crisis, capital is tight and prices are low.' The main shareholder in Road King is the Wai Kee Group chaired by William Zen who is staying with the company.

Souter sees Stagecoach's entry into the road tolling business as a parallel with buying Porterbrook: 'The clever thing was not to run the franchises but to own the trains. Same thing. The clever thing is to operate the roads rather than the buses.' Road King is more than a way of entering China as Souter hopes it will give Stagecoach a competitive edge on road tolling which he is certain will come to Britain: 'Governments are not going to want to build roads in the future because of the environmental issues. There's no UK company with interests in toll roads and it's too expensive to buy into the European ones. In the UK, thanks to privatisation, we're ahead on buses, trains, ferries, and airports, but we're behind on this road toll issue. Road King is an opportunity to look at the issue and get some intellectual property for the next period and see what happens in Britain.'

Although Road King has remained highly profitable and Souter reckons 'the investment will be paid off in three to four years', in the first year after the purchase, Road King's share price fell dramatically, leading to a halving of the value of Stagecoach's investment. Souter says this is a quirk of the Hong Kong Stock Exchange: 'Very few shares are being traded. There are two big private shareholders and we are certainly not going to sell at that price.' He would like to take the company off the market, as he has done with the later purchase, Hong Kong Citybus, but cannot do so. He also reckons that with about a dozen of these infrastructure companies in existence, there is room for consolidation, therefore Stagecoach may well expand its holdings in this industry. Despite Souter's arguments, the Road King investment has not impressed the City and contributed to the poor performance of Stagecoach's shares on the London market during 1998/9.

Prestwick is principally a freight airport – though Ryanair operates flights to Stansted from there – with plenty of growth potential as it came with 500 acres of undeveloped land and Souter expects it to be the first of several similar acquisitions of secondary airports. It was bought for £15 million by an entrepreneur, Matthew Hudson, from BAA in 1992 who has managed to make it profitable by operating on a low cost basis and forming strong links with local businesses. Souter hopes that Hudson will use his expertise to help Stagecoach Aviation buy other secondary airports and make them profitable.

Stagecoach had already expressed interest in Skavsta, Stockholm's second airport, and Wellington in New Zealand, both countries where Stagecoach already operates, but the bids failed. Since its acquisition by Stagecoach, Prestwick has expanded its freight operations and signed a deal with Ryanair to increase its range of services from the airport. Souter says he does not want to take the obvious step of expanding into airlines, though he did invest his own personal money in Suckling Airways, principally to ensure that it operated a service from Dundee to London City Airport. So rather than run his own jet like many executives, Souter has bought his own airline and it now runs four times per day between Dundee and London.

Stagecoach bought both Road King and Prestwick through private deals and Souter was attracted by the skills of Zen and Hudson, in much the same way that he liked Sandy Anderson of Porterbrook: 'These are both asset-rich deals where we are not just buying a stream of earnings. And both are run by entrepreneurs who have a real vision for the future of their business and part of the reason why the deal was a success, was because of the chemistry between me and these two guys, William Zen and Matthew Hudson.' Indeed, Souter had spent the Easter holiday in Florida with Hudson and their families and as *The Scotsman* reported: 'Effectively, Mr Souter liked the man so much he bought his company, giving Mr Hudson nearly £29 million in the process.'

After the Road King and Prestwick deals, announced simultaneously, the Virgin deal (described in Chapter 7) quickly followed and in August Stagecoach won its lengthy battle for Auckland's Yellow Bus. The company fought a successful campaign in the courts to be allowed to bid for Yellow Bus after initially being banned because it already operated some buses in the area. Stagecoach paid £37 million for the 532 bus operation which was being privatised by the local authorities. Souter likes New Zealand, so much so that he admits 'we paid a premium price for Yellow Bus' and it is significant that of the four major acquisitions in 1998, this was the only one which was obtained through an open tender. Souter feels that generally prices are too high in this situation and he prefers dealing with people he already knows: 'The deals where we get hits tend to be those where we are pally with a shareholder, because we know the people. It is to do with relationships and you have some trust built up. Even Yellow Bus we won because we had some local knowledge.' This shows how cautious Souter remains about paying over the odds for acquisitions and suggests, too, that new purchases may be fewer and further between than he would like. Critics also point out that obtaining deals like this mean that the assets are fundamentally undervalued and Stagecoach is taking advantage of this.

Another pattern of the deals is how Souter is now more prepared to work in long term partnerships with entrepreneurs such as Hudson and Zen, and Virgin's Branson. There is mutual admiration between these

The end of family Stagecoach

people and Souter. Hudson, for example, told the *Times*, 'Brian Souter is a throwback to the days when Britain was great. If you ask me, the problem with the world is that somewhere along the way we did not produce enough Brian Souters'. Yellow Bus was followed by a six month lull in purchases during which there were several failed attempts such as Stockholm's second airport and suburban rail operations in Melbourne.

However, Souter's first major acquisition of 1999 was particularly sweet as it was revenge over FirstGroup for Stagecoach's defeat in September 1998 over the purchase of China Motor Bus, the third largest company in the province. In March 1999, Stagecoach announced it was purchasing the second largest bus company, Hong Kong Citybus, for £181 million. Souter even donned a jacket and tie for the official announcement in sartorially-conservative Hong Kong and pointed out that FirstGroup had only bought a 26 per cent share in the franchises of their Hong Kong acquisition, while Stagecoach had bought the whole company. Two months later, Stagecoach bought a 45 per cent share in another bus company in the province, Kwoon Chung for £2 million and entered another European country, Italy, with the purchase of a 35 per cent stake in Sogin, the largest private operator which, as Sita, runs buses in half a dozen Italian cities, for £32.5 million.

And then, a few days later, on 14 June, came the announcement of Souter's blockbuster, its biggest ever purchase, the acquisition of Coach USA for £1.1 billion. The company had itself grown through acquisitions since its formation in 1995, built up by one of its founders, Larry King, a 42-year-old former Andersen accountant, who was pictured with his Brylcreemed hair playing buses with Souter. The company operates nearly 10,000 coaches, taxicabs and minibuses, principally charter but also some scheduled coach services, bus commuter routes and taxis. Kinski saw the acquisition as an opportunity to gain a toehold in the US where deregulation is expected to open up the market for local and school bus services. The deal was funded by a $2.25 billion loan with four banks, including both Bank of Scotland and Royal Bank of Scotland. Stagecoach said it would later refinance the loan through the issue of bonds and equity-related securities. Souter seems to have paid well over the odds for the company, whose shares had slipped to less than $14 from a peak of $45. However, Souter paid $42, a premium of 40 per cent over the price before speculation of a takeover led to a suspension a few days prior to the announcement. Again, Souter acquired a partner as King promised to stay on for at least three years with Stagecoach.

Souter reckons that Stagecoach is ahead of the field when it comes to bidding for companies abroad because, apart from Vivendi (formerly)

Compagnie Generale des Eaux), there are few international players as Britain deregulated and privatised first and Stagecoach's international experience is greater than that of its domestic rivals. The emphasis on overseas expansion is an inevitable consequence of Stagecoach's desire for growth in the face of a more mature market at home but it is also fraught with risks. Stagecoach has struggled, at times, in new markets. Most of its overseas operations, apart from Malawi in the early stages, and New Zealand have not been particularly successful. Canada was a disaster and Stagecoach has struggled in Sweden. Road King, as seen above, has performed badly on the Hong Kong Stock Exchange. Many British companies have foundered on American acquisitions, failing to understand that while the language may be the same, business practices are not. There is no doubt that acquiring Coach USA is one of Souter's biggest gambles, a view which was reflected in the press coverage of the purchase. The *Evening Standard* commented that 'it could be a bumpy ride' but that is not the first time such predictions have been made about the company.

Overall, too, Stagecoach faces a surprisingly uncertain future. Of course, in some respects, one could say that its main markets are stable and its profitability assured. Bus usage may be declining, but the process is slow and it is very easy to predict rates of returns from one year to the next. In terms of the SWT rail franchise, Stagecoach has begun to make serious money and will continue to do so until 2003 when the franchise ends. The Government's eagerness to discuss franchise renewal in a *quid pro quo* for extra investment makes it more likely that Stagecoach will retain SWT, though probably on much less favourable terms. And Porterbrook, with six to eight years left on most of its leases and the guarantees from the government still happily in place, will continue to be a generator of massive profits. Its medium term future has also been assured thanks to its massive investment programme which will generate a steady income for 30 years. Indeed, the very diversity of Stagecoach's business, which now ranges from airports in Scotland to toll roads in China, as well as buses and trains in Britain, gives the company a certain stability which is the envy of other transport companies whose portfolio is more dependent on a single aspect of the industry.

However, there is enough uncertainty in each of these just to smudge the horizon for Souter and his shareholders. On buses, there are flat margins, a shrinking market, despite efforts to stimulate organic growth, and other areas of doubt such as the new Competition Act and the effects of the Government's White Paper on integrated transport. On trains, there is Stagecoach's poor record initially with its franchise and the risk, though following the rail regulator's report in May 1998 largely receded, of regulation of the rolling stock companies. Nor has Porterbrook managed to expand overseas and its rivals have managed to begin to obtain new train orders. The Virgin investment, too, is fraught with the risks of any major infrastructure scheme as it is so dependent on the West Coast Main Line improvements being carried through in time. And, finally, the sheer ambition of the expansion programme, with Souter repeatedly saying he wants to double the size of the company even after doing so successfully several times, is, inherently, risky and uncertain. All this uncertainty contributed towards the poor share price performance in 1998/9.

It was Souter's awareness that the company needed a greater managerial input and stability in the light of its acquisition of a much wider portfolio that prompted him to seek a chief executive. For some years, Souter and, especially, Gloag had wanted a chief executive but had not found the right person. Mike Kinski was already a non-executive having been appointed in July 1997 when Souter had wanted someone who could advise the company on how to manage the process of change as it diversified. Souter began to realise that he could not keep all the balls up in the air simultaneously on his own and was aware that he was not as good at running companies as acquiring them. Kinski, who was executive director at Scottish Power in charge of integrating its acquisitions, Manweb and Southern Water, was feeling restless having been offered several other posts and asked Souter's advice about possible moves and whether his non-exec role would be affected. 'Why not come and work for us?' was the response and although Stagecoach was smaller, he was tempted by the opportunity of becoming boss of what was becoming a FTSE-100 company. He was also given a £250,000 golden hello on top of his £360,000 per year salary plus performance related bonuses.

Kinski is another self-made man, who like Souter and several of Stagecoach's key managers, came up through the ranks, starting as an apprentice for the East Midlands Electricity Board. His father, a Polish refugee, came to Britain just before the war and worked in the paint shop at Chrysler in Coventry. Kinski is a chunky fellow now, but was clearly lean in his youth as he played for Coventry City reserves and could have turned professional with Northampton but decided he wasn't good enough to make the grade. He spent a long time at Jaguar, during which time he gained engineering qualifications at night school, and ended up as personnel director. He joined Scottish Power in 1992 as Human Resources Director, an unusual background for a chief executive, and after a series of promotions, he was being groomed for the top job when he left to join Stagecoach in April 1998.

Kinski says his main skill is 'managing change' and he quickly set about reorganising the company to 'create a structure for a large organisation'. Kinski says Souter told him that Stagecoach was like a mid-teens athlete, good at sport but in desperate need of a coach: 'You will be our Arsene Wenger', he told Kinski. Stagecoach's structure had been reorganised in 1996 to reflect the declining importance of buses and in readiness for the push for international business. Instead of just having a main board and subsidiaries, a UK bus division was created because the business was becoming too unwieldy and possibly undermanaged, and other divisions covered SWT, Porterbrook and overseas. However, it was still a bit of a mess: 'For example, you had five people who ran UK bus businesses, and three reported directly to Brian for historic reasons. There was no common policy on things like group procurement, IT strategy and personnel development. Nobody knew how many computers we had, and whether they were compatible. Also, senior people kept on being taken from their normal task to look at a new business which means performance suffered.'

Kinski edged out a couple of senior managers, Neil Renilson, the chairman of Stagecoach Scotland and Jim Moffat of Fife Scottish, and restructured UK bus into three regions, each accountable to him. Then he set about strengthening the centre and filled what had clearly become large holes in the management of a major company. He appointed three men – Alan Bell, Robert Ballantyne and Alistair Smith – as, respectively, heads of human resources, corporate communications and information technology.

True to his roots, Kinski also quickly set up an open learning scheme, spending more than £1 million of the company's money on creating free courses for employees to develop their skills. Kinski's arrival has allowed Souter to concentrate on what he does best, seeking acquisitions and doing deals. However, he retains his post as executive chairman and still goes round the City talking to investors. Kinski, however, also has a role in the acquisition process. Souter now brings his deals to Kinski and to Keith Cochrane for approval before presenting them to the board.

Kinski, who lives away from his family in Rugby during the week and therefore laps up 12-hour days routinely, had an immediate effect on the company. The figures for the year to the end of April 1999 showed turnover going up by 15 per cent to £1,548 million but pre-tax profits rising 39 per cent, a performance that, for once, pleased the City. Margins on UK buses had continued to improve from 14.8 per cent to 15.8 per cent, helped, of course, by the good state of the economy, but even in troubled Sweden margins improved from 5.3 per cent to 6.3 per cent. Kinski's arrival has certainly, quite literally, paid dividends. South West Trains was becoming the *milchcow* that had been predicted, with profits of £34.4 million and performance was, at last, beginning to improve.

These changes and appointments mark the birth of corporate Stage-coach, a recognition that the structure of the small family firm grown big was no longer suitable for a major international transport business. Indeed, confirmation that Stagecoach had arrived by becoming an accepted part of the business establishment was its hosting, in June 1999, of the 16th Annual Scottish Business Achievement Award Trust lunch which raises money for charity as well as giving an award to the young business person of the year, a prize Souter won nearly a decade ago.

Souter had decided to hold the event in a muddy field near Dunferm-line, the site of the Scottish Vintage Bus Museum, rather than the more stately homes normally used. He also invited in local schoolchildren over the following week to teach them about enterprise. The buses were cleared out of the warehouse to create a stunning tiered auditorium seating some 650 business people under a tent, at a cost in excess of £100,000.

Souter chatted with Princess Anne at the top table as if a princess came to town every day. He was not wearing a tie (virtually the only man in the room not to be wearing one) and looked as if he had a bit of an accident with a razor that morning. His sister, Ann, decided to eschew the limelight, sitting on an ordinary table with her husband and confided to a colleague that she felt it was 'the end of family Stagecoach'. Gloag has largely pulled out of the company, concentrating on her charitable work. She had just bought an old Norwegian cruise ship for £7 million and asked me if I was good at fundraising, because she needed £13 million to fit it out. The idea is that it will sail around the world, stopping offshore in Third World countries for several weeks so that locals in need can be operated on.

Souter, however, saw the function as Stagecoach's belated acceptance as a major international company and clearly enjoyed himself when, rather reluctantly, he was badgered by the auctioneer into bidding £76,000 in the charity auction for a trip to Lapland in a private jet for his family and friends. With Souter's usual jokes and the mad party tricks (apparently a hardy perennial) of the organisation's president, Sandy Irvine Robertson, who gave the Princess a doll's outfit and various presents for her dogs, including coats with their crests, it was a rare occasion to see Stagecoach at play. Souter had even driven one of his favourite old Lodekkas from

Dunfermline station where his guests had arrived by steam train, and had some difficulty coaxing the veteran up the steep hill with a full load.

There was gossip about some big purchase, perhaps in America, and, indeed, three days later, the Coach USA deal was announced. Confirmation came through, too, that Stagecoach was moving out of its cramped Charlotte Street offices half a mile down the road to the five-year-old former HQ of Scottish and Southern, the hydro-electric company. Kinski points out that the company still only has under 50 head office staff, in addition to the 30 people working on insurance matters. There is, however, no disguising the fact that the company is now a global corporation, leaving Perth and, indeed the UK, behind.

12
Corporate cowboys or genuine geniuses?

The image of Britain's biggest start-up company of the Thatcher era is a public-relations disaster. When I told people outside the bus industry that I was writing a book on Stagecoach, the comments were, without fail, critical of the company. They would typically respond with comments like, 'They are a bunch of rogues, aren't they?', 'I hope you nail the bastards' or 'They're a ruthless lot, that brother and sister'. Nobody knows about Stagecoach's large investment programme or its fares-cutting exercises. It is seen as a monopolist, swallowing up rivals with ruthless disdain for the regulators and exploiting its dominant market position by driving small operators out of business through swamping areas with buses or cutting fares unfairly.

The bad image has been stimulated by widespread media coverage of the string of battles with the regulators, which came to a peak over the Darlington débâcle. The South West Trains fiasco also contributed to the public's hostility towards the company, especially as the row was stoked up by Souter's unwise comments about people complaining.

There is a deep ambivalence within Stagecoach about its approach to the media. On the one hand, there is a feeling that all publicity is good publicity. Souter clearly courts attention with his occasional clowning, ditties and entertaining speeches. For example, he attracted a bout of press interest in late 1997 when journalists belatedly picked a London Transport lecture he had given, which described his customers as the 'beer-drinking, chip-eating, council-house-dwelling Old-Labour-voting masses', contrasting them with the 'wine-drinking, courgette- and mangetout-eating, semi-detached-dwelling New-Labour-voting South' which were less frequent bus users. It was, in fairness, a comparison he had made many times previously but some City journalists reckoned he had done a 'Gerald Ratner'.

The very name of Stagecoach is much more catchy than its rivals' efforts, even the recently revamped Arriva and FirstGroup. There are so many good puns with Stagecoach for the headline writers. The fact that all the Stagecoach subsidiaries were required to adopt the familiar 'white-with-stripes' livery heightened awareness of the company throughout Britain, because people recognise their local buses as being owned by the same outfit causing mischief in Darlington.

On the other hand, there is a fundamental defensiveness about Stagecoach's attitude to the press, borne of an arrogance and deep conviction that the company is right and everyone else is wrong.

Stagecoach would not have achieved its notoriety without the efforts of John Mair, an energetic and somewhat obsessive independent TV producer who runs a company called Mair Golden Moments.

Between 1994 and 1996, Mair made four TV documentaries about Stagecoach, centring on its aggressive behaviour towards competitors, three for BBC regions – South, South East and Scotland – and a nationally screened *World in Action* on ITV. They brought the company's activities to a much wider audience than the press coverage as they were stuffed with footage of the bus wars and complaints by smaller operators about being hounded out of business by Stagecoach.

Mair explains that he came across the MMC reports and felt that they had not received sufficient coverage: 'I read the reports and reckoned here was a great story which hadn't been properly covered in the press. It was a story of raw capitalism. The law had been turned around. Nicholas Ridley had encouraged all these small operators to start up and they had taken him at his word, but then found that it was impossible to operate because of the tactics used by the likes of Stagecoach.'

When Mair worked on the first documentary, covering the south coast, he was amazed at how much anger there was among these small-business people: 'Every little town you went into, it took no time at all to find a small operator who had been driven out of business. Most were eager to talk. Their stories were all the same: predatory practices, blocking buses in, running buses either side, duplicating routes, cutting fares.'

Mair found himself being attacked by Stagecoach. While Brian Cox agreed to appear on the first programme, after that Stagecoach refused to have anything to do with him. When Mair went into an interview with the Scottish Traffic Commissioner, Michael Betts, he saw a fax on his desk from Jim Moffat, the managing director of Fife Scottish, accusing Mair of 'being a Trotskyite' and advising Betts not to take part in the programme. Mair is, in fact, an old Labour man.

Mair's 1996 *World in Action* programme for Granada, *Cowboy Country*, enlivened by some entertaining old footage from Westerns, was particularly hard-hitting. It showed a succession of small operators driven out of business by Stagecoach's aggressive response around the country, including the complaint that Trevor Brown, the director of one rival, Hylton Coaches in the north-east, was told by Stagecoach that they would 'flatten' his firm unless the directors sold out, a version of events accepted by the MMC despite Stagecoach's denials. There were tales from around Britain, including Peterhead, Thanet and Darlington, all focusing on the same story: Stagecoach's readiness to use its strength and size to attack any rival who was seen as a threat to its business. Most notably, the film showed how Stagecoach had run white buses called Jolly Roger against a firm called Roger's on the Aberdeen–Peterhead route. Faced with that kind of competition, the hapless rival withdrew quickly. In Thanet an earlier Mair film had shown Stagecoach buses with 'Fife Scottish' logos being sent down to compete with a small local operator, Thanet Bus. Now *World in Action* showed Stagecoach in Thanet using mysterious white 'ghost' buses marked 'relief', even though the existing services were not full, and a 'May madness' fares reduction, tactics which Mair says were designed 'to drive this poor fellow out of business'. The owner of Thanet Bus, Colin Wright, complained that it was, like the Souters, a family business: 'There's me, my wife, my son-in-law, my daughter and my granddaughter. It's her inheritance that they're trying to take away.'

Stagecoach made strenuous efforts to prevent the screening of the *World in Action* film. The company even took out advertisements in the Scottish press to counter the line taken by the programme. Stagecoach hired Peter Carter-Ruck, the aggressive libel lawyer, and Ann Gloag filed a complaint to the Independent Television Commission even before the programme was screened. Mair says, 'We were bombarded with faxes, almost daily, and they complained to everyone they could think of – the Broadcasting Complaints Commission, the ITC, and even the managing director of Granada, Gerry Robinson.' But despite intense pressure from Carter-Ruck, the programme went out as scheduled on 1 July 1996, with no interview from a Stagecoach executive because the company refused to put anyone up unless he or she was interviewed live.

The lingering footage in the film on Ann Gloag's grand home near Inverness, Beaufort Castle, shot from a helicopter because the red turreted building cannot be seen from the road, prompted Stagecoach into filing a formal complaint with the Broadcasting Complaints Commission (now the Broadcasting Standards Commission). Stagecoach had also originally complained about the Scottish programme on the grounds that it was unfair but did not proceed with the action.

There were two main areas of complaint against the *World in Action* film. The first was over the helicopter shots of Beaufort Castle which Ann Gloag had bought for £4.2 million in 1995. (She was by then so rich that she paid for it largely out of her dividends, without having to sell any shares.) Gloag argued this was an infringement of her privacy, even though she had not been there at the time. There was some desperate scraping of the barrel in seeking to build up the complaint. Her guests, a group of Canadian property developers, had been disturbed, the helicopter had flown close to osprey, and the film might alert the criminal fraternity to the existence of the castle. One letter to the BBC even suggested that, as the documentary makers would not fly over Balmoral, why were they allowed to do so over Beaufort? Stagecoach even sent Keith Cochrane to a Perth hotel to spy on Mair's researcher at work.

Mair argued that the castle was in the public domain and that there had even been a press release about the purchase. However, the complaint was partially upheld, 'in the making of the programme' because the helicopter had flown around the castle for seventeen minutes, which was considered excessively long, but not on the programme itself. It was a technical victory for Gloag, though a lawyer, a neutral observer, told me that Gloag's partial win was an attempt to appease a troublesome litigant 'with a sixpence'. In effect, Gloag's complaint was a way of warning other journalists to keep off her patch. The castle is remote, and few people in the neighbourhood ever see the new lady of the manor except when she buzzes by in her Bentley with the registration number ANN 1, allegedly bought from the Princess Royal.

The second complaint was more substantial, arguing that Stagecoach had not been sufficiently informed of the serious allegations made against the company and had not been able to provide a full response. This was rejected by the Commission, which said that it 'did not find any unfairness in the efforts Granada made to inform Stagecoach of the nature of the programme'. The Commission quibbled with a few details but did not uphold the complaint, largely because Stagecoach had not put up anyone to be interviewed.

More interestingly is what Stagecoach did not complain about. Apart from a few minor factual quibbles, Stagecoach did not take issue with the film's central theme, that the company had driven lots of smaller operators out of business by its hard-hitting tactics. The beginning of the film said that Stagecoach bought new buses and provided good reliable services to customers, but asked, 'Did they get there fairly?'

It is a good question. The conventional wisdom in the media holds that Stagecoach's success was built on its ruthless business approach and its managers' readiness to enter into grey areas of the law. In the film, Brian Wilson, the MP who was the scourge of Stagecoach until his elevation to the respectability of ministerial position in May 1997, is unequivocal. Wilson, a former journalist with an eye for a good story and something of a 'rent-a-quote' reputation in his opposition days, stoked up the criticism to Stagecoach (see Chapter 4) when he was Labour's transport spokesman during the Major government.

In the *World in Action* film, he accused Stagecoach of playing fast and loose with the rules: 'Competition law is just a joke. And Stagecoach cottoned early on to the fact that it is a paper tiger. What has happened repeatedly is that Stagecoach have gone into an area, done exactly as they liked, used whatever tactics suited them and then months or years later, along come the sort of plods from the OFT and the MMC and say this was really very wicked. By that time, Stagecoach are three counties down the road, doing exactly the same thing in another half-dozen areas.'

The arguments about Stagecoach's relations with the MMC were covered in Chapter 9 but Wilson also made another fundamental attack. He said, 'Stagecoach's wealth was founded initially on the cheap disposal of public assets, which they then sold dear. They sold off the bus stations for more than they paid for the bus companies. And now, they run almost entirely, in terms of profitability, on taxpayers' subsidy. It's a disguised subsidy, but it's a subsidy OK. And if everybody's profits were funded almost exclusively by taxpayers' money, then an awful lot of us could be multimillionaires.'

Indeed, Stagecoach did profit from the sale of the bus garages and stations in the early years and Souter admits that the sale of Southampton bus garage helped him emerge from debt for the first time since setting up the business seven years previously. However, Souter makes the point that the assets were sold on the open market: 'At the time we bought them, nobody wanted to buy them. And in actual fact, our getting involved early on in the [privatisation] programme made the government get more money. Once we were involved, others became interested, pushing up the values. Without us, they wouldn't have got 60 per cent of what they got.'

As for the ongoing subsidy, clearly much of Stagecoach's business is dependent on public money. South West Trains received £51 million in

1997–8 while around half of Porterbrook's income of £270 million is generated from public subsidy via the train operators. The domestic bus industry received a total of £913 million of state support in 1996–7. Almost half of the total is paid by local government for concessionary fares (mainly for pensioners), and the rest is for fuel duty rebate and tendered services (which are subsidised by local councils). While a precise estimate of Stagecoach's share of this is impossible, as the company has just under a fifth of the market, a total of around £180 million for Stagecoach's bus activities appears fair. Another source of subsidy is the fact that transport is zero-rated for VAT, a concession worth £400 million to the industry, £80 million to Stagecoach.

A thorough analysis of these figures is beyond the scope of this book and, in any case, would rely on a series of assumptions and judgements. For example, Stagecoach argues that the subsidy on concessionary fares helps the passenger and not the company. This is debateable since, without the subsidy, hundreds of bus routes around the country would simply not be commercially viable, just as rail lines could not be run without the direct subsidy from the Government. All the queues of old ladies at bus stops around the country at 9.30 a.m. are testimony to that.

In 1998–9, Stagecoach made total pre-tax profits of £219.9 million. However, to equate this figure with the level of subsidy is naive and meaningless. Most of Stagecoach's services used to be provided in the public sector and they have been bought by the company. Stagecoach's profits are a return on the investment by shareholders, which have replaced the government as owners of the assets. The subsidy that used to go to nationalised industries is now accruing to Stagecoach and its shareholders. The industry is also now much more efficient, though much of the extra productivity has been gained by reducing workers' wages and conditions and cutting the numbers of people employed in engineering and maintenance.

The fact that Stagecoach's margins are so high represents a constant temptation for Labour politicians. The Swedish model (see Chapter 6) has attractions for Labour politicians as profits are kept low through competition and regulation. Legislation emerging from the White Paper may change the rules of the game but Labour's three goals of improved public transport, better value for their subsidy and a squeeze on what are seen as excessive margins by fat-cat companies may prove impossible to reconcile.

Of course, Stagecoach owes its success partly to the fact that the company bought public assets cheaply and its growth has been helped by its aggressive response to competition. But there are a lot more factors that account for the company's phenomenal success. And unfortunately for business-studies students hoping to emulate the story, many of them are not replicable.

The first, although he will hate to see this in print, is Souter himself. Everyone I talked to in the industry laid responsibility for Stagecoach's success at his door. Even Mair, his TV foe, reckons 'Souter is a genius'.

No one who has come across Souter fails to be impressed by his talents as a businessman. Most mention the image of Souter shuffling into meetings, hunched and apparently timid, plastic bag in hand, but no one is now taken in by it. Steve Norris, the Tory Transport Minister, seems to have fallen in love with him at first sight: 'He has a nice ready smile and an attractive voice with a lovely Scots delivery. His certainty, his confidence and his encyclopaedic knowledge combined with the fact that he is an affable, pleasant, charming and very agreeable man, made him into an extremely engaging fellow. He turned up at the Department with a blue jacket, a white shirt and a yellow waistcoat of which the top button was clinging on a thread, a pair of pale beige chinos, trainers on his feet and carrying a white Sainsbury's plastic bag. No tie of course. He sat forward on the sofa with his elbows on his knees talking to me, and we began a discussion for which there was no agenda about how he saw the bus business developing. I was learning, at the time, and listening, and like everyone who encounters Brian, he lifted my sights quite substantially. It was Brian who made me realise what potential there was in the industry, what sort of enthusiasm there was for rail privatisation. His view was that he could translate what he had learned in bus on to rail.'

Souter was unique in the bus industry in that, unlike the people at the centre of the other big groups, he was an outsider, despite his experience as a clippie. As Norris put it, all the others who made fortunes out of the industry, such as Trevor Smallwood (Badgerline, later FirstGroup) or Harry Blundred (Devon General and Transit Holdings), 'were rather sharp busmen who realised that the thing crippling the bus industry was the enormous layer of bureaucracy on top of the garages and they cut it out. Brian was much more than that. He was the first one who undestood the scope of the deregulated industry. He decided he would take the whole business of a newly privatised and deregulated industry head on.'

Souter is that rare beast who combines accountancy skills with a wider business acumen and the ability to understand bus networks, the essential requirements of a good traffic manager. His ability to master detail is phenomenal. He picks up information from documents very quickly and his knack, as Derek Scott puts it, 'is to concentrate on the major issues, often three at most, and to overstate the pluses and understate the risks.'

It was Souter who ensured that Stagecoach was in there first at every stage of the privatisation and deregulation of the bus and rail industries. The ability to assess the risks before anyone else has done so was the key to every step in the Stagecoach expansion story. Souter is a deal maker and likes to do things personally. Apart from during the occasional hounding of TV documentary makers, Stagecoach has made very little use of lawyers and Souter has a personal antipathy to consultants, whom he sees as superfluous. All these people, according to Souter, get in the way and he likes to shake hands on a deal and proceed from there. No one who has been involved in a deal with Souter has ever accused him of reneging on a promise.

While Souter does not have much interest in money *per se* – unlike his sister, who clearly enjoys the trappings of wealth much more than he does – he has always been very careful with it and that has informed his business thinking: 'I've always had a very prudent approach to money. I've never bought a house beyond my means. That is not to say I'm avaricious or love money, but I don't like wasters and I think it's wrong to squander money.' His Methodist ethic shows through: 'The more that my wealth accumulates, the more I would give away because the money really doesn't have much use in itself. You can only eat one dinner, you know. The thing that drives me to continue to look after my money is the sense of responsibility that it needs to be looked after and dealt with responsibly, and the fact that the more I generate income, the more income can be given away.' Stagecoach gives away 0.5 per cent of its pre-tax profits to charitable causes and Souter's charity, the Souter Foundation, focuses on religious groups, social deprivation and children's charities. He has donated around £600,000 to £700,000 in each of the past two years, a figure Souter expects to increase substantially over the next few years, but he is reluctant to talk about it: 'What I'm giving away is a fairly substantial proportion of my income but you can't give away your capital.'

But his driving factor has not been to make money: 'Some people set up in business because they want to have a lot of money or they want a bigger house, and the things that money alone can facilitate, so they love money. That's never been a driving factor for me.' Souter, instead, is a true entrepreneur: 'I get fun out of taking risks. I like taking a risk and the returns are really a measure of success of the risk. So I get a kick out of doing deals.'

Indeed, both Souter and Gloag are brilliant deal makers, a skill learnt on their father's knee. Witness the large profits Souter made on both the 20 per cent divestments he was forced into by the MMC in Strathclyde and Sheffield.

The ability to size up the value of a potential acquisition has been a hallmark of the Stagecoach phenomenon. As one rival put it, 'It is a gift to be able to look at the same businesses as everyone else, assess their value, look at them in a different way and then make them into a major success but not through asset-stripping.'

Souter has also been ready to admit his mistakes. There have been several quite major ones such as Canada and Stagecoach Rail, but they have been dealt with quickly.

Without Souter's talents, Stagecoach would probably at best be a small regional coach and bus company, providing a few school and council contract services. Souter was never interested in running such a business. He had a vision right from the beginning and was constantly looking forward, seeking ways of growing the business. If one had to single out Souter's greatest attribute, it is his ability to think strategically – to, as he puts it, 'read the market'.

There are, of course, people within the industry – and even within Stagecoach – who are critical of Souter. One pointed to his arrogance and lack of public-relations savvy which damaged the company during the SWT fiasco. A Stagecoach manager questioned Souter's ability to run companies rather than acquire them: 'Look what happened at SWT. He is much better at doing deals and looking at innovations than the day-to-day running of businesses. He does not know the costs of his business as well as he should.' Souter, aware of this failing, responded by appointing Mike Kinski as chief executive in early 1998.

The 'Souter' factor is such an established fact that City analysts attempt to measure it. A study of the company by Merril Lynch in late 1997 estimates the Souter factor as 10 per cent of profits, or, at the time, 94p on the share price, thanks to his proven record 'in identifying opportunities, securing deals and efficiently and effectively integrating new businesses into the Group'.

The second component of the Stagecoach success story is the Ann Gloag–Brian Souter relationship. For the first decade or so of the company they sat nearly every day in the same office in what was an almost symbiotic relationship. They are now sharing an office again now that Kinski is on board. Souter says they have never lost their temper with each other: 'We've tended to calm one another down. If one of us is a bit fed up, we've tended to cheer the other up. We've encouraged one another on.'

Ann might have been the big sister but in business terms she was very much the junior partner and early on he taught her the basics of accounting and a balance sheet. She took on tasks like purchasing and dealing with staff right from the beginning. In the early stages, Ann and Brian worked interchangeably. They could substitute for each other on almost any task and, as Souter says, 'if someone was really hassling about dealing with women, I would take over, and if somebody really liked to deal with a woman, I'd get the heck out of it.' She does not have his visionary talents but Souter says she was able 'very quickly to share my vision. It would be unfair to infer that Ann wasn't capable of seeing the big picture or the big project.'

And they never disagreed publicly, which meant that the decisions they took could not be challenged by other executives, as Robin Gloag found out early on when they wanted him out: 'It was two to one. I couldn't say no.' According to Souter, 'Ann and I were very, very close and nobody could ever split us. There were none of the awful squabbles with members of the family being split, which happens sometimes in family businesses. There is a natural energy between us, a synergy that is almost a genetic thing or whatever, but we are just the same in many respects, like the kick we get out of doing deals.' Several other businessmen have told Souter, 'We really envy you and Ann because you've got one another. It's so lonely being in business on your own.'

Gloag may not have had Souter's spark of genius but she was amazing at getting things done. As Souter says, 'If I wanted something done, I know that when Ann starts a job, she'll always see it through. Right from the start, I used to develop the systems and Ann would monitor them.' She has enormous commitment and energy and she drives an incredibly hard bargain. Unlike Souter, who is universally seen as charming, Gloag has made enemies in the bus business and several people testified to her toughness.

Souter is touchy about this, aware of the criticism and fiercely defensive of his sister, pinning it down to a particular newspaper profile of her when the company was being floated: 'She's got great determination, and that may be interpreted by some people as toughness. I think a great deal of that is to do with one small piece that was picked up and replicated because there are tens of female journalists who want to create an Alexis Colby [of *Dynasty* fame] out of her. They want to create a stereotyped tough businesswoman who stamps all over people, and that's just not the case at all.'

Gloag is also more cautious than Souter. As a colleague puts it, 'Brian is the visionary, the ideas man. He also lets his emotions in sometimes, as he has in the Glasgow bus war. Ann doesn't do that. He said, "Let's get FirstBus", whereas Ann would have counselled him to be careful. If Stagecoach is a car, Brian is the driver, and Ann the brakes. She will slow the car down, he will shift it up a gear, and she will then brake again.' That is interesting because the launch of the Glasgow war (see Chapter 11) occurred after Gloag took more of a back-seat role and went part-time to concentrate on her charitable work and to enjoy life in her castle.

Indeed, throughout their relationship, Gloag has been the pragmatic one, occasionally knocking down Souter's ideas when they have been too far-fetched or optimistic. He has had to argue through his plans and she has been the sceptical one whom he has had to convince of their soundness.

While it is difficult to separate their individual contribution to the business, there is no doubt that Souter's contribution has been the more important but Gloag's should not be underestimated. As a colleague put it, 'If I had the choice, I would have Ann running my business rather than Brian. Brian is not that good at running businesses. Brian is the visionary, the ideas man, but he also lets his emotions in sometimes. Ann doesn't do that. Ann is half of Brian Souter, or at least 40 per cent.'

For a time, when Stagecoach deliberately put forward Gloag as the media person, she was seen as the powerhouse and Souter as the younger brother whose contribution was less important. This may have been partly a ruse to fool those on the other side of the negotiating table and it may also have been a way of giving the company a softer image and to increase the publicity value of the Stagecoach story, since women in business always attract media coverage. But it was false. Gloag's importance has been as a junior partner, a very important one, one without whom Stagecoach would not have been as successful, but nevertheless as the aide-de-camp to Souter's general.

Apart from the role of Souter and Gloag, Stagecoach's success can be attributed to a number of factors, none of which can be precisely replicated: opportunity, foresight, management skills, and dear old Lady Luck.

The opportunities were largely created by the policies of the Tory governments from 1979 to 1997: coach and bus deregulation, and bus and rail privatisation. Fortunately for Stagecoach, these were relatively evenly spaced out over a sixteen-year period which allowed the company not only to take advantage of each stage, but also to consolidate in time for the next one: coach deregulation in 1980, bus deregulation and NBC privatisation in 1986, Scottish bus privatisation in 1990, London bus privatisation in 1994, and rail privatisation in 1996. The other Tory policy that helped Stagecoach enormously has been the withdrawal of workers' rights through the Thatcherite reforms of the trade unions. Stagecoach has been able to boost its profitability through cutting wages, which would not have been possible in the industrial relations legislative regime of the 1970s. It was only by reducing wages – and cutting other costs – that Stagecoach and the other bus companies could make up for the huge withdrawals of subsidy by the government in the post-1986 deregulated era. But while the opportunity was there, everyone eschewed it apart from a few bus managers and Stagecoach. The foresight that has characterised Stagecoach has largely come from Souter and it has been an essential factor in the success.

Stagecoach's success has also been built on good management and effective delegation. There is widespread evidence that, of the emerging bus groups such as Go-Ahead, FirstGroup and Arriva, Stagecoach is the best managed and most efficient, as well as being, until recently, the only one to have established itself abroad. One passenger transport authority manager, who buys in services from several large operators as well as many small ones, says, 'Stagecoach is considerably better than its rivals, particularly in its approach to customers.' Stagecoach also responds better to criticism: 'When we had problems with one of the contracts, Stagecoach was quick to turn things round. Customer care, staff attitude, and cost per vehicle all significantly improved quickly.' Peter Huntley, a transport consultant with TAS, told the *Financial Times* that Stagecoach 'developed a strategy for running bus companies that is head and shoulders above those of the other private groups'. Barry Doe, a bus and rail industry consultant sums it up well: 'The media used to hate BR but now love to hate Stagecoach instead, despite its being by far the best of the large bus groups.'

Stagecoach has applied a set methodology after an acquisition: this has been the foundation of its cost-cutting strategy and its achievement of high profit margins. (It also brought about the SWT fiasco because of the failure to recognise the differences between the bus and rail industries.)

Barry Hinkley, the executive director, explains, 'When we buy a business, we look at management structure, then administration, then engineering staff, and the last one we look at is the traffic. In other words we say we have a network of services earning x amount of money. What we have to do is strip out the overheads in a systematic way, so that when we look at network, we are looking at it set against a cost base that we are happy with and that we understand. The last people affected in our restructuring processes are drivers. Once we have rationalised the network, we know exactly whether we are making money or losing it.' The companies acquired from the public sector had layers of unnecessary staff: 'The costs are far higher than they ought to be. Too many depots, supervisors, inspectors, people in the traffic office piling through statistics, people in the cash office. In any state-owned industry, the people are there and if you have managers with no interest in success, when systems change over time, they leave people in there even though they have nothing to do as a consequence of new technology.'

Souter's aim is always to cut down the number of managers so there are three levels above the driver or fitter – the main board, the four-person TEAM (Traffic manager, Engineering director, Accountant and Managing director) running the subsidiary and the depot manager. Interestingly, Stagecoach does not believe in having personnel or marketing directors. The white-collar staff superfluous to this structure are quickly made redundant. In addition, whole swathes of activity are cut out. For example, the huge engineering workshops so beloved of empire-building NBC managers are invariably closed down. According to Hinkley, 'They are a complete bind on the business. Unnecessary, things of the past. For the engineers of the past central works was their status symbol. How big it was, how many people were in it, but not how productive it was. I closed the one in Cumberland down in the first year. It was totally inefficient. Even in the remote north-west, I could buy in all the resources we needed, like engines and gearboxes, far cheaper than we could produce them. When you have a central works, you always have eight or ten vehicles awaiting engines or gearboxes, you are waiting for the works to produce them. I want an engine delivered, put in and the vehicle running and away you go.' Outsourcing is becoming standard in the bus industry, but Stagecoach led the way.

The closure of engineering works is part of another Stagecoach policy: getting rid of non-core businesses. Coach companies bought as part of bus firms were quickly disposed of and other activities were either closed down or sold. In Manchester, for example, there was a car repair shop, a driving school, a large computer system and a huge centralised bullion centre to count cash. Hinkley says, 'It was all non-core businesses. They all distract the management from what the task is. We get rid of anything that is non-core. That always saves money in the long run.'

Labour costs are looked at late in the process (see Chapter 10), after the other overheads have been reduced, and finally the network is examined and rejigged if necessary, a process that Souter says can take two years if services have been run down by cost-cutting managements in the past.

If Souter had one Blair-like motto, it would be 'investment, investment, investment'. Stagecoach invested in new buses at an early stage, even when it involved a considerable sacrifice in terms of Souter's and Gloag's salaries, realising that they were a key way of cutting costs. The fleet age has been reduced from the industry average of eleven to eight years by the end of the 1996–7 financial year. In the preceding four years, Stagecoach spent £244.6 million on new buses, against cumulative post-tax profits of £154.5 million in that period, but the pace of investment was slowing down as the optimum age of the fleet had almost been reached. Broadly, Stagecoach throughout its history has invested at around 1.8 times the level of its profits, a high figure for British industry.

Fleet sizes have invariably been reduced. Whereas in the past, companies kept 20 per cent above their 'peak vehicle requirement' – the maximum number of buses needed to operate the routes at peak times – in case of breakdowns, Stagecoach retains around 10 per cent spare capacity. This is partly as a result of having newer buses, which require less maintenance, but also because outsourcing ensures less time is spent on repairs. Buses are given an MOT-type inspection every twenty-eight days and are deliberately painted in the white-with-stripes livery because this ensures they are kept clean. Buses are all washed every night as part of the customer-care ethos. Drivers must be smartly turned out and customer-friendly, although passengers still often report that this is not always reflected on the ground.

While Stagecoach invests vast sums on new buses, it spends very little on marketing, arguing that buses are a visible product that needs no introduction. However, quality is seen as important. There is an emphasis on customer care, which has often been achieved but, at times, drivers have faced cuts in wages and conditions and this has led to disgruntled workforces.

Stagecoach also found it difficult in two years to turn round the railway culture of SWT, where Spanish practices and a jobsworth attitude can still prevail but eventually succeeded as the profits of £34.4 million in 1998/9 showed.

Hinkley is obsessive about quality: 'Quality is not like a menu with ten courses and you say, "I'll have course one, three, five and seven." If you do that, the chances are that the punter will not get the bus every day at the time you say he's going to get it. But if you deliver the full menu, you cut down the risks by 99 per cent of that bus not arriving to pick the punter up.'

Good management has been an essential part of the Stagecoach success story and the emphasis has been on building the company around a core of key players who have turned their hands to various tasks, often simultaneously. Brian Cox, when he first joined Stagecoach, was running Hampshire Bus and the Magicbus operation in Glasgow at the same time. Souter's policy has always been to leave managers in place initially, except for those immediately identified as incompatible with the Stagecoach ethos. Then, after a few months, there would be a reorganisation with the good ones having their careers advanced. Of course, many middle managers have left in the delayering process, but Hinkley, who has been the manager responsible for carrying out most of the restructuring, reckons there have been few mistakes: 'You have got to have the best at the top to make sure that your business is doing what it should be doing. It's no good having bits of dead wood lying in the senior echelons. We know who are the people who make it happen, and those who are just hanging on. We identify them very quickly and I've never regretted parting with anybody.'

One of Stagecoach's strengths has been its ability to make good use of the managerial talent it has picked up from acquisitions. Most of the senior people in the organisation – Barry Hinkley, Ben Colson, Roger Bowker – worked for acquired subsidiaries, or, like Derek Scott, Brian Cox and Keith Cochrane, have come through personal contact. Most of the senior executives who now find themselves millionaires are self-made people from working-class or lower-middle-class backgrounds. Many of the talented managers were found in the lower echelons of the acquired firms. Hinkley, who was only an engineering director when Stagecoach took over and was almost immediately promoted to managing director, says, 'We have a reputation for being ruthless, and that's unfair. What we have done is identify very quickly those people with talent and ability. What we are not prepared to do is carry people who are not making a contribution.' Very few senior managers have left Stagecoach since its creation and the composition of the board has been very stable.

Derek Scott says that Stagecoach expects managers to take responsibility and show leadership, but remember they are part of a group: 'They should not try to bullshit us over targets. If they can't make 15 or 18 per cent, they should tell us and we can work together. Managers who have an independent streak have difficulties. Managing directors who have not stayed with us have tended to be those who have taken initiatives of their own and the cardinal sin is to fail to consult with us. One, for example, kept on running a coach business even though we tried to dissuade him. He had committed the company to a full programme of summer and winter hotels in the north-west of England and didn't have a business plan to support it. Local managing directors have a stewardship job, rather than an entrepreneurial role.'

The philosophy has always been to delegate fully to local managers, giving them the power over a large range of decisions without reference to the main board or the tiny Stagecoach HQ, where there are just thirty central staff. Sometimes this has not worked, as with the Dawson Williams period at Hampshire Bus and the ill-fated Adamson and Low but usually the local managers, either the existing ones adapting to Stagecoach methods or the new ones put in by the firm, have succeeded. Souter deliberately sets his managers challenges: 'Our greatest management successes have come out of situations where we had to do things. Stagecoach, the animal, works well on challenges and being stretched a bit.'

The Stagecoach story shows that you can make millions without being perfect or inventing the wheel. Souter made many mistakes, and none of what he did was rocket science. He operated in a banal business with a declining market. Nor is it a very difficult or complicated industry. Yet he is Britain's most successful self-made millionaire of the Thatcher and Major eras. The recipe for any successful business person or organisation is, in no particular order: guts, opportunity, talent, hard work, luck and vision. Souter and Stagecoach had them all, as well as that ruthless streak and a readiness to flirt with the grey areas of the law which both, at times, tipped the balance in their favour and attracted the terrible publicity. Perhaps, with a bit less aggression, Stagecoach could have achieved the same ends without the opprobrium. But it is unlikely. Those two aspects of the business, the brilliant business skills and the ruthlessness, fit together, reflecting the two sides of Souter's character: the Christian family man who chats to the workers in the depot and has socialist instincts, and the hard-hitting businessman who drives his opponents off the road and demands total commitment from his staff.

The ability of Stagecoach to keep on growing depends enormously on Souter. He no longer has his sister at his side as she has largely eased herself out of the business, working only part-time and spending a lot of energy on charities. However, by appointing Kinski as chief executive he has cleared his decks to work more effectively on the acquisition programme.

Souter recognises that, to continue to grow, he has to cope with a more sophisticated market: 'more diverse, more geographically spread, simple privatisations, complex privatisations, tendering, concessions for twenty-five to thirty years and so on. Up to now Keith [Cochrane] and I have done business development as a sort of hobby, and we can't do that any longer. We must have more sophisticated due diligence and look at a wider menu in order to continue our diet. I'm going to concentrate on business development, which I like doing, and I'm better at doing, and Mike [Kinski] is a much better manager than me, and he will concentrate on making the biz more performance-driven. He's got a lot of corporate experience, and part of the development of Stagecoach from a family biz to a quoted company in the FTSE 100 is that we must have a more corporate structure than in the past.'

Porterbrook gives him a war chest to meet his target of doubling the size of the company by 2003. But it is going to be tougher. There are no more Porterbrooks in the offing and the opportunities abroad are more difficult to realise simply because they are more of an unknown factor. But with the recent successful acquisitions of Road King, Prestwick Airport, Citybus, Sogin and Coach USA, and the chunk of Virgin Rail under his belt, Souter laughs at the Jeremiahs, arguing that at every stage of its growth, the doubters have said that Stagecoach has overstepped the mark or will struggle to keep on getting bigger. He has proved them wrong every time until now and, by giving himself more time to work on the acquisition strategy, he has shown his determination to do so again.

With his millions, his four children and his dedication to the church, a less driven man than Souter would pull out at this stage. He spends a chunk of his earnings on his charitable work but concentrates more on Christian and evangelical causes than his sister, who is more eclectic and very generous in her giving. Like those old American entrepreneurs of the turn of the century, he will probably end his days happily doling out largesse from his Souter Foundation and being a non-executive chairman of Stagecoach. But he is only in his mid-forties and will remain very active in the company at least for a decade or so.

For the time being, Stagecoach does not face a succession problem but the venture into the US is undoubtedly Souter's biggest gamble. So far.

Epilogue

I met Souter just before Easter 1999 in another swanky London hotel lobby to discuss developments in the company for the paperback version of this book. This time he paid for the sandwiches, and he was now worth some £300 million, even though the share price had languished during the previous twelve months. He had just met with an Italian gentleman and said he liked doing business in hotel lobbies 'because if people come to my office, they may well be seen. This way it is anonymous.'

Although he says he mostly liked the book, he still insisted: 'I would rather it had never been written.' Despite this, 150 copies were handed to Stagecoach managers attending the 1998 group conference soon after publication in November 1998. In each one, Souter wrote a note:

'Robert Burns said:

> "O was some Pow'r the giftie gie us
> To see oursels as others see us!
> It wad frae mony a blunder free us,
> And foolish notion."

. . . and so I thought you'd be interested to get a signed copy of Christian Wolmar's new book about Stagecoach which was published last week. I'm afraid, however, you won't get Ann or I to sign this book!'

Index